MAKING POLICY MOVE

Towards a politics of translation and assemblage

John Clarke, Dave Bainton, Noémi Lendvai
and Paul Stubbs

First published in Great Britain in 2015 by

Policy Press
University of Bristol
1-9 Old Park Hill
Bristol
BS2 8BB
UK
t: +44 (0)117 954 5940
pp-info@bristol.ac.uk
www.policypress.co.uk

North America office:
Policy Press
c/o The University of Chicago Press
1427 East 60th Street
Chicago, IL 60637, USA
t: +1 773 702 7700
f: +1 773-702-9756
sales@press.uchicago.edu
www.press.uchicago.edu

British Library Cataloguing in Publication Data
A catalogue record for this book is available from the British Library

Library of Congress Cataloging-in-Publication Data
A catalog record for this book has been requested

ISBN 978-1-4473-1337-3 paperback
ISBN 978-1-4473-1336-6 hardcover

The right of John Clarke, Dave Bainton, Noémi Lendvai and Paul Stubbs to be identified as
authors of this work has been asserted by them in accordance with the Copyright, Designs
and Patents Act 1988.

Cover design by Clifford Hayes Design
Front cover image kindly supplied by Vanja Nikolic [vanja.nikolic1@zg.t-com.hr]
Printed and bound in Great Britain by CMP, Poole
Policy Press uses environmentally responsible print partners

Contents

Contents

Introduction

Policy moves. It moves from place to place: from the head offices of supranational organisations to the (more or less) grateful recipients in faraway elsewheres; or from the strategic stratosphere to the gritty encounters of the front line. Policy moves – and the fact of its movement makes things happen. What happens is not necessarily what was intended, or what was planned. Policy moves – and moves on, colonising new spaces and new settings with the promise of improving things. All of this is well-known – in the world of policymaking and moving, and in the world of policy studies. However, this book emerges from a sense of puzzlement: 'How does policy move?'; 'Who and what makes it move?'; 'What happens as it arrives and settles in those "elsewheres"?'; 'What keeps it moving?'; and 'What happens to it as it moves?' Linked to this sense of puzzlement – and the questions that preoccupy us – is a sense of frustration: why are these not the organising questions of policy studies? Why do the questions and answers of so much academic work on policy leave us cold? This mix of puzzlement and frustration brings us to this point: writing a book about making policy move.

Over the last decade, we have found ourselves in recurring conversations and collaborations, despite our geographically and institutionally distributed lives. Those conversations have continually returned to the puzzles and the frustrations that link us. In that time, we have shared our frustrations, exchanged sources of excitement and inspiration, and explored ways of thinking about how policy moves and what happens as it does. In particular, our conversations have led us to this collaboration – in which we try to see what happens if we use the ideas of translation and assemblage (and others) to think about policy moves. Doing a book is itself a practice of translation – in which we move from talking to ourselves (and small audiences at conferences and workshops) to addressing unseen others. Translation – as we suggest in the book – is a risky practice: much can be lost in translation and unanticipated meanings and effects can be gained. However, our hope is to recreate – reassemble, perhaps – both the spirit and the substance of our conversations. That means offering a way of thinking about policy in a spirit of conversation and collaboration. The book – and our approach – is necessarily unfinished. We could have gone through more and more cycles of discussion, reflection and revision. Some readers may think that we should, indeed, have done so, but we think that it is more important to start conversations than to finish them.

Conversations are supposed to include the possibility of 'talking back', rather than listening to a monologue. Equally, we believe that it is more useful to explore possibilities than to provide definitive answers, even if a book is a rather strangely formalised version of conversation and exploration.

We have tried to find ways of 'doing the book' in the spirit of our ways of working together. It mixes – both in substance and style – forms of collaborating. This begins with the jointly written first two chapters – the slow outcome of frequently circulated drafts, with many revisions, suggested changes and puzzled comments. However, they are, for now, the best we can do as a way of setting up our puzzles, articulating our frustrations and elaborating a way of thinking about the movements of policy. They are followed by four more substantive and more individually authored chapters, in which we each take up and make use of the collective conceptual framing developed in Chapters One and Two. The ways in which we use this framing are different, and each use adds to, stretches and develops it. Although they are 'individual' chapters, they have also been developed through collective discussion, and some of the traces of these discussions can be found in the interruptions that occasionally break into the chapters in which the other voices comment and reflect upon what is being presented. The final chapter is again collaboratively written, reflecting on the arguments of the book and exploring the possibilities and problems of trying to think and do things 'otherwise'. This interest in the possibilities of 'otherwise' is a critical element of our approach to studying policy.

We have several hopes for the book: that it proves interesting and engaging; that it is stimulating of thought and action; and that the spirit in which it has been conceived and written comes through the textual form. We have enjoyed the process of collaboration and we share a sense of playfulness that has shaped how we have worked together. It inflects our sense of doing academic work: our engagements with theory and practice, with established authorities, and with institutional and disciplinary boundaries tend to be transgressive. We think that such playfulness is productive: awed deference and confined subordination tend not to be good speaking or thinking positions. This orientation has certainly served us well, both individually and collectively, and the book could not have been conceived, much less written, without it. Nevertheless, all of those aspirations and orientations may well be also sources of frustration and irritation for readers. We can only say that we have found frustration and irritation to be productive forces too.

Trajectories and conjunctions

Before beginning the explorations in translation and assemblage in the coming chapters, we also thought it might be useful to set out some of the different routes by which we arrived at this joint focus on policy as translation, since they reveal some different but overlapping and intersecting trajectories.

Dave Bainton

Dave Bainton (DB) has been passionate about exploring and highlighting the ways that education, particularly education in the global South, is implicated in the realisation of impoverished and fragmented existence. The path has been taken through work in international education and attempts to find ways to retreat from complicity. Critique has been made possible through the many encounters – professional, ethnographic and personal – with other ideas and worlds that have been shared in translation. This journey has been taken via ethnographic (Geertz, Behar) and critical post-structuralist (Foucault) accounts of education and globalisation, and then, later, narrative analyses (Minh ha, Riessman, Polkinghorne), which tried to both repopulate the critical and understand how power operated at the level of experience.

Ultimately, these enriched and repopulated accounts of suffering remained too stable, and increasingly unproductive. Why was this? Was there something about the nature of critique, as imagined in Western academia, that was unfit to deconstruct the Western imagined educational structures and institutions? How might critique make purchase? Enter translation.

As an educationalist living with and transformed by the assemblages of education policies as they move and flow, a language of translation was meaningful. Texts, roles, relationships, buildings, hopes and ruptures all get translated as particular policy understandings of education are relocated. However, a language of translation found meaning not only in this more mundane sense of the management of childhoods and the nation. More than this, translation, in the sense that Iveković uses it, is a state of being. Where being in a state of permanent translation invokes an ontological instability in which transformation becomes possible.

But possible how? How might education policy be understood differently? Through the transformation of the mode of critique itself. Through the engagement of critique with indigenous (understood relationally, counter-hegemonically) ways of knowing. This journey

3

of critique, while working in Bhutan and Ladakh, highlighted the enormous silences within Western academia of non-Western theoretical frameworks and tools. While there has been, to some extent, an indigenising of research methodology, there remains largely unheard the insistence of indigenous theory in offering new ways to conceptualise educational policy and possibility. It is such a possibility that an engagement with translation offers.

John Clarke

John Clarke (JC) has had an obsessive interest in the ways in which meanings, power and politics combine since he entered the world of cultural studies in the 1970s when escaping management studies. Cultural studies tends to predispose its practitioners to two ways of looking and thinking in particular. The first concerns what Stuart Hall has described as the politics of articulation: how meanings are necessarily the focus of contending politics, in which forms of domination and subordination may be established – or contested and resisted. Second, cultural studies is oriented to what Larry Grossberg (2011) has described as contextual and conjunctural forms of inquiry: insisting that the particular formations in which meaning, power and politics are articulated are always specific. They cannot be known or diagnosed in advance or in the abstract.

JC first started using the idea of translation when teaching courses for those about to become managers in the 'reform' of public services in the UK, which were moving towards more manageralised forms of organisation, coordination and authority (Clarke and Newman, 1997). The concept of translation was used to help people think about the different discursive registers in which they would be working: on the one hand, the specific professional or occupational culture in which they had been formed (and which most of those that they would be managing still inhabited); on the other, the more abstract universalising culture of corporate management (into which they were being enrolled). Their new organisational roles were requiring them to mediate between these two cultures, languages and ways of thinking about service delivery: they were becoming translators – and it was important that they understood the tensions, risks and possibilities that such a location produced.

These experiences were grounded in an interest in how policy – and modes of thinking about organising policy – travelled: both across space (much of the managerialisation of public services in the UK drew on US management, organisational and policy thinking (Clarke and Newman, 1993); and within organisational settings, as actors were recruited to new roles, new ways of thinking and new orientations to their work and to the public that they were expected to serve. This set of interests predisposed him to find the work of Noémi Lendvai (NL) and Paul Stubbs (PS) immensely important and valuable when he first encountered them in 2003–05. These ideas – and the conversations in which they were embedded – made sense of many discomforts with the worlds of social policy and policy studies (including varieties of critical policy studies). From these encounters, the ways in which meaning, power and politics were at stake in moving policies became a focus of subsequent collaborations – including this one.

Noémi Lendvai

NL was born and raised in communist Hungary and studied social policy and social work soon after the regime collapsed and the disciplinary borders fully reopened to make 'Western European' welfare studies available and desirable in many Eastern European universities. After finishing an MA in political science at the Central European University, she started working for the Hungarian Ministry of Social Affairs as a policy consultant. In 2002, she started her PhD in policy studies, and, ever since, with a short interlude at the European University Institute (EUI) in Florence as a Max Weber Postdoctoral Fellow, she stayed at the University of Bristol, where she is currently a lecturer in comparative public policy.

For NL, translation appears a critical dynamic of policy ever since her time working for the Hungarian ministry and advising them on EU matters. Translation issues and their impact on social policies emerged throughout her work as a policy consultant and continued to occupy an important place in her academic work as well. In her doctoral work, JC's cultural turn on welfare and PS's post-colonial and ethnographic approach to welfare have been very influential. The tentative conclusion in NL's doctoral thesis, which pointed towards the need to move away from the policy transfer and the catch-up convergence literature, and towards an approach of policy as translation, and policy as meaning-making, led to the collaborations with JC and PS, and later with DB. For NL, translation has been fundamental in interrogating 'policy' as forms and practices of knowledge production, as colonisation within the EU, and as part of an agenda towards critical policy studies. It has also been an academic agenda of interdisciplinary engagement: departing from social policy, venturing into political science, fascinated by anthropology, influenced by human geography and cultural studies, reading translation studies, settling into policy studies, and holding on to social policy again. Translation has been and continues to be a fascinating and difficult, but rewarding, intellectual journey.

Paul Stubbs

PS began a journey to a more critical, post-structuralist take on social policy while still in the UK; however, his move to Croatia in 1993, and collaborations with Croatian anthropologists, made him much more aware of the importance of symbolic and cultural representations and translations. A 'new wave' of Croatian anthropologists working in the Institute of Ethnology and Folklore Research, in Zagreb, on issues relating to *War, exile, and everyday life* (see Jambrešić Kirin and Povrzanović, 1996), introduced him to the work of James Clifford (esp 1997) and Katherine Verdery (1996). Together with the book *Welfare and culture in Europe: towards a new paradigm in social policy* (Chamberlayne et al, 1999), PS was encouraged to rethink his 'on the ground' experience as an activist–researcher–consultant in the post-Yugoslav space through an exploration of the 'cultural' conditions and lived experience of welfare as a set of complex, folded and contested social relations. The article 'Globalisation, memory and welfare regimes in transition: towards an anthropology of transnational policy transfers' (Stubbs, 2002), a long time in the making, in retrospect, failed to escape the straitjackets of concepts of 'welfare regimes' and 'policy transfer' and move towards more productive thinking around concepts of 'welfare assemblages' and 'policy translation'. The statement that the story of global welfare reform is 'complex and contradictory', accessible through ethnographic methods underpinned by an 'anthropology of policy' (Stubbs, 2002: 328), was at least a marker for future work. The encounter with the work of NL (see Lendvai, 2004), based, originally, on a shared geographical focus, later led to further collaborations, including: a programmatic statement on the need to move from 'policy transfer' to 'policy translation' (Lendvai and Stubbs, 2007); an empirical study of the role of intermediaries in social policy reform in South East Europe (Lendvai and Stubbs, 2009a); and a conceptual critique of much of mainstream 'global social policy studies' from a 'post-colonial' perspective (Lendvai and Stubbs, 2009b). PS's rediscovery of JC's work (esp 2004) reconnected his interests in social policy and cultural studies and, again, served to embolden his concern to bring anthropological approaches to the study of policy.

Working collectively

This book was conceived over a long, and very satisfying, breakfast in Montréal, Canada, at the end of the annual meeting of the American Anthropological Association in November 2011. All four authors had contributed to a panel convened by Catherine Kingfisher, called 'Tracing Policy: Translation and Assemblage', under the auspices of the Interest Group on the Anthropology of Public Policy, chaired by Janine Wedel. The subsequent making of this book has been a complicated social and spatial process, with the challenges of getting ourselves together in a place for long enough to talk, think and write being overlaid onto the usual problems and pleasures of working collaboratively. Some of our earliest collaborations, involving three of us, came from a series of workshops in Croatia funded by the Friedrich Ebert Stiftung, exploring topics such as 'Multi-level Governance' and 'Neo-liberal Governmentalities' in South East Europe, where we formed a group concerned with researching 'Intermediaries and Translation in Interstitial Spaces'. Attending and presenting at a number of European Social Policy Analysis Network (ESPAnet) conferences also solidified our collaborations, not least in a growing shared awareness of the problems of orthodox and mainstream approaches to social policy.

It is, perhaps, within the framework of the American Anthropological Association annual conference and, in particular, the Interest Group for the Anthropology of Public Policy (now the Association for the Anthropology of Policy) where the ideas in this book began to be formulated, particularly in two panels: 'Beyond Policy Transfer: Transnational Translations and the Reconfiguring of Technocracy and Politics' (in 2009, in Philadeplhia, organised by Janine Wedel and Tara Schwegler); and the one organised by Catherine Kingfisher in 2011. Later, in the process of writing this book, sessions at the International Studies Association in San Francisco in 2013, organised by Rianne Mahon, and a panel at The Interpretive Policy Analysis conference in Vienna in 2013 were of considerable importance. We are grateful to the organisers, participants and publics at these different events for trying to help us think better.

Individually, we have used classes, courses, workshops and other invitations to develop, refine and occasionally overthrow our thinking before the next moment of collaborative exchange. JC worked on some of the issues explored here in a graduate class on critical policy studies in the Department of Sociology and Social Anthropology at Central European University and would like to thank all those who took the course and made life interesting. We have also been supported by the

Open University and the University of Bristol to organise workshops through which the arguments were rehearsed and developed (held in Milton Keynes in May 2013 and in Bristol in October 2013).

Finally, we owe thanks to many individuals for their engagement with our enthusiasms, excitements, doubts and anxieties. In particular: Wieger Bakker, Bojan Bilić, Bob Deacon, Richard Freeman, James Ferguson, Eric Gordy, Jeremy Gould, Elissa Helms, Vesna Janković, Alexandra Kaasch, Vjeran Katunarić, Catherine Kingfisher, Olivier Kramsch, Tania Li, Janet Newman, Reima Ana Maglajlić, Matko Meštrović, Maja Gerovska Mitev, Mariella Pandolfi, Jasmina Papa, Maja Povrzanović Frykman, Prem Rajaram, Ešref Kenan Rašidagić, Christophe Solioz, Janine Wedel, and Siniša Zrinščak.

We owe special thanks to the anonymous reviewer for Policy Press, whose comments and suggestions both supported us in our endeavour and urged us to do better: we have tried! A debt of gratitude is also owed to Vanja Nikolić, whose painting provides the image for our cover.

Finally, thanks to Emily Watt at Policy Press for thinking that this might be a good idea!

ONE

Moving policy studies

Settling and unsettling policy and its study

Policy matters. In part at least, this is because policy involves social processes that are intertwined with people's lives, often in very profound, sometimes oppressive, and even violent, ways. This book is concerned with policy movement, including the mobility of policy across borders and boundaries. Associated in different ways with the dynamics of globalisation, the role of supranational organisations and agencies, or the spread of 'best practice', the trans-border, trans-boundary, movement of policies is visible on a large scale – whether this is the spread of Conditional Cash Transfer policies (see, eg, Ferguson, 2010; Lavinas, 2013), the rise of 'austerity' (Clarke and Newman, 2012; Blyth, 2013) or the propagation of the United Nations' Millennium Development Goals (Gabay, 2012).

When policy moves, it is always *translated*: that is, it is made to mean something in its new context. Policy is never a singular entity: it is put together – or assembled – from a variety of elements that are always in the process of being reassembled in new, often surprising, ways. This concern with movement, translation and assemblage is central to our challenging of more conventional views of policy mobility, such as 'policy transfer', 'policy diffusion' or 'policy learning'. Our concern is with the limitations of what we see as a conventional and linear approach to the policy process that too readily treats policy as a finished object. Instead, we will suggest that policy always involves practices of translation as policies are interpreted, enacted and assembled. Hence, we share, but also attempt to go beyond, a conception of policy as moving horizontally, across sites, and vertically, from policymaking centres to 'implementation' on the front line. As Kingfisher (2013: 3) argues:

> [T]wo insights – policy as a power-laden artifact and architect of culture, and policy produced not only officially but also in myriad unofficial ways – serve to displace models of policy as rational, neutral and acultural, as well as to trouble visions of policy as something that can be implemented in any kind of straightforward, top-down,

unmediated, and transparent manner. Instead, these insights invite us to envision the life of social policy – a process rather than a thing – as complex and convoluted, tracing and leaving traces of meaning and power as it travels across sites and through persons.

The movement of policy is not new, of course. Machiavelli's handbook on governing (*The Prince*; Machiavelli, 2003 [1532]) travelled (in Italian and in translation) around Europe. In a different way, the Catholic Church acted, and still acts, as a supranational organisation, defining policy at the centre and seeking its implementation through local offices. The organisation of European colonialism involved policy movement, both the directives from the metropole on how the periphery should be ruled, and the innovations of policy and practice in the colonies that made their way back to the centre – from counter-insurgency policing to governing through community and communal identities (Pandey, 2005, 2006; see also Clarke, 2014). Timothy Mitchell's (1991 [1988]) study of British colonial rule in Egypt shows how power and control over subject populations was precisely articulated through 'civilising' and 'modernising' policy innovations in public health and hygiene supervision, model villages, schooling, and army training, always coupled with the threat, and often the use, of violent force. Later, Mitchell (2002: 41) traced, in the same period, the rise of 'techno-politics' as a 'new politics based on technical expertise'.

Policy has also always moved from 'conception' to 'implementation'. Orthodox studies of the policy process (eg Hill and Hupe, 2009) have drawn attention to the processes of implementation and the slippages that are possible between the grand idea and the practices 'on the ground'. A whole sub-literature deals with the 'unintended (and unanticipated) consequences' of implementation (following Merton, 1936). As the geographical and organisational distances over which policy moves have become larger, and possibly more complex, so the 'implementation' of policy attracts new interest, not least in the idea of 'governing at a distance', which is associated with the rise of what has been variously defined as audit culture, audit society, performance management, the evaluative state or the competitive–evaluative nexus (see Power, 1997; Neave, 1998; Pollitt et al, 1999; Strathern, 2000; Clarke, 2005).

Social scientists, including policy scholars, are particularly prone to identify and proclaim the 'shock of the new', demonstrating in the process that they are not very good historians. As a consequence, the 'historical amnesia' (Clarke, 2012) that surrounds policy performs important political 'work', rewriting history to edit out inconvenient elements, and reinforcing a need to be seen to be 'doing something' in a constant drive to newness and innovation, which has been termed 'policy hyperactivity' (Pollitt, 2013). It may well be the case that there are different issues and intensities in the movement of policy in the present conjuncture that warrant greater attention. Is the mobility of policy increasing, both in terms of frequency and distance? Can it be argued that, today, more policies move, and move more quickly, over greater distances than ever before? Jamie Peck (2011: 773–4) suggests that there is something qualitatively and quantitatively different about 'contemporary policy making processes', which:

> seem to be accelerating, as measured by the shortening of policy development cycles and the intensity of cross-jurisdictional exchanges. Today's 'fast-policy' regimes are characterized by the pragmatic borrowing of 'policies that work', by compressed reform horizons, by iterative constructions of best practice, by enlarged roles for intermediaries as 'pushers' of policy routines and technologies, and by a growing reliance on prescriptively coded forms of front-loaded advice and evaluation science. On the face of it, policy ideas and techniques have become mobile in entirely new ways – exhibiting an extended reach as well as a diversity of registers.

Such claims need to be treated with some caution: there may be a difference between the addition of new elements and the argument that the processes are entirely new. It is true that, today, the policy space seems 'denser' or 'thicker' than ever, with policies appearing to pile up on one another in the urgent drive to 'improve' people, places and, indeed, policy processes themselves. Today's policies should be 'smart', 'evidence-based', 'efficient' and 'effective', even (to borrow from production processes) developed and implemented 'just in time'. As we argue throughout this book, however, policy spaces are often more contradictory and unstable than this description allows for. Time and space, as we note later, involve contested understandings that are mobilised in different ways as policies move. Such understandings appear in narratives that locate policies in relation to failed pasts or promised futures, or identify the places of 'success' that should be followed or imitated in the pursuit of new directions (on the significance of Finland in recent educational policy reform, see, eg, Waldow et al, 2013).

We begin from the urgent need to think about the ways in which making policy move necessitates moving policy studies, and, thereby, identifying a number of ways in which conventions of policy studies are in the process of being challenged, reworked and themselves put into motion. An interest in how policy moves unsettles taken-for-granted conceptions of 'policy' itself, rendering strange that which is generally considered to be familiar. Our route through this field in this chapter is, of necessity, selective and partial. It reflects, first, our own sense of deep dissatisfaction with a policy studies orthodoxy that treats policy movement in terms of policy transfer, policy diffusion and policy learning. We argue that these concepts tend to stop us grasping certain aspects of policy that seem to us to be crucial. We then turn to work on policy as meaning, which has been important to us as a foundation for a more critical policy analysis. Increasingly, however, we see this work as a stepping stone, or a take-off point, enabling us to get to our current position, rather than a satisfactory end point in itself. Finally, we explore concepts of space, scale and time and their usefulness in a critique of both 'methodological nationalism' and 'methodological globalism' in policy studies. In this way, we aim to 'clear the ground' for a fuller exploration of our interest in translation and assemblage in Chapter Two.

While noting a number of points for our departure from a policy studies 'orthodoxy', this is by no means an exhaustive inventory, representing only some of the preoccupations that have shaped our diverse individual and collaborative work. It is also worthy of note that what we call 'the orthodoxy' is by no means as monolithic as we imply. Indeed, between some of our initial interventions in the field and the completion of this book, we have seen the idea of 'policy translation' being increasingly woven into more orthodox policy studies approaches (eg Stone, 2012; Ozkan, 2013; Mukhtarov, 2014).

Our attempt to 'think differently' about policy and its movement involves, then, an exploration of what is involved in thinking of policy as translation. We attempt to explore this question through a range of conceptual and analytic resources that are introduced here and pursued in greater depth in Chapter Two. These ideas are then developed, albeit unevenly, in the four substantive chapters that follow. In this way, we present what can be seen as a *provisional* conceptual repertoire for the study of policies and their movement viewed through a lens of translation and assemblage. A concluding chapter explores the ethical and political implications of our approach and the possibilities of thinking and doing 'policy otherwise', hinting at prefigurative or alternative practices that can be developed by making policy translation more visible and, thereby, contestable.

Unsettling policy as transfer

The dominant set of approaches to the movement of policy within policy studies is organised around ideas of 'policy transfer', 'policy diffusion' and 'policy learning'. Notwithstanding refinements over time, and riding roughshod over disputes and diverse trajectories within these approaches, we see this literature as extremely problematic. It has, indeed, been critiqued from many different directions. Much of this literature originates within political science: it adheres to positivist/rationalist epistemologies, and, in many ways, even draws on 'neoclassical economics and orthodox communications theory' (Peck, 2011: 775). Crucially, it tends to operate with an unreconstructed map of the world in which 'policy' moves between different places, whose position, boundaries and history are both understood and understandable within an objectivist epistemology and ontology. As Dolowitz and Marsh (2000: 5), still among the main proponents of the approach, note:

> While the terminology and focus often vary, all of these studies are concerned with the process by which knowledge about policies, administrative arrangements, institutions and ideas in one political system (past or present) is used in the development of policies, administrative arrangements, institutions and ideas in another political system.

This analysis, symptomatic of the approach as a whole, sees mobility as a property of the policy, understood as comprising eight different categories: 'policy goals, policy content, policy instruments, policy programs, institutions, ideologies, ideas and attitudes and negative lessons' (Dolowitz and Marsh, 2000: 12). Crucially, they see the places or sites between which such movement takes place as, in and of themselves, unproblematic: policy simply moves between different 'political systems', spatialised and bounded conveniently as nation-states or, sometimes, as (sub- or supranational) regions. These are the 'container' versions of nations that underpin many political and sociological conceptions of the nation as a site of social inquiry – leading to a view of flows as 'cross-national' (Stubbs, 2005). More puzzlingly, the actors that feature in their accounts as the agents of transfer, learning and so on tend to be mobile or border-spanning, be they consultants, non-governmental organisations (NGOs), international agencies or others, although this does not appear to impact on their analytical approach in any significant way.

The list of key questions asked within the policy transfer literature seems rather limited and, certainly, one-dimensional and linear. Dolowitz and Marsh (2000: 8) suggest the following questions:

> Why do actors engage in policy transfer? Who are the key actors involved in the policy transfer process? From where are lessons drawn? What are the different degrees of transfer? What restricts or facilitates the policy transfer process? And how is the project of policy transfer related to policy 'success' or policy failure?

In an earlier text (Dolowitz and Marsh, 1996), they go so far as to construct a typology of policy transfer based on a continuum from 'voluntary' to 'coercive' transfer, with processes in the middle judged as 'negotiated'. This, argues Peck (2011: 780), is an 'analytical gaze' that conjures up policies 'willed into motion by searching and learning subjects ... evaluated in terms of universalizing models of rational or satisficing behavior ... floating in abstract analytical spaces, or boxed inside descriptive taxonomies'.

In much of the 'policy diffusion' literature, an actor-centred perspective of sorts is replaced by an image of policies willed into motion by broad, and strangely often broadly benign, structural forces, such as development, Europeanisation, globalisation, industrialisation, regionalisation or, even, modernisation (see Tews, 2005). Here, a model of 'convergence' or 'catch-up' familiar in the Europeanisation literature (cf Lendvai, 2007) is combined with the idea of the emergence of a 'world society' (cf Meyer et al, 1997), which focuses less on agents and more on supposedly 'larger cultural processes, logics, and mechanisms' (Tag, 2013: 30). A literature on 'lesson learning' or 'lesson drawing' (cf Rose, 2005) focuses more on understanding the conditions under which policies operate in their 'home' jurisdictions in order to produce guidelines that can be used to make lesson-learning more 'successful'. This is, of course, both a highly 'normative' and astonishingly 'apolitical' move to make (Mukhtarov, 2014: 73), reflecting as it does the mutual dependency between some policy scholars and the policy environments that they are studying, perhaps most clearly seen in work on 'multi-level governance' within the European Union (EU) (Stubbs, 2005).

What is common to all this literature is the rather linear notion of movement being described. Policy ideas or models are rendered as 'objects' to be loaded up on a truck at point A and unloaded at point B. Those doing the loading and unloading, and the truck itself, are of little scholarly interest. The terrain on which the truck travels is largely seen as smooth and unproblematic. The truck only moves from A to B, never back the other way. When unloaded and unpacked, the object, akin to a 'product' perhaps, is 'picked over selectively by a faceless elite of continuously learning policy-makers' (Peck, 2011: 791; see also Kingfisher, 2013). It is this, rather than the supposed 'immutability' of policy ideas in their movement (Mukhtarov, 2014), that is most at issue. In a rational-linear conception of policymaking, a policy is simply put together and announced. After that, it may be implemented more or less well; hence, a scorecard of success and failure can be drawn up, with any 'unanticipated' effects noted for future lessons to be learnt. The 'object' will still be largely the same or, at least, the same order of things. For Deborah Stone (1988: 8), in one of the first texts to critique a framing of policy only in terms of rational choice, the process can be likened to an assembly line:

> The model of policy making in the rationality project is a production model, where policy is created in a fairly ordered sequence of stages, almost as if on an assembly line. Many political scientists, in fact, speak of 'assembling the elements' of policy. An issue is 'placed on the agenda,' gets defined; it moves through the legislative and executive branches of government where alternative solutions are proposed, analyzed, legitimized, selected, and a solution is implemented by the executive agencies and constantly challenged, refined and revised by interested actors, perhaps using the judicial branch; and finally, if the policy-making process is managerially sophisticated, it provides a means of evaluating and revising implemented solutions.

In short, viewing policy as an object involves seeing it as a finite and finished product. It has been made, and can be investigated, traced, analysed and known in relatively straightforward ways. When it travels, only the aforementioned lorry is needed. Instead, we want to suggest a view of policy as always in the making, or under construction. As it moves from one place to another, from one site to another, from one level to another, it is revised, inflected, appropriated and bent in encounters of different kinds. A policy, then, is never a completed object. Indeed, in the process of policy movement, sites and levels themselves may also become unsettled, reformed and reconnected in new ways. This does not mean that each moment makes something new or different, but that the outcomes of these movements and moments cannot be wholly prescribed from its starting point. Indeed, understood in this way, policy is always subject to revisions and inflections, which opens up a politics of translation in which there are always possibilities at stake. Policy, then, is necessarily unfinished.

In contrast to a policy transfer orthodoxy, then, our concern with translation seeks to reveal processes of re-representation and reordering. Translation is a process of displacement and dislocation (Callon, 1986), raising questions about transferability and translatability that are rarely addressed within the orthodoxy. Indeed, an understanding of policy translation considers the displacement or suppression of dissenting voices; in contrast to the orthodoxy's focus on 'goodness of fit' (cf Lendvai and Stubbs, 2007), we are concerned with that which is *'unfit to fit'* (Gebhardt, 1982: 405). As two of us argued in an early piece (Lendvai and Stubbs, 2007), a move from 'policy transfer' to 'policy translation' is, not least, a shift in 'register' or 'vocabulary' to explore more fluid, dynamic and messy processes. In other words:

> Policy translation goes beyond policy transfer since the world cannot be reduced to binary notions of stability versus change, or adaptation versus resistance, determined by the 'goodness of fit' (based on the distance or gap between the original policy and policy in the recipient country). The mainstream literature operates within a perspective that has a narrow conception of power primarily in terms of institutional veto points or veto players, and their ability to block change.... By reconsidering our understanding of the policy transfer process from the point of view of translation we would argue instead that the policy transfer process should be seen as one of continuous transformation, negotiation, and enactment ... and as a politically infused process of dislocation and displacement. (Lendvai and Stubbs, 2007: 180)

Unsettling policy as meaning

For a number of scholars, including some of us in our earlier work, one of the first movements away from a policy transfer orthodoxy, with its view of policy as having a given, fixed or essential character, was towards a concern with *policy as meaning*. Framing policy as a meaning-making process derives from a broad constructivist turn in social science and, particularly, from work in policy studies, especially in North America, which paid close attention to the meanings that specific policies contain, carry and distribute. The idea of policies as 'meaning-making' and 'claims-making' processes (Yanow, 1996), always 'layered by implicit meanings' (Innes, 2002), forces much greater attention onto the 'constant discursive struggles' over the definitions and boundaries of 'policies' as constructed, as well as over criteria for their 'classification and assessment' (Stone, 2002b: 60). Policy becomes seen as an 'interpretive process', with policies seen to express 'values, feelings and ... beliefs' (Yanow, 1996: 8), and even 'emotions' (Stone, 2013), which are communicated to, and read by, 'various audiences' (Yanow, 1996: 9) in varied ways.

The question of meaning forms a crucial point of intersection in the development of policy studies – and, in particular, for those approaches to policy that have emerged in opposition to rational choice and positivist views of policy. Various 'turns' can be condensed together here: the argumentative turn (Fischer and Forester, 1993; Fischer and Gottweiss, 2012); the interpretive turn (Yanow, 2000, 2007); the linguistic turn (Fraser, 1995); the discursive turn (see, eg, Howarth, 2010); and even the cultural turn (Clarke, 2004). Each of these 'turns' takes up the production, circulation and consequences of meaning as a central focus, albeit in different ways. Each 'turn' also contains variants – articulating different epistemological, theoretical and methodological orientations. Not all studies of 'discourse' take up and make use of 'discourse' in the same ways, as is clear, for example, when we note the distance between Howarth's (2010) attempt to construct a post-Marxist discursive model of 'hegemony' for policy studies and Schmidt's (2008; 2013) rather belated incorporation of discourse into forms of institutional theory within political science. All share, to an extent, Dolowitz and Marsh's (1996) admission, which still holds true, that the literature on 'policy transfer' was 'too positivist' and too little engaged with constructivist approaches. Mukhtarov (2014: 7) takes this as an entry point for the idea that policy translation, with its focus on language and meaning, constitutes 'a social constructivist approach to the travel of ideas'. While that may be true for some work on policy translation, there is much more to work on policy translation than this suggests (including, we hope, this book).

Our own interest in many of these themes derived from anthropological approaches to policy which suggested that policy is always 'in the business of the production and reproduction of meanings' (Jenkins, 2006: 7). Policy, then, like politics, in this case, even setting aside that many language groups use one word to cover both English words (Lendvai and Stubbs, 2007), is deeply 'ideological' in the sense of making 'claims about how the world is and about how it ought to be' (Jenkins, 1997: 84). Jenkins (2006: 7) goes on to suggest:

> Policy, of whatever sort, constitutes and is constituted by meaningful practices, codes and categories, on the one hand, and may call into being new or modified meaningful practices, codes and categories, on the other. It may not be too much to say that, in the modern world, policy processes are among the most important vehicles and instruments – along, perhaps, with formal socialisation and mass communications – for the production and reproduction of the collective meanings which frame and imbue everyday life.

Work within an 'anthropology of policy' approach, marked initially by an edited collection of essays of the same title (Shore and Wright, 1997a), made an important contribution, as exemplified by the book's subtitle: *Critical perspectives on governance and power*. Here, policies are seen as 'most obviously political phenomena', disguising their political nature through the 'objective, neutral, legal-rational idioms in which they are portrayed' (Shore and Wright, 1997b: 8). Shore and Wright (1997b: 14) suggested that anthropological approaches to policy should rely less on 'traditional' approaches to policy studies and more on 'traditional' approaches to anthropology, focusing on a concept that appears to most of those involved in its making as 'axiomatic and unproblematic' and exploring its different meanings and the work it performs as 'an organizing principle of society'. At the same time, an anthropology of policy opened up possibilities for a 'radical reconceptualization of "the field"' as 'a social and political space articulated through relations of power and governance', together with a focus on 'analysing policy documents as "cultural texts"' (Shore and Wright, 1997b: 14, 15). What followed in the three main parts of the book – a focus on language, discourse and power; a focus on the cultural construction of identities; and a focus on the technology of neoliberal rationalities of governance – faced criticisms that it was 'too Foucauldian', allowing 'too little space for individual agency' (Shore and Wright, 2011: 17). The more recent collection, perhaps, oscillates between a continued focus on governmentality as well as attention to the all-pervasiveness of 'the micro-physics of disciplinary power', and a group of texts that address, in diverse ways, 'the reflexive capacities of political subjects' (Shore and Wright, 2011: 17, 18). We share the plea in the book that there is a need not only to pose the question of 'how a policy means' (Yanow, 1996), but also to address how policies change and become 'as they enter into relations with actors, objects and institutions in new domains', and how they are implicated in constructing subjects 'as objects of power' (Shore and Wright, 2011: 20).

Much of this 'meaning'-centred work is important in critiquing 'conventional wisdoms' about policy, which turn out to be conventions within orthodox approaches to its study, too. First, the approach through meaning insists that policies cannot be understood outside of the 'sociocultural contexts' in which they are 'embedded and understood' (Wedel et al, 2003: 43). Second, it suggests that policies rely upon 'ideologized discourses' (Wedel et al, 2003: 43) that tend to mask complex social relationships and interactions. Third, it shows how public policy, and its analysts, rely on many 'flawed dichotomous frameworks' (Wedel et al, 2003: 43), such as 'state and society', 'public and private', 'local and global', 'top–down and bottom–up' and 'centralised and decentralised', which need to be unpicked. In short, this set of approaches seems well placed to explore 'the complexity, ambiguity and messiness of policy processes' (Wedel et al, 2003: 44). At its best, such work addresses the profoundly unsettling effects that policies and policy actors may have on supposedly stable boundaries: institutional, organisational or professional. Janine Wedel, for example, has explored how 'transactors' (Wedel, 2004), utilising 'multiple roles and identities' (Wedel, 2004: 156) and operating in multiple intersected and intertwined institutional and organisational sites, 'play' and, thus, transform the boundaries 'between national and international; public and private; formal and informal; market and bureaucratic; state and non-state; even legal and illegal' (Wedel, 2004: 167).

For us, the turn to treating 'policy as meaning' was of vital importance, and was, without doubt, one of the foundations for much of the work of critical policy analysis that followed. Yet, by itself, a concern with meaning is not enough. Several of the 'turns' noted earlier have expanded the possibilities of policy studies but without always pursuing what we would see as the critical 'edge' of critical policy studies. In many of the studies to have emerged around language/meaning/discourse, meanings are 'made safe': they circulate, rather politely, in arguments and deliberative processes, or they are securely installed within the confines of institutions. Such meanings rarely appear as troublesome, turbulent or disruptive – either in the specific field of policy or in the mode of analysis. This may be what Jessop (2013: 438) implies when he suggests that the 'argumentative turn' has become 'normal science'. For us, meanings are more interesting than this: they are a focal point because they point to the constructed, conjunctural and contested character of policy. Meanings are usually in motion – they only rarely become crystallised and solidified. When they do, such moments are the result of intense effort to normalise and naturalise a particular cluster of meanings, for example, meanings about the naturalness of forms of inequality, about the desirability of progress or about the inevitability of market rule. Meanings, as Jenkins suggests, matter because they are wrapped up in practices of making and remaking the worlds that people inhabit. Such practices, however, are typically contested by different meanings, different possibilities and different projects that seek to realise one possibility, to make it come true and to have it accepted as normal and natural. For us, then, meanings matter because they are a point of contestation, and it is the analysis of this contestation that is important. Meanings are inextricably linked with forms and relations of power and authority and are implicated in the making and remaking of social worlds. Policy, then, can be conceived as a particular setting in which meanings are made, installed, naturalised, normalised and, of course, contested. Policy can also be seen as a particular genre of meaning making – there are conventions associated with the writing and communication of policies, with their review and revision, and with their replacement by newer, better or more 'modern' policies. What we take forward into later chapters of the book is this underpinning: the 'turn' lets us grasp policy as a setting and a genre in which meanings are made, contested, installed, naturalised and normalised, and in which power is organised, challenged and rendered normal or even invisible, through the work of making policy move.

Unsettling policy in space and time

A related movement away from a linear notion of policy transfer seeks to unsettle conventional ideas of both space and time, introducing a different set of concerns beyond a focus on policy as meaning. It is not just that we seek, with Peck, to 'contextualize policy-making behaviors in more historically and geographically sensitive ways' (Peck, 2011: 791). Perhaps, geography and history, and, crucially, their interconnections, need to be conceived not as prior to, but as integral components of, policies and their translation and assemblage. Space and time, then, are actively enrolled and reassembled within policy. They help, separately and together, to constitute the social world of policy. As Peck (2011: 793–4) goes on to argue, even though 'cross jurisdictional flows' are now commonplace:

> this does not mean that once-distinct policy-making 'worlds' are simply dissolving into the global space of flows. Rather, new geographies of policy are being shaped, and new modalities of time–space policy compression are at work, as mobility and mutation proceed in tandem.

David Harvey (1989: 226), in *The condition of postmodernity*, argued that time and space, together with money, forms 'a substantial nexus of social power' in money economies in general, and capitalist societies in particular, since 'command over spaces and times is a crucial element in any search for profit'. Harvey reserves the concept of 'time–space compression' for a particular space and time, Europe in the crisis of 1847–48, when the certainties of the Enlightenment project began to be questioned. Resting on a particular economistic reading of Kern's (1983) study of *The culture of time and space*, Harvey makes a case for the idea that modernism, and, with it, a certain modernising view of policy, was, in part at least, a response to a crisis of experience and representation of space and time. His concern with 'the production of space' and 'the ordering of time' echoes Giddens' (1990) concern with the 'recombination of time and space' and the 'zoning of social life'. Giddens (1990: 17; but see also Thompson, 1967) argued that the invention of the mechanical clock permitted 'the precise designation of "zones" of the day'. For Giddens (1990: 19), modernity tears space away from 'place' by fostering relations between distant others, such that locales are structured not just by 'that which is present on the scene'. This understanding of time and space and the concept of 'time–space' is productive for an unsettling of policy orthodoxies since it recognises that the recombination of time and space, as in the timetables or timelines of policy implementation, are neither natural nor technical, but deeply social, political and contestable. At the same time, a notion of 'time–space distanciation' as inevitable, helping to form 'a genuinely world historical framework of action and experience' in which social relations are 'lifted out from local contexts and restructured across indefinite spans of time and space' (Giddens, 1990: 21), leans too far towards what we would term a 'methodological globalism', which appears to be in danger of replacing 'methodological nationalism' as the cornerstone of policy studies.

It is true that, conventionally, policy studies has treated policies as exclusively national phenomena, attached to a particular place and polity – and model of the nation and nation-state. Policies were seen as occurring in different, but consecutive, historical times. Such a view enabled comparative studies as a process of looking for the similarities and differences between national systems and/or over time. This view of the national space of policy, although perhaps not so much the linear time of policy, has been increasingly challenged. To some extent, this is reflected in growing attention to new domains and dynamics of policy, and, in particular, those associated with perceived processes of globalisation, regionalisation and Europeanisation. These processes are understood to have unsettled the unities of place, people and policy associated with methodological nationalism. Saskia Sassen has argued that the taken-for-granted unity and coherence of the national space concealed the contingencies of how different elements were 'bundled' together – and those contingencies have been revealed and even 'unbundled' to some extent by contemporary social dynamics:

> The theoretical ground from which I address the issue is that of the historicity and the embeddedness of both categories, citizenship and the national state, rather than their purely formal features. Each of these has been constructed in elaborate and formal ways. And each has evolved historically as a tightly packaged bundle of what were in fact often rather diverse elements. The dynamics at work today are destabilizing these particular bundlings and bringing to the fore the fact itself of that bundling and its particularity. Through their destabilizing effects, these dynamics are producing operational and rhetorical openings for the emergence of new types of political subjects and new spatialities for politics. (Sassen, 2006: 80; see also Clarke et al, 2014)

The assumed fit between the concepts of 'policy', 'state' and 'nation' has been challenged across both spatial and scalar dimensions. Space and scale cannot be taken for granted as unproblematic; rather, they are contingent, complex and constructed. There can be no prior presumption of the territorial integrity and stability of national spaces and their configuration in fields of international relationships. At the same time, there is a need to be concerned with 'the production, reconfiguration or contestation of particular differentiations, orderings and hierarchies *among* geographical scales' (Brenner, 2001: 600, emphasis in original), often misconceived as 'multi-level' governance, involving levels supposedly 'above' and 'below' the nation-state. Again, anthropologists have been in the vanguard of this challenge, developing understandings of the 'trans' – transnational and translocal – as ways of coming to terms with the mobilities of people, objects and ideas and the spatial imaginaries that connect and locate them (eg Basch et al, 1993; Gupta and Sharma, 2006; Amelina et al, 2012). Similarly, geographers have argued for a more relational understanding of space and of places as sites in which many relationships intersect and are condensed (Massey, 2004, 2005). Places, then, are made – rather than passive points of departure or arrival. These contexts matter: they shape how policy is imagined and interpreted as it travels from one context to another. However, these places – these spatial contexts – are reworked in the process of policy movement. Centres of power gain authority and legitimacy as their policy models are adopted (eg think of supranational organisations such as the Organisation for Economic Co-operation and Development [OECD] or the EU, which provide models for issues ranging from pension reform to education systems). At the same time, the power of such centres may also be identified as a reason for challenging or resisting policies (eg in Latin America's resistance to the 'Washington Consensus' on structural reform and the neoliberalisation of economies). Policies also change places as they travel, though not always in the direction intended. Equally importantly, travelling policies also have the capacity to change relationships between places as they travel, establishing relations of dependency, profitability or antagonism – as beneficiaries try to throw off their former teachers or advisors, or as policy donors become disenchanted by the lack of 'progress' or 'gratitude' in the recipients.

As a result, transnational policy flows are never linear transfers from one place to another, but involve 'multi-scalar networks' (Jones et al, 2004: 104) that organise space in ways that enable – and constrain – the movement of policy. As we argued earlier, we fear that the concepts of policy transfer, diffusion and learning remain excessively attached to methodological nationalism or only escape its stranglehold to fall prey to either lumpy models of multi-level governance (see Stubbs, 2005) or a methodological globalism that imagines the world as a uniform and borderless space across which policies flow uninterruptedly.

It is certainly the case that what have been termed 'internationalisation', 'globalisation', 'glocalisation' and 'transnationalisation' are both political and academic discourses that attempt to grasp a complex set of social practices, and, hence, pose distinctive challenges to the traditional boundaries of the field of policy studies. As political discourses, they are mobilised by governments, agencies and organisations to explain the need for policy change and innovation – in particular, discourses of internationalisation and globalisation have been much used by governments to explain what must happen (to 'keep up' or to succeed) and to explain what cannot happen (we cannot control, we lack the authority, etc). As academic discourses, they have brought into question the centrality of the nation-state as a primary and confined unit for social and public policies, but they have also brought new epistemological and ontological notions, such as 'spatiality', 'governmentality', 'hybridity', 'fluidity' and 'disjunctions', that decentre our conceptual understandings and highlight the impoverished vocabulary of mainstream policy analysis. If we focus, for a moment, on critiques of mainstream social policy, which can stand for a wider range of policies, it has been argued that in a globalised and transnationalised world, 'important differences are not properly captured by the concept of social policy that is used ahistorically to represent state actions in both developed and developing societies, regardless of their different histories and different social conditions' (Baltodano, 1999: 14). Transnationalism, therefore, points not merely to 'the intensified international struggle to shape welfare regimes' (Jessop, 2002: 204), but also to the need to deconstruct the taken-for-granted conceptual apparatuses around 'social policy' and 'welfare regimes' developed in the Global North (Midgley, 2004) and to be vigilant against Western imperialism (Gupta, 2006: 230). In short, time and space remain in need of being unsettled in policy studies.

As a consequence, we want to argue for the importance of locating the trajectory of the nation-state in changing *transnational* conditions and processes, rather than seeing it as moving from a national to a 'post-national' form (or merely staying national). In the process, we might come to see specific nation-states as temporarily constructed achievements. Some of these constructions are more visible than others – whether this is the constructed unity of a UK, the persistence of the 'Southern question' in a unified Italy, the post-Soviet remaking of Central and Eastern Europe, or the complex transitions of South Africa through the 20th century. While such visibility is relative, even the most apparently settled, unified and organic nation-state represents a constructed and naturalised achievement, rather than a state of nature (Gupta, 1998).

The transnationalisation of social policy, in Ferrera's (2005: 207) terms, results in 'the redefinition of the boundaries of social sharing'. Ferrera maintains that three distinctive processes constitute these changes: the proliferation of levels of governance; the complex web of different coalitions between multiple actors; and the significant expansion of both 'locality' and 'vocality' options. Similarly,

Leibfried and Zürn (2005) argue that the previously known national 'constellation' of the state has been dispersed along territorial lines with far-reaching organisational changes, leading to complex, diverse and competing processes.

Transnational frameworks also have the effect of decentring state-centric approaches, and explicitly challenge the 'methodological nationalism' of much mainstream policy studies. At the same time, an emerging orthodoxy of 'global policy studies' needs to be questioned since it remains based on a crude global–national dualism (cf Robinson, 2001). Rather than merely a 'scaling up' of objectivist knowledge, there is a need to emphasise the interactions, the complexity and the liminality of encounters between actors, sites, scales and contexts. On the one hand, following Ferguson and Gupta (2002: 994), 'it is necessary to treat state and nonstate governmentality within a common frame, without making unwarranted assumptions about their spatial reach, vertical height, or relation to the local'. On the other hand, the ability of actors to 'jump scale' should not be considered as unproblematic or universal, not least since 'different languages, rhetorics, ideals, justifications and rationalities circulate at different scales' (Gould, 2004b: 283). Above all, actors cannot be predefined prior to their engagement in particular practices and the researcher needs to constantly be open to the possibility of new organisational topographies and surprising alliances. The boundaries between state and non-state actors are breaking down, progressively producing a reallocation and reinvention of authority (Sinclair, 2000), and a new complexity of scale.

Despite such developments, we fear that concepts such as 'flows' and 'mobilities' remain excessively attached to methodological nationalism, or, more precisely perhaps, only escape its stranglehold to fall prey to methodological globalism, which imagines the world as a uniform and borderless space across which objects flow uninterruptedly. Our interest in the transnational and translocal aims at seeing how flows flow, how they are interrupted and how they come (differentially) to rest at particular places and times. In addition, we are interested in what happens in – or to – the places where such policies come to rest: how are they remade or reshaped by this new arrival? Our concern with such interactions of policy and place extends – through the lens of translation and assemblage – to asking what policies become in the process. There is a danger, even in critical policy studies, of assuming the effects of policies as they travel from global centres to peripheral recipients. While we understand the wish to grasp the relations of power that structure fields of international, national and local formations, we need to be careful not to treat policy in practice as always fixed in the intentions or interests that can be discovered at the point of departure. In short, 'making policies move' is not the same as 'making sure that policies are implemented'. Repertoires of refusal, resistance and recalcitrance must be allowed for as part of the dynamic, complex and contradictory processes through which policy moves.

This more productive view of space and scale is also relevant to the ways in which policy is put into practice – in the changing social and organisational landscapes that were once simply, and certainly too simplistically, grasped as the state. Ideas of 'governing at a distance' have become increasingly significant for thinking about how policy works through multiple agents in multiple settings. Sometimes referred to as the shift from government to governance, these processes have been taken up in other analytic framings, such as Foucault's concept of governmentality. For example, Rose (1999: 50) has written about 'governing at a distance' as involving new technologies of government:

> Political forces instrumentalize forms of authority other than those of 'the state' in order to 'govern at a distance'. In both constitutional and spatial senses – distanced constitutionally, in that they operate through the decisions of non-political modes of authority; distanced spatially, in that these technologies of government link a multitude of experts in distant sites to the calculations of those at the centre – hence government operates through opening lines of force across a territory spanning time and space.

This has proven to be a useful concept, being deployed in a diverse array of studies, including those in which states have been finding ways to govern the social and varieties of social provision without direct lines of command and control. Both organisations and individuals have, it seems, been increasingly invited to imagine themselves as responsible, auditable or inspectable performative selves (see Power, 1997). However, there are some problems regarding the way in which 'distance' is imagined in this view (Allen, 2003), and whether distance is only spatial (might there also be social, organisational and cultural distances across which government tries to work?). One example, of how such shifting alignments of policy, authority and publics reorganise our conceptual frameworks might be found in the idea of the 'front line'.

The concept of the front line derives from both images and studies of 'integrated' organisations (the military, state bureaucracies, corporate enterprises). So, for example, the interest in 'street-level bureaucrats' as policy actors in underdetermined organisational spaces (Lipsky, 1982; see also, eg, Bovens and Zuoridis, 2002; Meyers and Vorsanger, 2007 [2003]) understood them as working at the end of a chain of command. In most of the areas that we are interested in, the integrated organisation is no more; rather, a variety of more or less connected organisations form networks, partnerships and the like to produce or deliver new forms of policy. Front-line workers are, at least, more distant organisationally from the centres of policy and strategy and may be only loosely coupled by a variety of organisational devices (contracts, targets, performance management techniques, etc). This would apply, for example, to subcontracted domiciliary care workers. However, other 'front-line workers' are 'volunteers' in some sense (primary carers, workers in NGOs, etc), or they are the citizens/users/consumers of services – the active, self-regulating, co-producers of service outcomes. In the 'expert patient', the 'knowledgeable consumer', the 'self-starting entrepreneurial self' and more, the site of the front line is – possibly – internalised in the citizen, who becomes the worker, the self-surveilling agent and the citizen in one moment.

The disintegrated state produces many front lines and multiplies varieties of front-line workers – from partnership workers who do the labour of joining up government, to the recovery entrepreneurs in Robert Fairbanks' (2009) study of post-welfare Philadelphia. New occupations flourish (eg 'community safety workers' or the workers in new labour market activation programmes), and new ethics of practice are mobilised in NGOs, or what Aradhana Sharma (2006) identifies as GONGOs (Governmentally Organised Non-Governmental Organisations). In these emergent divisions of labour, there are also new or reworked genderings, as women become valorised as particular sorts of subjects with desirable skills or capacities (Newman, 2013a).

In sum, contemporary policy movements make the spaces of policy both more visible and more problematic. We cannot (or, at least, should not) presume that the existing vocabulary of policy studies – particularly nation-states and the field of international relations on the one hand, and the hierarchical modelling of 'levels' on the other – can provide adequate or productive analytical resources for studying policy as it moves. Although we do not want to argue the opposed positions (globalisation means the end of the nation-state, or governance means the end of government), we do think that doing policy studies means being much more attentive to the changing formations in which policy moves, their changing alignments and the emerging relationships that are in play within and across them. We take this up further in the later chapters.

The changing landscapes of policy – especially those brought into view by moving policies – have unsettled the conventional models of space and its organisation in policy studies. Less obviously, they have also unsettled the taken-for-granted notions of 'time' in policy studies (Pollitt, 2008). Perhaps the unsettling effects have been less obvious because time has tended to be a taken-for-granted concept in the field – linear, universal and subject to periodisations (eg the simplifying distinctions of past and present that Clarke and Fink [2008] have called 'sociological time', the recurring declarations of the 'end of' things, or the identification of Golden Ages and Declines). As noted earlier, studies of policy mobilities have reintroduced the question of time in concepts such as 'fast policy' (Peck, 2002). Nevertheless, we think that the idea of 'fast' movement adheres to a certain essentialist idea of 'time' and assigns particular emphasis and connotations to 'time'. Fast policies may not always be as fast as they first appear, or, by extension, emphasising the speed of policy transfers may cause us to miss some of the rather more obscure, and often rather slower, processes through which policy unsettles and resettles particular social landscapes. Time in policy is constructed, mobilised and, above all, contestable. Policies often construct a myth of a problematic 'policy past' in need of, more often than not, 'urgent' correction in order to create a more glorious 'policy future'. Policy is 'planned' using temporal notions of 'the policy cycle'. New policies are often based on 'action plans', which set out 'deadlines' that should be met. Policies are 'monitored' and 'evaluated' over intervals of time, allowing for taking stock and the setting of new goals for the future. In consultant–civil servant encounters, the consultant's time is measured in working days, whereas the civil servant may feel that she or he has 'time on their side', having waved goodbye to groups of consultants who leave nothing behind but their reports to be allowed to rot in drawers. Transnational development organisations often take much longer than intended to plan interventions, themselves usually time-limited 'projects' and 'programmes' that, again, almost inevitably, are said to need to be implemented 'urgently'. 'Change takes time' is a maxim often invoked by transnational development actors seeking to obtain longer contracts from international donors for their interventions.

Yet, thus far, policy studies has not really taken time seriously. It has been argued, rightly, that much of the policy transfer literature tends to render the process ahistorical (Stone, 1999). There has been little attention to the difference between time and temporality, or to the ways in which different conceptions of time may be at work within policy processes. Different ideas of time are being invoked when we refer to a 'policy age' or a 'policy culture' akin to a kind of '*Zeitgeist*' of policy ideas. The use of favoured 'actants', or of 'techniques' and 'technologies' of policy, may also vary over time, as Gasper (2000) has shown regarding 'logical frameworks'. Policies are often implicated in 'telling the time' (Clarke, 2007: 245) and constructing future aspirations (Dussauge-Lagune, 2012): they categorise pasts, presents and futures; they are replete with the languages of progress and modernisation; and they may position different sections of the population in particular time modes (old-fashioned thinking, forward-looking, etc).

Time and temporality, like 'space', are complex and multidimensional, and certainly not reducible to Westernised 'clock time' (Adam, 2005 [1998]: 8). Policies do not merely pass 'through time', but are constituted by time (Oke, 2009: 311). Fabian (1983: 17) has pointed out that societies tend to be placed not in equivalent times, but on a 'temporal slope', so that so many of the policy keywords, including development and modernisation, are derived as operating in 'evolutionary time'. Indeed, Oke (2009: 323) argues that within globalisation discourses, space and time re-converge through notions of the West and the non-West, with the latter reactive to, but not strongly constitutive of, processes of globalisation. Many of the processes that we address in this book reveal the interpenetrations of different 'rhythms' or conflicts of time and temporality. Unsettling the 'temporal qualities' of policies is an important task since 'the times of and for … policy are … interwoven with other times, and embedded within individual and collective experiences of time' (Coffey, 2004: 102, 103). Policy times, then, are 'complex and multiple', consisting of both 'temporal rhythms and ruptures' (Coffey, 2004: 104, 105). While Adam (2005 [1998]: 10) suggests that 'timescapes' may be understood as 'the embodiment of practiced approaches to time', this needs to be fluid enough to allow for the ways in which policies are embedded 'with/in different times, temporalities and temporal rhythms' (Coffey, 2004: 107).

This is suggestive for us: policy might be produced within particular timescapes (the conventional conception of the political/electoral cycle or the urgency demanded by 'crisis' and the 'speed' of the global), but its movement might bring into contact different rhythms and senses of time (eg as the local meets – and resists – the global) that cause problems of coordination (cultural 'lag' or people who want to 'rush ahead'). Policy also tries to organise time, for instance: telling stories of failed pasts and promised futures; establishing implementation timetables, reporting points and milestones; and offering models of the 'life cycle' of policies and projects. This is a particular sort of policy work, which tries to organise different times and temporalities by treating them as if they are singular and linear. Of course, such a view of policy time rarely succeeds in eliminating other conceptualisations.

Resettling policy: performance and practice

The field of critical policy studies has often attempted to reveal the 'real' or 'true' intentions that underlie, stand behind or are concealed by policy texts. The language of policy thus comes to be treated as a sort of smokescreen or rhetorical cover for the real intentions of policymakers (or even the real intentions of those whose interests stand behind the policy process and policymakers). The process of 'unmasking' has a certain satisfying quality, particularly when the language of policy is so often painfully neutral – and neutralising – as it celebrates its objective, technical, distant or apolitical character. However, we are not convinced by this tactic – a move towards what we might call 'dirty realism' in which the unmasking of 'real' interests or intentions is enough for a critical analysis. The turn to discourse has been one way of refocusing analytic attention on the work that language does – in policy as in other fields (eg Fischer, 2003; McDonald and Marston, 2006; see also Newman, forthcoming). From these turns, as noted earlier, we take the productive capacity of language (rather than its smokescreen quality) as a crucial analytical gain. However, it must, as we argued, always be linked with a recognition of the conjuncturally contested possibilities of discourse – the multiple (or heteroglossic, to use Mikhail Bakhtin's [Holquist, 1981] term for the simultaneity of many contending voices) ways of thinking and speaking that are at stake.

However, our own work stresses two further issues. First, that the 'productive' effects of discourse cannot be assumed: the identifications, positions and practices that are sought in particular discursive strategies may not materialise (Clarke et al, 2007). Discourse-analytic studies of policy need to look beyond texts and statements, to policy in practice, or even policy as practice. Second, however, we think it may be important to move beyond the Foucauldian conception of language as productive so as to treat policy discourses as performative – presented to real and imagined audiences, attempting to make specific proposals or projects appear as if they are logical, innovative, necessary, obvious and so on. In such processes of policy talk, policy is both made and made meaningful in performance.

Hence, policy is always 'unfinished', always open to having its intentions, its meanings and its substance bent, or re-appropriated. Here, we want to emphasise the importance of moving policy from being a singular object of study to something that is always in the making, emerging in processes of *assemblage* (Li, 2007; Newman and Clarke, 2009). Although we will discuss it more extensively in the following chapters, the idea of assemblage (borrowed through complex chains of connection and translation from the work of Deleuze and Guattari) is important for us because it draws attention to the heterogeneity of elements that go into making policy, for example, people (more accurately, particular types or categories of agent), objects (forms, guidance documents, computers and programs), places (officially defined territories, buildings, offices, meeting places, etc), as well as different sorts of texts (manifestos, official statements, media commentaries, guidelines for implementation, action notes, training leaflets and more). Even before policy is put into practice, all these elements have at least to be represented as forming a coherent and intelligible programme designed to achieve specific objectives.

As it moves, policy is vulnerable to processes that are best captured in the language of the 'linguistic turn': it can be inflected; its meanings can be rearticulated; or it can be translated into new forms. We will return to these terms and their implications in the following chapters, but we think it important to emphasise just how disruptive or unsettling their implications are. The policy, as conventionally conceived in the policy studies field, can only ever be one moment in a process – it is the apparently definitive announcement (the text that expresses purpose or intent, that sets out the methods, techniques and devices through which its purpose will be achieved, etc). However, a different reading of the 'assembly line' would show us something different – the policy is assembled from multiple resources (intentions, ambitions, discourses of legitimation, anticipated 'delivery agents', political and organisational alliances, and more). These may not fit comfortably together; indeed, here, the streamlined and integrated model of the assembly line gives way to more handicraft images of things being cut and pasted, or bodged together, in processes of what Levi-Strauss (1966), in his studies of totems, called 'bricolage'. Coherence – as Carmel and Paul (2010) have argued in the case of EU migration policy – is a narrative accomplishment in policymaking, rather than the expression of a singular principle:

> The creation of an EU socio-political space for consideration
> of migration matters brings into the political imaginary a
> bounded, populated territory, market space and social
> realm comprising the EU. But it also creates a political
> dynamic to make possible and plausible a consideration of
> the Union as a legitimate and appropriate regulator of the

population of that territory, as well as of its economic and its social relations. This is the case even if the regulations impose not order, but uneven, patchy and contradictory rules. From our perspective, the search to imagine and articulate a 'coherent' policy field of 'migration' is central to that ordering. (Carmel and Paul, 2010: 17)

By this, we mean to draw attention to two related phenomena. One is that policy involves work – labour of different kinds (Clarke, 2012). The types of labour include: the cultural work of imagination – the problematising, appropriation or borrowing of other policy framings, discourses and themes; the political work of articulation – vocalising or ventriloquising different perspectives, building alliances, and aligning interests and constituencies; the organisational work of coordination – crafting the discourses, techniques and technologies that try to ensure implementation, compliance and commitment; and, not least for our purposes, the work of translating – giving the policy life and meaning as it moves from context to context. As we have already emphasised, policy moves in different dimensions – crossing borders and boundaries of different kinds, in which each crossing involves the practice of translation, whether this is across bounded political spaces (nations, localities, etc) or organisational spaces (from the 'strategic' core to the 'front line' – and beyond). Although we share the rejection of rational 'policy transfer' models, a focus on policy as meaning and, indeed, policy space and time is not enough for us. A concern with translation and assemblage takes us away from the 'epistemic modernism' of mainstream policy analysis and some of its critiques. In Chapter Two, we explore in more detail the implications of this focus on translation and assemblage.

TWO

Translation, assemblage and beyond: towards a conceptual repertoire

Introduction

The chapter offers a set of concepts that we have found useful in rethinking policy and its movement beyond orthodox 'policy studies' approaches. We are, of course, not alone in trying to escape the limitations and assumptions of this orthodoxy; indeed, critical alternatives have been proliferating over the last 30 years or so. In different ways, these have tried to unlock or displace the rationalist, linear, positivist and depoliticising tendencies of the world of policy studies. We share many of these concerns and have a strong sense that our own development is inextricably intertwined with interpretivist, Marxist, feminist, post-structuralist and other strands of critical thought that have reworked the task of studying policy. Yet, we are also struck by a puzzle that emerges in critical approaches.

One of the recurring dynamics of critical policy studies is the unlocking of the narrow confines within which 'policy' is conventionally enclosed – the rational, technocratic world of policymaking, policy implementation, review and reflections on the 'unintended consequences' or 'unexpected failures' of the original policy objectives. The 'scene' of policy in these orthodox approaches is an orderly one: predictable groups of actors (political representatives, government officials, consultants, advisors, state employees and more or less grateful recipients) populate this scene. Critical approaches to studying policy have disrupted this scene: exploring how economic, social and political forces come to affect the making of policy; suggesting that states are more complex and contradictory entities; asking how populations are imagined and enacted in policy; questioning the ways in which policies position and discipline categories of people; and examining how policies work to enact or advance some social interests despite their technocratic neutrality. In such views, policy is rarely rational, never merely technical and always political in some larger sense. Interests, identities and intentions are intimately entwined in the processes and practices of policy.

The puzzle, though, emerges at this point: is policy merely the carrier of such interests, intentions or identities? If we know that a policy furthers the interests of capital, advances a neoliberal conception of the subject and enacts patriarchal authority, then attention tends to move away from policy to these larger forces, tendencies or dynamics. What is distinctive about policy – either as a genre of acting on the world or as a specific domain of intervention? If policy is only the ventriloquist's puppet, it is of little interest in itself. In our work, we are interested in making the critical move without losing sight of policy itself. This has three implications for our work:

1. We have to pay attention to the *making* of policy, not merely read off dominant interests, ideologies or intentions.
2. We have to think about policy as a *genre*: as a way of imagining the world as an object of intervention; as a way of enrolling subjects into a process of acting; and as a practice that seeks to produce effects, including the act of 'taking the politics of out things' (what Tania Li [2007] calls 'rendering technical').
3. We have to think about what happens as *policy moves*.

This last point informs our work in many ways. It forces us to think about policy as always 'unfinished', rather than merely embodying a singular objective, interest or desire. It asks us to think about the different sorts of agent and agency that are in play as policy moves. It requires us to think about outcomes as separate from, and possibly even different from, intentions. In this chapter, we aim to walk this fine line between a critical analysis of policy's place in making and reproducing a world of domination and subordination, in creating and managing forms of inequality, and in enabling and enacting forms of violence on people and places, and attention to the shifting, mobile and contested forms that a policy can take as it moves.

Our aim is to expand the analytical repertoire of critical policy studies by borrowing and deploying concepts from beyond policy studies (and from beyond the established lines of critical policy studies). Many of the concepts are borrowed from alternative critical literatures and approaches, some of which have 'policy' as a central object of study, others of which do not. We anticipate two critical reactions: from within policy studies, there may well be complaints about this importing of 'trendy' concepts from elsewhere; at the same time, such borrowings may well be seen by adherents of their original critical schools of thought as 'inappropriate expropriations' as we treat these concepts, both singularly and in articulation with each other, in ways that stretch them beyond their normal usage to create a vocabulary for policy studies. This commitment to 'bending and blending' (Lendvai and Stubbs, 2007) is definitely not 'the last word' on what might be a new line of analysis in the field of 'critical policy studies'. It is also, explicitly, not an attempt to create a new 'school' ready to be named, abbreviated and canonised; rather, we advocate an approach to theory and method that is sensitive to contexts and provisional. Such an approach, we hope, is also mobile – travelling, adapting and being recurrently renewed. Our aim in this chapter and in the book as a whole is to convey, perhaps more explicitly than many supposedly 'neater' or more finished accounts do, the process of intellectual enquiry that is involved in 'making up' an approach to policy studies.

Mobilising translation

Translation provides us with both an orienting metaphor and a conceptual lens through which to examine the movement of policy. The idea of translation is associated with a variety of 'turns' in policy studies (and the wider social sciences), including the 'interpretive', 'constructionist/constructivist', 'linguistic', 'cultural' and 'discursive' turns. The concept has, itself, travelled far beyond linguistic theory, being adopted and adapted in different ways, within policy studies, cultural studies, anthropology and post-colonial studies. In some of its appearances, it makes up the core of a theoretical framework – as in the sociology of translation – in others, notably, post-colonial studies, it represents a key aspect of theorising, while elsewhere it is used more as a metaphorical expression, or a sensitising tool, making other relationships and dynamics visible. In all cases, the use of the idea is animated by its linguistic inheritance, pointing to the work (the labour, the practice) of translation that is the condition of moving meanings from one context to another and indicating why translation may not be a simple transition, but involve possibilities of difference that have to be negotiated (Morris, 2006). Minimally, then, translation refers to making a meaning (or set of meanings) move from one linguistic or cultural context to another. More importantly, it marks a space of possibility because the practice of translation is rarely a simple act of like-for-like substitution (replacing one term by its equivalent in another language). Rather, translation is a selective and active process in which meanings are interpreted and reinterpreted to make them fit their new context. Like the concept of 'assemblage' discussed in the next section, translation serves to remind us of the fluid and dynamic nature of the social world, encompassing 'displacement', 'dislocation', 'transformation' and 'negotiation' (Callon, 1986). As Latour (2005: 21) puts it:

> Like all sciences, sociology begins in wonder. The commotion might be registered in many different ways but it's always the paradoxical presence of something at once invisible yet tangible, taken for granted yet surprising, mundane but of baffling subtlety that triggers a passionate attempt to tame the wild beast of the social.

Sociologies of translation: association, uncertainty and agency

Translation has been a central concept for those approaches known variously as Actor-Network Theory (ANT) and Science and Technology Studies (STS). These approaches have subsequently taken many analytical lines and pathways, but the interest for us here is the underpinning emphasis on displacement and dislocation, which enable the movement of things and people into new alignments. These approaches foreground processes of association and assemblage, as well as a concern with radical uncertainty about the effects and outcomes of such processes: 'To translate is to displace ... [and] the notion of translation emphasizes the continuity of the displacements and transformations which occur ... displacements of goals and interests ... devices, human beings, larvae and inscriptions' (Callon, 1986: 18). Displacement and dislocation, the continuous negotiations, and the enrolment of both actors and actants make up the 'social' for ANT. ANT treats translation as an index of movement – pointing to practices of *translocation* in which people and objects change places, coming to rest (temporarily) in new networks and assemblages. The continuous metamorphoses and transformations are key to actor networks, in which 'there is no in-formation, only trans-formation' (Latour, 2005: 149). As Latour (2005: 34–5) asserts, if the social is associated with inertia, stability and durability, such stability cannot be achieved without vehicles, tools, instruments and materials, that is, associations and assemblages. In a very strong sense, stability or inertia is not a normal or natural condition, but has to be created: 'If the sociology of the social works fine with what has been already assembled, it does not work so well to collect anew the participants in what is not – not yet – a sort of social realm' (Latour, 2005: 12). The social in the making, however, always takes place in a world of pre-existing fields of power, such that translation necessarily mediates between what is and what will become. Translation, then, is a form of exercise of power, even if not all ANT analysts make the concept central to their work. Actor networks are associations of heterogeneous elements, groupings that have to be made, or remade; as Latour (2005: 39) argues, 'no society to begin with, no reservoir of ties, no big reassuring pot of glue to keep all those groups together'. Importantly for our book, ANT asserts that when 'norms' have been set, 'normalisation' does not automatically follow (Mol, 2010: 263). Nevertheless, we might disagree with Latour about what exists before a specific act of network assembling takes place. While understanding his discomfort with the big structural versions of society, we doubt the sense that the fields in which assembling takes place are empty of pre-existing forces, arrangements and dispositions.

We wish to underline that translation is not a process of arbitrary 'free association' in which things can be made to mean anything; rather, it is a deeply politicised process that is concerned with 'the building, transforming or disrupting of power relations' (Sakai, 2006: 71–2). Thinking through translation disrupts conventional assumptions about policy as an object, treating it instead as 'a bearer and generator of meanings' (Johnson and Hagstrom, 2005: 370). Richard Freeman (2004, 2009) has suggested that the concept of translation enables two important insights into the policy process: first, translation highlights the constructed and communicative character of policy – policy exists and acts through language; and, second, translation identifies policy as emerging through processes of representation and association:

> what we call translation, or the replacing of terms in one language with those in another, is also a substitution of one set of relationships or associations with another. These may be similar to the original but can never be identical. To translate, therefore, is to make new associations, to reassociate or perhaps to reassign. (Freeman, 2004: 7)

This view of policy in translation centres on language and language work, and, in some versions, locates language in fields of relationship, association and articulation in which power is organised and enacted. Policy, in Fischer's (2003: 543) terms, 'is not only expressed in words, it is literally "constructed" through the language in which it is described'. It is vital to go beyond this notion of language as 'descriptive', and to assert that policy is inscribed through language and cannot exist outside of language. This process of representation is, however, never neutral or technical, but, rather, as Bourdieu and Wacquant (1992: 142–3) insist:

linguistic relations are always relations of symbolic power through which relations of force between the speakers and their respective groups are actualised in a transfigured form. Consequently, it is impossible to elucidate any act of communication within the compass of linguistic analysis alone. Even the simplest linguistic exchange brings into play a complex and ramifying web of historical power relations between the speaker, endowed with a specific social authority, and an audience, which recognises this authority to varying degrees, as well as between the groups to which they respectively belong.

Bourdieu and Wacquant (1992: 143) suggest that linguistic relations are 'unintelligible' outside of the 'totality of the structures of power relations', though whether, as they go on to suggest, these are usually rendered invisible in linguistic exchanges is open to question, particularly in the case of transnational policy (Lendvai and Stubbs, 2007). Translation, then, speaks simultaneously to the content, movement and contexts of policy. The concept opens up the content of policy, inviting us to study the processes of its making and remaking through language, through the practices of association and articulation. 'Association', as we have seen, is a central term for ANT and related versions of translation, pointing to the ways in which it is the relationships of association that give meaning and weight to such things as policies. In contrast, 'articulation' has been a central term in cultural studies (see, eg, Slack, 1996; Clarke, forthcoming), where it brings multiple senses of connection into play: articulation as association (connecting X and Y to make something new); articulation as bringing to voice (articulating a position or point of view); and articulation as mobilisation (connecting social agents into alliances, blocs or political projects). We will return to the idea of articulation later in this chapter.

Post-colonial translations: representation, violence and power

For post-colonial scholars, 'translation' is a core concept – and is understood both literally and metaphorically. It highlights the power surrounding linguistic and geographical-cultural translation that produces the often violent restructuring of the worlds of the colonised (including the concepts, images, words and practices, and the relations they represent). 'Translation' has multiple meanings in post-colonial studies. Most broadly, 'translation' refers to the process of 'reordering', which tries to make the colonised more comprehensible and manageable to their masters (Kibberd, 1995). Colonial powers both accumulate knowledge of the 'local' and translate that knowledge into the ways of seeing, hearing and knowing that enact colonial rule (on colonial ways of seeing see, eg, Mitchell, 1991 [1988]). Colonial rule also instructs colonial subjects about how to understand themselves. What are translated are not only words, labels and images, but the colonised person herself – where the colonised self becomes translated into a colonial object – a servant/subordinate/person of colour – and, in so doing, becomes alienated, displaced from themselves (Fanon, 1965). For Niranjana (1992: 2), translation is a significant site for representation, power and historicity, where 'translation depends on the Western philosophical notions of reality, representation and knowledge. Reality is seen as something unproblematic, "out there"; knowledge involves representation of this reality, and representation provides direct, unmediated access to transparent reality'. Such colonial translations also function as part of a strategy of containment, serving to reinforce hegemonic versions of the colonised and their place in the world. This capacity to know – and to define the terms through which reality can be known – is a critical element of colonial rule. However, post-colonial approaches have explored translation as a double process – a relationship – rather than simply an element of the power of the coloniser. For example, Vazquez (2011: 27) argues that translation has two different meanings:

> translation as erasure, speaks of the coloniality of translation: that is, the way in which translation performs a border-keeping role and expands the epistemic territory of modernity. The second, translation as plurality, speaks of the configuration of dialogues and the thinking of the borders that challenges the modern/colonial system of oppression.

This double significance of translation points to the coexistence of its capacity to produce, reproduce and re-inscribe domination and also its potential to create the conditions and spaces of possibility for thinking and speaking 'otherwise' and doing so dialogically (in contrast to the monological quality of colonial rule). In drawing on post-colonial studies in this way, we do not presume that the only significant formations and relationships are colonial – the varieties of domination, subordination and exploitation are too rich for that to be true. However, the post-colonial understanding of the centrality and productivity of translation illuminates our approach to policy in movement.

In particular, we want to emphasise the view that, rather than translation being deterministic and unidirectional, translation should also be understood as contested, and, as such, translation inevitably includes the possibility of retranslation, of redefining and resisting, of 'talking back' to dominant understandings, or taking back the possibility of self-naming. For example, bell hooks (1989: 28) has identified language as a site of both domination and resistance:

> We are rooted in language, wedded, have our being in words. Language is also a place of struggle. The oppressed struggle in language to recover ourselves – to rewrite, to reconcile, to renew. Our words are not without meaning. They are an action – a resistance. Language is also a place of struggle.

This view of language as a site of contestation and struggle around domination and subordination transforms the interest in meaning that has been at the heart of the 'interpretive' or 'argumentative' turn in policy studies (Fischer, 2003; Fischer and Gottweiss, 2013). There, as we argued in Chapter One, meanings are produced, circulated and consumed throughout the policy process, but they are not the object of fierce contestation or subtle reworkings. Drawing on the work of Barbara Godard, Simon (2000: 32) suggests that research should be understood as writing that is engaged in 'extending and developing the intention of the original text' – a transformative act where, in the context of the divide between the Global North and South, the need for 'rewriting' dominant global understandings is critical. Translation, then, is also a call for a critical interrogation of academic knowledge production and its radical inequalities. For Vatanabadi (2009: 796), there is a danger that 'translation posits a continuity in the geo-political hierarchies and the production of knowledge', and she highlights the need for sustained scrutiny of disciplinary works (in post-colonial studies, cultural studies and translation studies) that continue to reinforce those hierarchies.

In post-colonial studies, the work of Spivak and her politics of translation has been extremely influential, taking translation far beyond the confines of literary studies. For Spivak (2000: 320), translation is 'the staging of language as the production of agency'. In post-colonial studies, language is always enmeshed in relations of domination and subordination, but it is also the condition of possibility for naming and resisting such subordination. Working in this line of thinking, Pratt (1999: 34) has developed the idea of 'contact zones': 'social spaces where cultures meet, clash, and grapple with each other, often in contexts of highly asymmetrical relations of power, such as colonialism, slavery, or their aftermaths as they are lived out in many parts of the world today'. We have found this idea very illuminating – drawing attention to the moments of contact in which policy (among other things) might be translated from one 'culture' to another. Pratt insists that this is a moment that is both pre-structured (formed out of highly asymmetrical relations of power) and yet unpredictable in its outcomes. Certainly, the asymmetries of power create tendencies towards the reproduction of domination and subordination, but they cannot guarantee this reproduction – it is always at risk of challenge and contestation. In the moment of contact – or, as we frame it, in the practices of translation as policy moves – other possibilities emerge. They might not be realised. They might, indeed, be repressed, ignored or reworked back into familiar patterns. However, the consequences of contact and translation are always unknowable in advance.

Such a view of contact – and the approach to translation that it implies for us – works with a complex understanding of borders: as powerful demarcations; as always being traversed; and as always at risk of being erased, redefined or re-inscribed. Neither contact nor translation is an easy process of free exchange or equivalence. The act of moving across a border or beyond a boundary is always entangled with the 'asymmetric relations of power' that Pratt foregrounds, but movement takes place nevertheless in ways that both assume and bring into question the naturalness, stability or desirability of the particular borders and the distinctions that they mark (see, eg, Rajaram and Grundy-Warr, 2008; Kramsch, 2010, 2011).

A further resource that we borrow from the domain of anti-colonial approaches is Paulo Freire's critical transnational pedagogy, to which we return in Chapter Seven. Despite obvious difficulties in addressing contradictory experiences of oppression, and the divided experiences and differentiated positions that are central to a radical politics of difference (cf Weiler, 1994), Freire is nevertheless concerned with some of the same issues of language in post-colonial settings:

> [L]anguage is inevitably one of the major preoccupations of a society which, liberating itself from colonialism and refusing to be drawn into neocolonialism, searches for its own re-creation. In the struggle to re-create a society, the reconquest by the people of their own word becomes a fundamental factor. (Freire, 1978: 176)

In this section, we have tried to draw out from post-colonial studies the double significance of translation as both an act of domination (the means through which power, hierarchy and rule are re-inscribed) and a condition of possibility in which dialogue, talking back and building connections and solidarities (Spivak, 2000) become possible.

Translation, plurality and emergence

Translation, situated at the point of intersection and exchange of languages, offers a way to think about and interrogate the 'unfit to fit': those policies, projects and political programmes of 'improvement' that find it difficult or impossible to remake their intended object, or can only 'work' at the expense of disruption, disorder and both symbolic and material violence as they try to make the new place 'fit' the plan. In such moments, the lens of translation enables us to see forms of otherness (which are at risk of being denied or suppressed), the invisible (that which cannot be seen or made visible in the colonial view) and the beyond (which persists outside the dominant as alternative possibilities of being). Arturo Escobar (1995), puzzled by the monotonous discourses of 'modernity', 'globalisation' and the stubborn failures and devastations of development, argues that the task at hand is not only to critique and deconstruct development as a regime of representation – which 'has been linked to the economy of production and desire, but also of closure, difference, and violence' (Escobar, 1995: 214) – but also to work towards a new, plural, political ecology of knowledge, with a 'strategic move away from conventional Western modes of knowing in general in order to make room for other types of knowledge and experience' (Escobar, 1995: 216). The claim to knowledge that insists on a single and incontestable 'reality' is itself an exercise of power and an attempt to re-inscribe power by suppressing other possible knowledges. For Escobar (Escobar, 1995: xxxiii), a 'pluriverse' names a new imagined space marked by a plurality of knowledges, in which:

> pluriversal studies would ... discover the forms adopted by the multiple worlds that make up the pluriverse, without trying to reduce them to manifestations of known principles. Pluriversal studies will focus on those processes that can no longer be easily accommodated in the epistemic table of the modern social sciences. This is why pluriversal studies cannot be defined in opposition to globalization studies, nor as its complement, but needs to be outlined

as an altogether different intellectual and political project. No single notion of the world, the human, civilization, the future, or even the natural can fully occupy the space of pluriversal studies.

For Escobar, there is a critical distance between the monological certainty of modernity's project (to make everywhere the same because the founding European template is the goal for all to aspire to) and the pluriverse, made up of multiple points of view, models of knowing and ways of seeing and speaking. This concern with plurality is echoed in the call by De Sousa Santos to work with the multiplicity and variety of social practices, offering another important challenge for policy studies:

> Translation is the procedure that allows for mutual intelligibility among the experiences of the world, both available and possible, as revealed by the sociology of absences and the sociology of emergences, without jeopardizing their identity and autonomy, without, in other words, reducing them to homogeneous entities. (De Sousa Santos, 2005: 16)

We return to the question of 'emergences' in Chapter Seven, but, here, we can see the persistent tension between the threat of domination (through homogenisation) and the possibility of mutuality – exchanges (in translation) between ways of knowing, thinking and being. This analytic project – grounded in ideas of plurality and multiplicity – goes beyond the historical or even contemporary analysis of how particular translations have functioned. It points to the need to dwell in the translation process itself in order to enable *active* choices about how different policies might be effectively translated – choices that are attentive to the political and ethical issues at stake in translation. The idea of 'beyond' points to a particular temporality – invoking a sociology, in De Sousa Santos's terms, of 'emergences', or a sociology of the 'not-yet'. Such a sociology takes not what exists as its object, but rather the possibilities of what might be that are at stake in the present. In seeking to make choices about the multiple possible policy translations that would bring into being alternate policy assemblages we need an analytics of what might be. As De Sousa Santos (2004: 24) puts it:

> The concept that rules the sociology of emergences is the concept of 'Not Yet', [a] more complex category because

it expresses what exists as mere tendency, a movement that is latent in the very process of manifesting itself. The Not Yet is the way in which the future is inscribed in the present. It is not an indeterminate or infinite future, rather a concrete possibility and a capacity that neither exist in a vacuum nor are completely predetermined. Indeed, they actively re-determine all they touch, thus questioning the determinations that exist at a given moment.

This is the sociology of the beyond – beyond the now, beyond the normalised, naturalised and taken for granted, beyond, in the case of policy studies, a narrow formulation of how to govern or manage public services, welfare provision or populations. But what is beyond? Is participation merely another governmental technology to incorporate 'ordinary people' into the logics of being governed? Is giving choice to citizen-customers merely another enrolment into being 'responsible' (Brown and Baker, 2012)? Our concern here is always with the double potential of translation in studying policy. This means being attentive to the ways in which policies – as they move – may imagine and inscribe positions, hierarchies, relations of domination and subordination, and forms of power and authority. Policies do so even – or perhaps especially – when they come to speak in neutral, technical or administrative vocabularies. However, we also insist on the importance of distinguishing between ambitions and outcomes: depoliticising tactics are vulnerable to re-politicising practices and claims; ordinary people can 'turn nasty' rather than behaving responsibly; and contradictions may be suppressed but rarely go away. If we are to take translation as a sensitising tool to direct attention to the multiple, the plural, the contradictory and the awkward in the policy process, then we need to see 'unintended consequences', 'unforeseen scenarios' and 'unanticipated reactions' not as unfortunate by-products, but rather as systematic features and likely consequences of policymaking in its conventional form. This, we think, is a necessary analytic commitment to a double orientation to the movements of policy and power: to recognise plans and projects, but to be attentive to their interruptions, disjunctions and failures.

This attention to the possible uncertainties and contestations of policy in translation emphasises a politics of translation that departs from the notion that translation is a simple matter of communication and transfer in a singular epistemological and ontological world. The political character of translation is important because both the relational and the multiple dimensions of translation imply unequal and uneven relations and negotiations as policies move. Translation, then, is always a political act that works across different cultures and unequal, always negotiated, relationships (Palmary, 2011). As we noted earlier, for Pratt, contact zones form the settings in which asymmetrical relations (difference structured by power) are played out – with an emphasis on the improvisational and interactive dynamics of such encounters:

> contact zone is an attempt to invoke the spatial and temporary co-presence of subjects previously separated by geographical and historical disjunctures, and whose trajectories now intersect. By using the term 'contact', I aim to foreground the interactive, improvisational dimensions of colonial encounters so easily ignored or suppressed by diffusionist accounts of conquest and domination. (Pratt, 1992: 7)

For us, this emphasis on the interactive and improvisational character is profoundly important. Pratt combines our concern to make visible the structured inequalities of power between places and people with an attention to how things work out (unpredictably) in practice. Knowing the inequalities that structure the 'contact zone' is vital (these are not spaces of free and equal exchange), but that knowledge does not allow us to predict the outcomes. In a similar vein, Apter captures relationality and sites of translation as 'translation zones'. She argues that:

> [i]n fastening on the term 'zone' as a theoretical mainstay, the intention has been a broad intellectual topography that is neither the property of a single nation, nor an amorphous condition associated with postnationalism, but rather a zone of critical engagement that connects the 'l' and the 'n' of transLation and transNation. (Apter, 2006: 5)

Attention to political dimensions and dynamics also implies understanding processes of both translation and non-translation, that is, the production of voices as well as silences (Tymoczko, 2006a). The attention to the political also implies the interrogation of what Tymoczko (2006a: 447) calls the epistemic dimension of translation, that is, how translation not merely reflects existing knowledge, but rather is a form of knowledge production itself, where translation is a text about text, a form of 'metatext'. Translation is also political as it is 'a significant medium of subject re-formulation and political change' (Apter, 2006: 6), or, as Tymoczko (2006a: 459) reminds us, 'translation has a potentially radical and activist edge, that is driven by ethical and ideological concerns, that it participates in shaping societies, nations, and global culture in primary and central ways. Translation can change the world.'

Rada Iveković (2009: 52) has explicitly stressed the importance of translation within a 'new political economy' concerned with identities as, themselves, a translation of 'the without into the within'. For Iveković (2002), translation as 'a whole field of degrees, nuances, divergences, a range of (im)possibilities of traversals of meaning ... represents a kind of "opening up of meaning" without "the promise of exhaustiveness"'. Her argument that 'what is to be translated is not texts, but contexts' (Iveković, 2002) opens the study of hegemonic practices as a set of attempts to maintain 'the codes of exclusive translation', a series of more or less unsuccessful attempts to eliminate alternative translations. Translation is, in this sense, 'the act of differing without there being a definite origin or a definitive culmination' (Iveković, 2002). Politically, a focus on translation opens up 'a way to revisit the question of citizenship and of political subjectivity *beyond the European metaphysics of the subject* and beyond reductive political economy' (Iveković, 2008, emphasis in original). In a sense, she suggests that '[t]ranslating means being/putting in transition: transition processes (post-socialist; post-colonial; post-war; postpartition; post-dictatorial; post master-narratives; globalization etc) are processes of translating political programmes, institutions, cultural narratives, economic and juridical systems, practices' (Iveković, 2009: 49). Like languages, 'political agendas or forms ... intersect, host and transmit each other' (Iveković, 2009: 50). Ultimately, '[t]ranslating guarantees a certain social and political fluidity and flexibility, while the lack of translating willingness usually signifies some reserve of possible violence' (Iveković, 2009: 51).

In such ways, attention to translation expands the possibilities of what might be studied and how it might be studied. The lens of translation draws attention to the 'colonial' work of capturing, ordering and disciplining, while also making visible the incompleteness of colonial visions. Translation points us to the 'other voices': other ways of thinking, acting and being that persist and sometimes interrupt the dominant. The idea of translation also points to the dynamics of social and political relationships and the politics and ethics of engagement – an issue to which we will return later.

Policy as translation

Translation, then, is never neutral: some terms are translated, and some are not; some meanings are inscribed, while others are silenced. Policy translation, operating as it does on the borders between different epistemic territories, is caught up in this endless struggle between uniformity and multiplicity. On the one hand, we have translation as an act of oppression, where dominant ideas are translated across the border into the language and territory of the subaltern, bringing epistemic violence in its wake. On the other hand, we have translation as resistance, a space where the dominant loses control over the meaning-making process, and where talking back is possible. To put it differently, even as translation inscribes a process of erasure as meanings are untranslated or are made invisible, so the possibility of a critical difference between what is and what might be opens up. We do not see these alternate conceptions of translation as competing. Rather, we understand both tendencies as being in play. We argue that, typically, unreflexive translation of a 'monocultural' policy can lead to social rupture through the expansion of 'modernist' policy practices. At the same time, we see the creative and interpretive dimensions of translation to be able to be called into play in the service of making visible and contestable alternative policy creations and, with them, the possibility of transfigurative social practices.

A translation perspective, then, treats policy translation as a process of *potential* struggle. The idea of 'policy as translation' questions, as we addressed in Chapter One, the concept of 'policy transfer' as a linear process of policy diffusion or transplantation, challenging assumptions of an objectified or commodified knowledge 'extrapolated from its context' (Yanow, 2004: 15). Indeed, a sociology of translation provides a way of exploring 'the interrelation of discourse and agency' (Newton, 1996: 731) since translation requires translators, acting within 'actor networks' of humans and non-humans (actants) (cf Latour, 1987). 'Translation' is a crucial part of an anthropology of policy that emphasises the 'messiness and complexity of policy processes' (Shore and Wright, 2011: 8), seen as a set of imaginaries or narratives 'moving through time and space' non-linearly, with attempts to embed policies as authoritative, normative, forms (enacting the claim that 'There Is No Alternative'), opening up new spaces of contestation ('there is a crack in everything, that's how the light gets in').[1] The attempt to render policies

---

[1]   Lyric taken from the Leonard Cohen song 'Anthem' from the album 'The Future' (1992).

as universal through the 're-transcribing' (Venn, 2006: 82) of socio-economic, administrative, bureaucratic and political practices, usually viewed in terms of a transnationalising, even globalising, 'neoliberal' discourse, has limits to its logic, tending to produce 'hybrids, paradoxes, tensions and incompatibilities' (Clarke, 2004: 94). Along with Larner and Laurie (2010: 225), we would argue for the need to open up new lines of research that can capture the complexities of 'multiple actors, multiple geographies and multiple translations involved in the processes of policy transfer'. While policies exist within 'domains of meaning' (Shore and Wright, 2011: 1), the study of the creation of 'new alignments' or 'new social and semantic terrains', involving what Shore and Wright (2011: 2) call 'redomaining', is also crucial.

Policy 'transfer' may take place in ways that are insensitive to context, and create social ruptures in the process. Yet, translation processes are always anchored in local contexts, suggesting that translation always holds the possibility of the specific rather than the general, diversity rather than uniformity, and divergence rather than convergence (Johnson and Hagstrom, 2005). As a result, 'the translation process often should be regarded as a battle between competing interpretations vying for supremacy' (Johnson and Hagstrom, 2005: 375). In that sense, translation is always a political project, with a need for a critical research agenda to uncover what gets transferred, who gets to translate and who the losers and winners are within the travels of a particular policy. In this sense, translation is a process where some things are made visible while others are hidden or erased, and a critical policy research agenda must seek to trace these processes.

Translation calls attention to the mobility of 'policy', where, as Cowen (2009) puts it, as policies, concepts, institutions or actors move, they morph – changing their shape or character. This morphing is inevitably linked to change, slippage, breaks in the smooth reproduction of knowledge and new associations among the actors involved in such processes. It is a fundamental break with a linear, chronological and rationalistic understanding of the policy process. Policies travel and move; however, the immense mobility and motion that has been associated with globalisation and global connections are far from smooth. The mobility of policy is not free-flowing, but rather, as Lowenhaupt Tsing (2007: 4) argues, geared by friction, which, for her, entails the 'awkward, unequal, unstable and creative qualities of interconnection across difference'.

Translation also changes how we might think about the contexts that are at stake in the movement of policies in at least two ways. Contexts are neither the 'background' from which policies emerge nor the receptacles into which policies arrive. Rather, contexts *animate* translation in different ways (Clarke, 2013). Contexts are productive of associations and articulations: they generate spatial and scalar imaginaries of how policies *should* travel (coded in ideas of learning, exchange, sharing, etc). Contexts are active (if selective) recruiters, enrollers and translators of policy, rather than mere passive recipients. Translation implies thinking again about the conventional spatial and scalar fields across which policy is understood to move, perhaps towards a more 'folded' understanding of proximities and distances (Allen, 2011), as well as time and temporalities (Adam, 2005 [1998]). Finally, contexts involve fields of relationships that are themselves realigned in the process of translation – as established orderings of power, knowledge and position are reworked.

Assembling and reassembling policy

Our interest in this particularising and contextualising understanding of agency has led us to the concept of 'assemblage', which emerges from the work of Deleuze and Guattari (1988) and has been widely taken up (albeit in widely differing usages – or translations). It has proven productive because it provides a way of emphasising aspects of multiplicity and movement. As Venn (2006: 107) argues, it draws attention to 'complex becoming and multiple determinations ... sensitive to time and temporality in the emergence and mutation' of phenomena. Equally, the sense that assemblages involve 'ensembles of heterogeneous elements' (Ong and Collier, 2005: 5) is a critical part of its analytical value as a way of underlining the different things that might be brought together to enable particular courses of thinking and action. For us, it is important to explore the ways in which specific assemblages may, or may not, become stabilised or made to cohere into particular 'regimes', but which should never be reified as 'final or stable states' (Marcus and Saka, 2006: 106). Such an analytic orientation emphasises the contingent character of any particular assemblage (requiring attention to what makes it hold together). Analysts using assemblage as a key concept have also stressed the conjunctural contingency of particular assemblages as both constructing and acting on 'problem spaces' (Ong and Collier, 2005: 4). For example, Palsson and Rabinow (2005: 93) talk about the 'specific historical, political and economic conjuncture in which an issue becomes a problem'. The concept of 'problem-space' has also been developed by David Scott, who argues that:

A 'problem-space', in my usage is meant first of all to demarcate a discursive context, a context of language. But it is more than a cognitively intelligible arrangement of concepts, ideas, images, meanings and so on – though it is certainly this. It is a context of argument and therefore one of intervention. A problem-space, in other words, is an ensemble of questions and answers around which a horizon of identifiable stakes (conceptual as well as political-ideological stakes) hangs. That is to say, what defines this discursive context are not only the particular problems that get posed as problems as such (the problem of 'race', say), but the particular questions that seem worth asking and the kinds of answers that seem worth having.... Problem-spaces alter historically because problems are not timeless and do not have everlasting shapes. In new historical conditions old questions may lose their salience, their bite and so lead the range of old answers that once attached to them to appear lifeless, quaint, not so much wrong as irrelevant. (Scott, 2004: 4)

It will be clear that Scott's interest in the framing of discursive-linguistic spaces of dispute and argument is relevant for our interest in the possibilities of translation, highlighting as he does both 'argument' and 'intervention'. Here, we want to underline Scott's insistence on their temporal specificity: policy assemblages are elaborated, developed and deployed in specific times and places as 'solutions' to the defined problems of those times and spaces (even when they may be represented as timeless and universal). Assemblage is a productive concept for interrupting such transcendent or universalising claims – both in the languages of policy and politics and in some of the analytic framings of travelling policy (eg the archetypes of globalisation or neoliberalism, from which all things flow).

As we noted in the first section of this chapter, assemblage has been a key concept in ANT and the related practice of STS as a way of marking the organisation of (heterogeneous) elements in a network or configuration, in which it is the assemblage that makes each element effective or active. One advantage of the concept (cf Chapter Four, this volume) is that by underlining the contingent character of apparent unities, it is possible to make more visible the ways in which *things* and people are put together, thus providing leverage that an over-attention to the words (language, discourse, etc) may miss. Assemblage draws attention to the ways in which meanings are materialised in practices, in settings, in the ordering of things and in how such conditions shape the possibilities of thinking and acting. As usual, we find ourselves walking a delicate line: wanting both to rescue the significance of language and meaning (eg via translation) and to insist on the importance of how, when and where the words are materialised and put into practice.

A concern with practice – the work or labour of making things happen – is also important to our understanding and use of assemblage. Newman and Clarke (2009: 9) argue that assemblage points to:

> the idea that the institutionalisation of specific projects involves the work of assembling diverse elements into an apparently coherent form. In the context of studying publicness, the idea of assemblage points to the ways in which policies, personnel, places, practices, technologies, images, architectures of governance and resources are brought together and combined. Assemblage does two particular things for us.... It draws attention to the work of construction (and the difficulties of making ill-suited elements fit together as though they are coherent). And it makes visible the (variable) fragility of assemblages – that which has been assembled can more or less easily come apart, or be dismantled. In a period where we have seen the vulnerability and mutability of what appeared to be solidly established institutionalisations of publicness, the idea of assemblage allows us a way of working with this double dynamic of solidity and fragility.

Latour and Deleuze/Guattari have focused less on 'mundane states' and more on radical transformations, the struggle of new paradigms to emerge and, above all, on controversies that question the stability of 'political', 'technical', 'scientific', 'cultural' or 'ethical' domains. Any phenomena that have 'a distinctive capacity for ... abstractability and movement' tend to produce equally distinct 'lines of mutation' (Ong and Collier, 2005: 11, 18) through the de- and re-articulation of elements. This suggests a strong preference for studying specific spatial-temporal moments or 'conjunctures', produced by the coming together, often in 'perverse confluences' (Dagnino, 2006), of diverse trajectories, trends, pressures and forces (Clarke, 2010a). As McFarlane and Anderson (2011) assert, an important aspect of assemblage is the ways in which it captures the radical uncertainty, non-linearity and contingency of change. Too often, in critical policy studies, there is an emphasis on what Raymond Williams (1977) termed 'the epochal', reducing the complexity of a historical moment to the 'rolling out' of a dominant tendency in which 'the usual suspects' play the leading role, be they 'globalisation, neo-liberalism, modernity (or post-modernity), post-Fordism, or the needs/interests of capital' (Clarke, 2004: 3). Such forces seem to re-emerge endlessly and to repeat the same scripts with the same conclusions.

In contrast, both translation and assemblage point to the danger of deciding, too early, that we know what something means, and of making decisions that provide closure to the research process. Such closures – whether theoretical or methodological – limit the possibilities of a continued dialogue across and between research sites, ideas and participants. This cautions against attempting to develop 'a truly global understanding' (Midgley, 2004: 217) of policies that rests upon decontextualising fundamentally contextualised (Northern and Western) concepts such as social welfare, social policy and the welfare state. Attention to the particularities of time and space – and how they are being configured in a specific set of policies, politics and practices – seems more important to us.

Seeing moving policies as a folded set of transnational processes working through practices of translation in multiple, emergent and entangled assemblages might offer new ways of understanding knowledge, power and politics. Policy is always a multi-actored process: for example, social policies involve, at least, policy élites, planners and managers, welfare providers, community organisations and welfare recipients (see Kingfisher, 2013). Such multi-actored and multi-sited processes are hard to contain within the linear narratives of 'path-dependent regimes' and 'policy transfer'. The gap between research on 'how policies reconfigure the lived realities of the people they affect' (Lendvai and Bainton, 2011) and a classificatory literature on 'regime typologies' is rather large, and not easily bridged. Ideas of assemblages and translation offer a way into seeing how the production and reproduction of knowledge enables certain agendas to emerge while others are actively silenced. The subject positions to which Kingfisher refers are themselves complex constructions, both enabling and silencing, constraining and empowering, in highly selective, but always deeply conjunctural, ways.

Towards a vocabulary of policy in motion

In our attempt to think differently about policy and its movement, ideas of translation and assemblage provide analytic resources that have proven valuable in many ways. Translation and assemblage offer ways to think through the process of how power and policy operate within the dynamics of societal transformation. In exploring translation and assemblage in this way, we have begun to accumulate a range of conceptual and analytic resources to build a vocabulary that provides us with ways of 'coming to terms' with the challenges of studying policy as it moves. These terms – borrowed from different sources and orientations – have developed as a necessary shared vocabulary between us. We have tried to find – and appropriate – analytic tools that were sensitive to the articulations of power, policy and practice, that were productive of alternative ways of doing policy studies, and that might inform the possibilities of doing policy 'otherwise'. Such a vocabulary is necessarily provisional and unfinished – it is both shaped by the places and times of its construction and is open to being remade and reassembled in the process of being put to work – as the following chapters will show. Each of the substantive chapters draws from this shared commitment, but inevitably emphasises different, if overlapping, aspects of this vocabulary. We view the tentativeness of this accumulated but unfinished vocabulary and the diverse ways that it is taken up in the different chapters as part of a critical policy analysis that is capable of exploring the multiple contexts, sites and scales of complex and contested global processes. This vocabulary itself reflects our view of 'bending and blending' as intrinsic features of the process of policy movement – and is built through the same principles. We have borrowed, bent and blended conceptual resources from a diverse range of analytical approaches because each of them offers a particular kind of analytic grip, while they together constitute a rich repertoire for conducting policy studies. However, let us emphasise, again, that we view them as a vocabulary or repertoire rather than seeing them as a complete and coherent theory of policy in motion. In the following subsections, we offer sketches of clusters of words/concepts that we have found particularly useful, and try to indicate something of where we have borrowed them from, and why.

Articulation, contradiction and paradox

It should, we hope, be obvious by now that our commitment to thinking contextually means refusing monocausal and linear accounts of agency and action. Examining the productive effect of how multiple, plural or heterogeneous contexts combine to create new conditions of possibility offers a different way of approaching social explanation. Paradoxically, thinking about action in this way requires us to think about how any specific action is always both *overdetermined and underdetermined*. It is overdetermined in the sense that the French Marxist philosopher Louis Althusser (2005 [1965]) developed in his famous essay on *Contradiction and overdetermination*, in which he argued that social phenomena – in that case, revolutionary moments – are the product of multiple and combined forces and cannot be understood outside of their heterogeneous conditions of existence. In thinking of forms of social action, such as policy in motion, we also need to be attentive to their overdetermination – examining the coming together of many contexts whose combinations generate the conditions of possibility for particular agents (individual and collective) to perform specific actions. However, agency is simultaneously *underdetermined* in the sense that how it is enacted/performed cannot be predicted in advance. Even when we accumulate knowledge of many contexts, we will never be able to explain fully or predict the specific outcome. The *combination* of multiple contexts (and their potentially incoherent or contradictory logics of action) means that particular forms of agency always contain the possibility of acting differently, of failing to follow the script or of refusing the rules (see next section).

This has an important connection with our continuing interest in the analysis of *articulation*: the mobilisation of discursive and political connections into dominant formations and blocs (and thus the production of subordinated discourses and groups). For us, this concern with articulation as a set of political and discursive practices has been an enduring contribution of cultural studies to the analysis of contemporary processes and projects (see, eg, Hall et al, 1978; Hall, 1986; Slack, 1996). The concept of articulation denotes the political-cultural work that has to be done to mobilise both meanings and people in order to realise a project (and the work of disarticulation and demobilisation that is necessary to shut out other projects). As a result, we are particularly concerned to explore the attempted closures around dominant political-cultural logics of rule, and the attempted co-options of such logics for other purposes (not necessarily 'resistance', but, rather, other purposes that inflect, twist or borrow from dominant logics). We stress 'attempted' closures and co-options because, as we have argued earlier, it is important not to assume that projects, plans or strategies necessarily achieve the results they seek. Equally, being attentive to 'other purposes' is important because the fields of meanings and mobilisations in which policy moves form sites in which emergent identifications, affinities and alliances, and the means through which they are expressed and enacted (sites, practices, spaces, cultural representations and institutional norms), are projected, contested and – sometimes temporarily – institutionalised (Newman and Clarke, 2009: 8–9).

An analysis of attempted processes of closure leads us to an interest in paradox and contradiction. Paradoxes are relatively simple juxtapositions of things in which we are invited to contemplate two opposed (or difficult to reconcile) thoughts, possibilities, trends and so on. Being able to observe such different possibilities is helpful as a point of entry or as analytical leverage in studying policy in motion. Paradoxes, we think, are different from contradictions, where there is an internal relationship between the one thing and its opposite, and – in dialectical materialism – the contradiction is dynamic, driving historical change. For example, the relationship between the capitalist and labouring classes is both antagonistic (a matter of opposed interests) and contradictory because capital is always driven to socialise the means of production (including labour) even as it extracts and appropriates surplus value in private form. The contradiction is productive of historical development (and not just of class struggle). The historical development includes the emergence of more contradictions as capital seeks to create new possibilities for capital accumulation and also seeks to stabilise the social and political conditions in which such accumulation can take place (including attempting to contain the contradictions and antagonisms that it generates). Such attempted stabilisations have been variously described as spatio-temporal fixes (Jessop, 2002), as 'settlements' (Hughes and Lewis, 1998) and as hegemonic moments (Hall et al, 1978). What all of them share is understanding of the temporary quality of such fixes, settlements and moments, and their tendency to come apart under the pressures that they attempt to contain.

Performance and performativity

We turn now to a rather different register: that of performance and performativity. Bringing the performative dimension of policy into view allows us to focus on sites of practice – of acting, speaking, feeling and doing – and on 'the repetition or citation of a prior, authoritative set of practices' (Butler, 1993: 227) by diverse actors. Policy actors have to manage 'backstage' as much as 'front-stage' performances (Goffman, 1959), in a kind of 'expanded theatricality'. Going beyond Goffmann's rather artificial separation of the performer from the performance, what Butler terms 'iterations', mainly speech acts in her terms, but used more widely here, actually bring certain categorisations into being. Hence, Butler suggests, the focus on performance comes out of dramaturgical sociology in general and, in particular, Goffman's view of social life as composed of a multiplicity of performances by actors. Performativity leads directly to Judith Butler, and it is her reading that we are taking here: that even though there may be 'scripts', actors do not perform them consistently – there is slippage, forgetfulness, improvisation (Mangham, 1978) and innovation. However, the performative derives from Lyotard's (1984) observations about the rise of the 'performative principle' in contemporary society – a principle which demands that value must be demonstrated and validated through visible, measurable, auditable performance. Lyotard's analysis finds many echoes in the realm of policy, not least in contemporary demands for transparency and accountability (eg Cowen, 1996; Ball, 2003).

The performative works with a notion of 'lived and embodied conception of "doing" rather than interpreting or implementing policy' (Newman, 2013b: 527). As policy worlds are performed, policies 'are mediated and translated, refused, inhabited or reworked by those they summoned' (Newman, 2013b: 2013: 527). The performative also implies the presence of simultaneous dynamics of creativity and constraint, activism and incorporation, and retreat and proliferation. It is also a world with 'multiple spaces of power and resistance with which actors engage – pragmatically as well as politically' (Newman, 2013b: 527). The performative is an important analytic framing for us because it reconfigures some of the taken-for-granted notions in which policies are often framed in more orthodox accounts, such as intentionality, rationality, consequentialism and directionality. The performative also cuts across 'illusions of order' and an assumed consensus about policies, what might be termed 'the consensus on consensus'. The 'consensus on consensus' names a particular moment when all (or most) participants in a scene (from national politics to a policy-drafting meeting) believe that all (or most) of the others are in agreement. It is a moment that is produced by various devices (from naming 'public opinion' as if a singular and coherent public exists, to the discursive use of a presumptive 'we' to identify an imagined collective subject). It is also a moment whose effects are often profoundly silencing because of the difficulties of challenging such a presumed consensus. It is precisely this consensus on consensus that moves policies into the taken-for-granted and silenced spaces and draws the focus away from potential dissent and disorder.

The performative also frames the possibilities of agency found within the slippage of particular enactments. As a result, it is preferable to treat agency as something that always takes particular forms. It is worth considering what it might mean to think about agents and forms of agency contextually. This argument assumes that, following

Michel Foucault's work, we can no longer operate with a notion of 'agency in general'. On the contrary, Foucault was devoted to revealing the particular forms in which subjects, subjectivity and agency were constituted. Such particular forms, in our terms, always arise contextually – in specific points of time/space. In Foucault's work, we always encounter the ways in which specific forms, relationships and practices of power are being produced: agents are always empowered to do something in particular. This represents a radical, and irrecoverable, break with sociological notions of agency as a generic property of human beings, which is often in play during debates about structure versus agency (see also Clarke, 2013).

This argument about agency might be developed further in at least two other directions. On the one hand, the view of specific forms of agency is developed in ANT approaches, particularly around the concept of assemblage or *agencement* (for a discussion of the translation of '*agencement*' as 'assemblage', see Phillips, 2006). We turn to these issues in the following section. On the other hand, this concern with the contextual particularity of agency also appears in one strand in the sociology of work, echoed in some aspects of policy studies (notably, that which focuses on 'street-level bureaucrats'; see Lipsky, 1982), which is interested in 'unreliable' agents, workers who: do not work as they should; exhibit unexpected or unpredictable forms of agency; or perform acts of resistance, recalcitrance or subversion (see, eg, Collinson and Ackroyd, 2005). We are interested in whether this 'unreliability' of agency can also be understood by treating the agent as a point of condensation of multiple, heterogeneous and possibly contradictory forces. Particular locations condense different forces, pressures and logics, whose combination might induce specific forms of indeterminacy that require agents to resolve the resulting tensions, paradoxes and contradictions or to perform the work of translation between the logics. To put it another way, such indeterminacy might appear in locations where there are too many 'scripts' to be followed, such that actors/agents have to 'bend and blend' and improvise.

Emotion, affect and 'structures of feeling'

> It is that we are concerned with meanings and values as they are actively lived and felt, and the relations. We are talking about characteristic elements of impulse, restraint, and tone; specifically affective elements of consciousness and relationships: not feeling against thought, but thought as felt and feeling as thought: practical consciousness of

a present kind, in a living and inter-relating continuity.
(Williams, 1977: 132)

Policy studies may have moved – in part – from rational models to interpretive approaches – a development in which there is a strong focus on speech, language and texts – but it has yet to make a move into fully confronting issues of emotion, affect and feeling, despite some work around emotion and welfare organisations (eg Hoggett, 2000; Froggett, 2002). This cluster of terms marks out a really important set of issues for policy studies. It does not seem to us that it is possible to think about the forms of relationship, power and action that we are engaged in without attending to their affective/emotional aspects. There are troubling questions about how we can engage with these without recourse to psychoanalytic reductionism and, above all, without lapsing into a psychologistic or biologistic essentialism, as in Massumi's (2002) idea of affect as somehow 'pre-social' (but see Wetherell, 2012).

If we take the 'realm of affect' as a realm of 'bodily intensities; emotions, feelings and passions' (Gould, 2009: 3), then feeling and emotion are fundamental to policy, not, as often argued, as interfering with reason and deliberation, but as constitutive of policy practice per se. For Gould (2009: 17), 'emotion ... is ... a crucial means by which human beings come to know and understand themselves and their contexts'. Emotions are those parts of affect that get 'actualized or concretized in the flow of living', such that 'emotion is structured by social convention, by culture' (Gould, 2009: 20). The relation between the two is not temporal, but is, perhaps, akin to a translation. Gould (2009: 22) prefers the concept of 'sentiment' to feelings, to 'connote bodily, felt experiences'. The conceptual architecture is further complicated by her use of the concept of 'emotional habitus' to encompass both affect and emotions, providing members of a group with 'an emotional disposition ... a sense of what and how to feel ... schemas about what feelings are and what they mean' (Gould, 2009: 22).

Recent interest in the affective reprises Raymond Williams' insistence that culture included historically specific 'structures of feeling'. It is a phrase that Williams returned to frequently, in part, to talk about the emergent, not yet fixed, character of experience (as opposed to fixed or reified 'world views' or 'ideologies'): 'For structures of feeling can be defined as social experiences *in solution*, as distinct from other social semantic formations which have been *precipitated* and are more evidently and more immediately available' (Williams, 1977: 133–4, emphasis in original).

We think that it is difficult for critical policy studies to proceed productively without paying attention to the dimensions of emotion, affect and feeling because of the ways in which they shape and animate the fields of policy and practice. However, we are conscious of two dangers associated with trying to ride the 'affective turn'. The first is that the emotion–affect–feeling cluster displaces other concerns and concepts, despite arriving as a supplement that adds to and enriches the analytic repertoire. Some never make it back from the affective turn. Our hope is that our somewhat promiscuous approach to thinking analytically can weave the attention to emotion/affect/feeling into our repertoire, rather than succumbing to them. However, there is a reverse danger, identified by Newman (2012), who argues that such terms cannot simply be appropriated to conventional ways of theorising politics, policy and practice. In particular, she argues that conventional conceptions of rational choice-makers and deliberative subjects may borrow the languages of emotion and affect without them making any difference to how actors, processes and relationships are conceived. In what follows, we try to walk the fine line between these two dangers.

Moving policy: translation, assemblage and beyond?

Mainstream policy transfer literature has relied heavily on new institutionalism, which has emphasised institutional isomorphism and homogenisation as a result of diffusion (for a critical overview, see Beckert, 2010). What we might call the 'illusion of similarities' had an important role in driving institutionalism in assuming, discovering and reinforcing isomorphism. As Towns (2012) points out, there is also a widespread belief among mainstream International Relations scholars that policy diffusion rests upon 'norms', yet norms are undefined and unexplored, both conceptually and empirically. In such stuttering moments, the possibility of studying policy through the lens of translation becomes more significant. Models of policy transfer rest on such assumptions about spaces and places (usually political communities, understood as nation-states), on assumptions about the balance of agency (agentic transmitters and passive recipients), and on assumptions about the transportability and transferability of knowledge across borders, boundaries and languages. So, a critical point here is the unpacking of the assumed singularity of underlying norms, content, effect and work of moving policies. In contrast to these assumed singularities, a view through translation implies a multiplicity of policies: as policy travels across languages, sites and scales, it is produced, assembled, enacted and populated differently.

Translation implies multiple voices, plural trajectories and perhaps the possibility of making policies 'otherwise'. As Escobar (2010) argues, our understanding of the world of globalisation is hugely monolingual and unilinear: singular terminologies collapse complex social realities into a uniform conceptual and academic framework. 'The modern ontology of One World' (Escobar, 2011), the assumptions of a universal, 'free-flowing' space, has crowded out more relational, plural understandings: the 'pluriverse' in his terms. Literatures on policy transfer, globalisation and global policy diffusion show similar traces to that of Escobar's critique: a discourse of globalisation as a unified global space, fully economised and delocalised, which constructs particular forms of knowledge while disregarding, disposing of and silencing other forms of knowledge. For many, then, 'development otherwise', or 'International political economy otherwise' (Rojas, 2007), is a methodology that is able to open up the discussion towards more plural understandings, a point to which we return in Chapter Seven.

In a fascinating article, Ingrid Palmary (2011) delves into the politics of meaning that inevitably surrounds translation. In her feminist research into gendered violence in times of conflict, she interviewed women living in South Africa who had been displaced through armed conflict from Rwanda and the Democratic Republic of Congo. Much of the interviewing was done in French by a professionally trained female interpreter (from the Côte d'Ivoire) while some interviews with women who spoke Kinyarwanda (but not French or English) were done by an untrained man from Rwanda. Palmary found that, in contrast to the French interviews, which provided a polished, 'transparent' translated text, paradoxically, the Kinyarwandan interpreter, precisely in not normalising any 'correct' translation for Kinyarwandan words, not only made visible the range of possible meanings, thereby opening up a space for negotiation of that which was untranslatable, but also shone a light onto the limitations of her own linguistic repertoire for understanding the experiences and accounts of these women. It is precisely this moment, when translation transcends linguistic and methodological territories and becomes essentially epistemological and theoretical, that its counter-hegemonic possibilities are manifested.

Translation, in this sense, is not a one-way process. A translation can never be a replica, can never simply be a new context for an old policy; it is a new understanding of the world. As such, reflexive translation has the capacity to do much more than make us sensitive to the politics of policy transfer, offering a greater possibility of holding up a mirror to new critical possibilities of social change. It is this dialogue between the different possibilities of the world that is the true insight that a translation frame offers. For Palmary, the making visible of possible translations created a reflexive moment where the very categories of her research framework were brought into focus.

This reflexive mirroring brings issues around visibility and erasures into sharper perspective, and sheds important light on policy as a process of knowledge production and its internationalisation. In the context of global policy agendas, Widerberg's caution seems highly relevant. Reflecting on the unproblematic and widespread usage of the term 'gender', she writes:

> I saw, when rereading my Danish article, how influenced we Scandinavians have been by the debates and research in the US. Through the internationalization of knowledge and the dominance of the English language as its mediator, we have been made to share understandings to a higher degree than we have been made to share actual social arrangements. We might live in countries and cultures that are quite differently organized, but our intellectual tools are very much the same. (Widerberg, 1998: 135)

She takes translation further by arguing that:

> when we go deeper, we see that translating understandings of gender from one culture and language to another also implies eliminating certain concepts and contextual understandings expressed in the one language, and introducing instead, in the other language, concepts expressing other (contextual) understandings. 'Going international', wanting to participate and be understood in the international feminist debate, thus implies changing the voice as well as the story. However frustrating this issue may be when experienced in the process of translation, there are always insights to be gained, not least about the 'positioning' of understandings of gender. (Widerberg, 1998: 133)

Even as translation has been responsible for changing the voices and stories she is able to tell, insofar as other voices can be heard, the limits of dominant understandings of gender are also made visible. A similar idea has been expressed regarding the translation of some of Freire's central ideas from Portuguese into English:

[H]is language is loaded with his feelings, since he never provided a dichotomy between reason and emotion. Paulo was a radically coherent man: what he said contained what he felt and thought and this is not always easy to translate. There are emotions whose meaning can only be well perceived, understood and felt inside a certain culture.... I think it is difficult for translators who have only studied the Portuguese language, albeit accurately, to express Paulo in all his aesthetic and even cultural-ideological richness. (Nita Freire, quoted in Mayo, 2004: 9)

Policy transfer, in its structured directionality, cannot avoid consideration of an encounter between the dominant and the marginal – an encounter that is fundamentally political. Within this encounter lie enormous possibilities for the reproduction of inequalities, or, worse, for increased marginalisation, violence and abjection. At the same time, it may be helpful to consider the degree to which, in this encounter, 'global policy' might itself be transformed so as to provide genuine alternatives. As scholars and practitioners engaged in our own translation practices, we have the option to open up the spaces to make visible policy translation, as Palmary does. What we do with the voices that are talking back is the bigger challenge.

What follows

In this chapter, we have tried to establish the elements of an approach to viewing policy as translation. In the following four chapters, we try to put this way of thinking to work in relation to four more substantive issues, each drawn from our individual work. They indicate something of the range and potential possibilities of viewing policy as translation precisely because of their differences. Each chapter makes the translation perspective work in a particular way, addressing specific formations, contexts and assemblages. Their objects and sites of study – which might be crudely represented as: 'social and child protection reform' in the post-Yugoslav space; the 'new public management' in higher education in England; 'social inclusion' in Hungary and the EU; and 'education for all' in the Indian Himalayas – are both spatially and temporally diverse and provide the possibility for different conceptions of both 'policy' and 'movement'. Each chapter is individually authored but is marked by deliberate forms of interruption. Footnotes are used where the author wishes to digress from the main line of analysis and/or to establish a dialogue with herself/himself. Throughout the four chapters, the other non-authors 'talk back' on a number of occasions, marked by differently formatted, right-justified, texts. These interruptions may be digressions, points of disagreement or signals of possibilities that are considered by their writer to be important but that were not incorporated into the final version of the text. They are meant to resemble comments on a text in the way that a reader might scribble in the margins. The 'non-author' may be one or more of us. Our intention is to reveal more of the process of debate, discussion and dialogue and to break down, to an extent, the distinction between writing texts and reading texts.

Chapter Three (by Paul Stubbs) offers an auto-ethnographic reflection on social policy and childcare reform efforts in Bosnia-Herzegovina and South East Europe, conceived as complex, multiple, liminal and fluid spaces. Exploring reform in so-called semi-peripheries, the chapter examines the ways in which, in a crowded playground, flexible actors, including consultants, may generate, occupy and transform new and emergent policy spaces. Their activities produce and reproduce a range of ambivalent effects in a continuum between opposition and acceptance, and imitation and rejection, in-keeping with the idea of the region's 'semi-otherness'. A policy translation perspective goes beyond policy transfer's template of modernisation to explore the dynamic and contradictory nature of these processes. In tracing the nature of reform encounters, and exploring who is silenced and who is empowered to speak, the chapter explores the multiplication and reworking of diverse policy imaginaries between the universal and the particular, and between the political and the technical.

Chapter Four (by John Clarke) explores how a new language – managerialism – enabled the transformation of power and authority in universities. The processes of managerialisation are explored through the changing regime of English higher education, drawing on vignettes from practice and other case-study materials. At stake is how the internal architecture of power is remade to enable the 'right of managers to manage', while the language of managerialism simultaneously enables the translation of emergent external political objectives and programmes into the 'business' of the corporate and competitive university. The chapter takes up translation in a very specific sense: the capacity of a specific way of thinking and speaking within what appears to be a common language (English) to transform institutions, rework social relationships and remake forms of power and authority into new assemblages.

Chapter Five (by Noémi Lendvai) takes translation as a complex intersection between languages, policy agendas and policy actors in the context of the European Union's (EU) governance of social inclusion. The chapter considers the entanglement of the linguascapes of 'EU English', the 'techno-zone' of EU inclusion governance and the repertoires of Hungarian translations and policy responses within these complex policy spaces. Translation allows the conceptualisation of these dynamics not as policy transfers with an assumed epistemic modernism, where Europeanisation is seen as a modernisation project, but rather as operating within translation zones in which multiple speakers speak multiple languages, producing multiple regimes of inclusion. The chapter argues that the Hungarian translation of inclusion as 'togetherness', or 'closed up', are the result of the fiction of the language of EU inclusion policy, the fiction of the Hungarian translation and the fiction of policy texts produced in the process of 'deliberative governance'. As such, translation enables us to access spaces of contestations, resistances and sites of policy productions, capturing the complexities of travelling policies.

Chapter Six (by Dave Bainton) frames translation as a process of displacement and erasure, reassembling and silencing in the process of reconfiguring individual subjectivities and identities. The chapter considers how particular Westernised translations of 'education' in Ladakh, Northern India, are materialised as a complex assemblage. Critically, the analysis traces the reassemblage of the social, the familial and forms of livelihoods that are often subjected to processes of displacement and erasure. A translation perspective is utilised here to open up the potential alternative translations of education by looking at how indigenous ways of knowing might become articulated in less violent ways. Themes of narrative, landscape, sculpture and Buddhism suggest that there is a need to translate 'within the silences' that surround dominant translations of education – both in the sense that indigenous ways of knowing are typically silenced within modern education, and to draw attention to the limitations of 'wordy' ways of knowing.

In the final chapter, again written jointly, we turn our attention to some of the issues that emerge from treating policy as translation – the analytical, ethical and political challenges that confront us in trying to think and act 'otherwise'.

THREE

Performing reform in South East Europe: consultancy, translation and flexible agency

Paul Stubbs

An introduction

This chapter is born out of the ambivalence[1] I confess to feeling as a result of having undertaken a range of tasks covered by the term 'consultant' for a number of international organisations in South East Europe[2] and beyond since about 1997, reaching a peak in the early 2000s, mainly concerned with aspects of social welfare reform. It reflects on the limits of the 'consultancy' role, building on earlier works that, using different registers, explored the growing salience of consultancies in transnational social policymaking (Stubbs, 2002, 2003). I continue to argue that engaging in consultancy gave me access to material that, as a researcher, I was highly unlikely to be privy to,[3] and provided much-needed insights into the 'black box' of policy

---

[1] Ambivalence, as 'the simultaneous existence of contradictory feelings in relation to a single object', is both socially structured and operates 'at an unconscious level' (Gould, 2009: 12, 13). As an emotional reaction, it 'incites, shapes and is generated by practices of meaning-making' (Gould, 2009: 13).

[2] The term 'South East Europe' is used here as a broad, catch-all, geographical term to cover the successor states and territories of the former Yugoslavia, plus Albania, Bulgaria and Romania. Some definitions of South East Europe may include Turkey and/or Greece. Elsewhere, I have argued that regions are 'socially and politically constructed and subject to diverse and contested meanings ... contingent on social practices and social networks' (Solioz and Stubbs, 2012: 17). Any naming is, therefore, a political act, and the term 'South East Europe', while avoiding the orientalism of the term 'Balkans' or even 'Western Balkans' (cf Todorova, 2009), simultaneously denies the importance of the region's 'translational transnationalism' (Apter, 2001: 66) and complex histories of contestation and cooperation across shifting borders.

[3] A recent account of the making of the United Nations' (UN's) 'Social Protection Floors' initiative suggests that:

translation missing from more institutionalist accounts. Subsequently, my involvement, with others, in a critique of the very programmes that I had helped to put in place, however, merely served to compound ambivalence upon ambivalence.

This text revisits some of my consultancy experiences and examines them through a translation lens, suggesting that transnational reforms are always translated and never merely transferred or transplanted. The chapter reflects some of my current concerns with understanding reform attempts in the 'semi-periphery' of South East Europe as arenas of struggle, neocolonial 'contact zones', sites of diverse performances, on- and off-stage interactions, and improvisations marked by 'radically asymmetrical relations of power', containing elements 'ignored or suppressed by diffusionist accounts of conquest and domination' (Pratt, 1992: 7).

The chapter explores two broad sets of reform efforts in which I was involved. The first relates to a relatively minor role I had as a consultant on a United Nations Children's Fund (UNICEF)-led Regional Consultation on Child Care System Reform in South East Europe, culminating in a conference in the Bulgarian capital, Sofia, in 2007. Here, I use material first prepared, jointly, with Reima Ana Maglajlić, who was a consultant on the same programme (Stubbs and Maglajlić, 2012, 2013). The second relates to the UK Department for International Development's (DFID's) efforts in the early 2000s to reform social welfare systems in Bosnia–Herzegovina (B-H), discussed in a paper co-written with Noémi Lendvai (Lendvai and Stubbs, 2009b). The main body of the chapter, then, contains the two sets of empirical cases, described and developed from two very different vantage points.

On auto-ethnography

The phenomena being described, compared and analysed here occurred quite some time ago. Insights from consultancies that I was engaged in were gathered haphazardly and not primarily for the purposes of research. While engaged as a consultant, however, I continued to be,

---

If I became aware of anything about the problems of researching processes such as these it was that even being resident does not give the researcher insight into the myriad informal meetings, lunch-time and toilet conversations, telephone calls and email exchanges that take place and *do* influence events and policy content. *Researchers are impossibly outside the loops and those in the loops do not see from inside one loop other equally significant loops and rarely have the time to reflect on their own role.* (Deacon, 2013: 6, emphasis in original)

perhaps first and foremost, a researcher, so that a certain critical research sensibility was always present. The use of consultancy experiences and their translation into research raises ethical issues, many of which I continue to struggle with.[4] The chapter is an attempt to remember and compile a coherent and plausible story based on uneven participations, scattered observations, fragmentary interview material and a rereading of a number of documents. The method used is, broadly, ethnographic in the sense of being 'a layered and evocative ... presentation of located aspects of the human condition *from the inside*' (Willis and Trondman, 2000: 7, emphasis in original).[5] As a form of 'hunting and gathering' (Gould, 2004a), an ethnographic sensibility 'encourages the thought that one cannot predict at the outset of an inquiry where it will lead or what will turn out to be relevant to exposition' (Strathern, 2013: 207).

Gould's (2004a: 2) question '[C]an ethnography grasp a phenomenon that is constituted at multiple scales?' leads, inevitably, to discussion of the 'positionality' of the researcher in the sprawling, multi-scalar and multi-sited 'field' of policy reforms. How can one reconcile a structural and historical political economy of social welfare and its reconfigurations across space and time with the paradox that reform

---

[4]   A coherent case can be made for the abandonment of the classical anthropological ethic that the 'first responsibility is to those whose lives and cultures we study', particularly in cases of 'studying up', where anthropologists study 'powerful institutions and individuals of complex societies for purposes of understanding and even contributing to public policy choices' (Wedel and Kideckel, 1994: 37). However, I may have breached these same authors' exhortation that researchers need to utilise journalistic ethics so that 'we must first represent ourselves accurately to our informants' and indicate 'who we work for and in what capacity and the ends for which our information is gathered' (Wedel and Kideckel, 1994: 37). At the same time, not only is it the case that 'it is not possible to be transparent concerning the research topic when the researcher knows that she will be developing and changing the nature of her inquiry during the research process' (Eyben, 2005: 3), but this is even more the case when the research identity comes later. Indeed, despite David Mosse's (2005) attempts to 'depersonalise' his account of an aid project on which he had worked, the response of some colleagues was still a feeling of 'betrayal' (Eyben, 2009). In a sense, what remains here is a covert account of my own practice, situated in a context in which other individuals are not directly identified, but may be rather easily identifiable, and the organisations for which they work are identified directly.

[5]   While sharing a preference for 'theoretically informed' ethnography, it is important to acknowledge that 'discourses/ideologies' cannot be assumed to equate always with 'lived outcomes', and that ethnography can contribute to 'the critique of over-functionalist, over-structuralist and over-theorized views *and* to the positive development of reflexive forms of social theorizing, allowing some kind of voice to those who *live* their conditions of existence' (Willis and Trondman, 2000: 7, emphasis in original).

'has no empirical objectivity irrespective of the position of the observer' (Gould, 2004a: 6) and, yet, at the same time, 'the range of things we can know first hand ... is extremely narrow' (Gould, 2004b: 283)? A focus on positionality suggests that the presentation of research as if 'from above or from nowhere' (Marcus, 1995) is, at best, unhelpful and, in many ways, dishonest. My use of 'auto-ethnography', then, involves giving priority to direct involvement, embodied participation and emotional reactions (Ellis et al, 2011: 9). The tendency to present oneself as 'heroic', always trying to 'do the right thing' but blocked at every turn by 'others', is, perhaps, the most problematic potential pitfall here. Auto-ethnographers, in broad-brushstroke terms, seek 'to produce aesthetic and evocative thick descriptions of personal and interpersonal experience', through 'facets of storytelling (e.g., character and plot development), showing and telling, and alterations of authorial voice' (Ellis et al, 2011: 14). Using auto-ethnography, I share Bilić and Janković's (2012: 29) view that 'social scientists should be flexible and open to new forms of scholarship that would be more personalised and ... thus transcend hierarchies and divisions that mainstream sociology sometimes creates'.[6] In auto-ethnography, the individual self, in co-presence with others, is the evidence, raw data as it were, from which, via interpretation, knowledge can be produced. Using translation, seeking to achieve a kind of 'critically reflexive location' in which a plural sense of self is created, an epistemic–aesthetic tension can be used to craft 'a critical cultural story', a kind of *understory* of hegemonic

---

[6] Blagojević and Yair (2010: 342) may be overstating the case, somewhat, when they argue that:

> semiperipheral settings constitute ripe settings for exposing scientists to extreme forms of social change, and hence for deep understanding of social life. Furthermore, plunged into a survival mode of life, social scientists in 'transition' settings are challenged to deconstruct the forces that engulf their lives and rock their careers. Having been exposed to institutional and organizational earthquakes, they become sociologically privileged: they learn to deconstruct interests and assess reforms; they clearly see the rule of arbitrariness and perceive the ways of power with naked eyes. Consequently, social scientists in semiperipheral areas may be said to 'enjoy' epistemic advantages relative to their peers in the centers of science – who work in stable locations – because they were witnessing – much to their distraught at times – the positive and negative repercussions of profound and fast social change.

Blagojević's concept of the 'semi-periphery' is discussed in the following. In terms of my own positionality, it is important to remember that as a UK citizen, albeit one who has lived and worked in Croatia and the wider region since 1993, I may be seen as 'in' but not 'of' the semi-periphery.

systems' (Spry, 2009: 603–4, emphasis in original). This can only ever be a partial, more or less plausible, story, however, capable of being added to, refined or contradicted.

The task at hand, then, is how to reassemble rich auto-ethnographic evidence in ways that can most usefully contribute to a broader understanding of policy reform as translation and assemblage. Concentrating on particular sites and/or particular agencies has to contribute to an understanding of how socio-economic, political, administrative and cultural practices are performed and 're-transcribed', translated and reassembled. A commitment to 'reflexive ethnography' as an entry point for the analysis of policies as translation rejects classical anthropological notions of ethnography as 'intensive fieldwork' and a kind of professional *rite de passage*, in favour of a 'bending and blending' approach (Lendvai and Stubbs, 2007: 183), in which boundaries between research and other roles are broken down, and in which different positions and perspectives are combined.

Through 'thick description', 'schematic and compressed' accounts of events can contribute to improved understandings of sociocultural reform practices. At the heart of thick description is auto-ethnography as a constructed reading of events (Geertz, 1973). In treating 'the models and language of decision-makers as ethnographic data to be analysed' (Shore and Wright, 1997b: 13), 'vignettes' can be created where fragments of research materials and recollections become a key component of a 'peopled ethnography' (Fine, 2003). The 'bending and blending' of different roles and the salience of reinterpretations is presented, thus, not as a problem, but as an opportunity to translate an event experienced as a 'consultant' meaningful to 'critical researchers'. 'Collapsing scale' by focusing on the human scale of social interaction and on actors 'irrespective of their socio-spatial position' holds a danger of downplaying both 'hierarchical variables of status, power and mobility' and 'structural forces and more aggregated processes' (Gould, 2004a: 18). What is crucial is the act of writing, then, as a purposeful, if by no means objective, reassembling, itself akin to a work of translation, which seeks to connect processes observed with a theorisation of context as an attempt to track across scales and sites. Gould (2004a: 20) is surely correct, however, in arguing that, in and of themselves, 'the situational intuition and embodied knowledge of the ethnographer are inadequate tools for situating … observations in a broader social, political and economic context'.

Dave Bainton (DB): I am wondering to what extent ethnographies and auto-ethnographies are themselves inscribed in the act of translation. We are used to understanding our own writings, these chapters included, as politically enrolled in our case studies (after Clifford and Marcus, 1986), thereby 'blending' not only research/praxis, but also our own involvements in them. To what extent, therefore, should we see texts such as these as (potentially alternative) translations of policy dynamics – with the political possibilities that this affords to narrate alternative imaginaries. The auto-ethnographic account is both revealing of, and delimited by, the encounters and processes of the policy space, and begs the methodological question of how we might go beyond the flows that lead to the creation of fragile consensus, to the translations of the other voices that are silenced in these assemblages.

Paul Stubbs (PS): I agree completely. Indeed, I think that there is a real need for an auto-ethnographic method to be conceived as operating across complex notions of space and time so that the auto-ethnographer is increasingly drawn to seek out and understand those silenced other voices, as well as to explore as many of what later in this text I call the 'elsewheres' of policy- and reform-making. Even with this, auto-ethnography is still necessarily limited, and I do think that exploring how to rescue, through a lens of translation, ideas of 'collaborative action research', working alongside those silenced or marginalised, is also needed.

South East Europe: contexting/contesting the semi-periphery

It is rather hard to convey, in a short but meaningful way, elements of the 'social, political and economic context' of 'South East Europe'. Certainly, one of my main concerns is the active construction or translation of 'South East Europe', and particular symbolic locations within it, as a site of 'complex social and political engineering' (Lendvai and Stubbs, 2009b: 681). The issue of whether patterns and processes found here are 'unique' and 'specific' or 'universal' and 'generalisable' – most likely, as always, the answer is somewhere 'in–between' – is not the main focus of this chapter. It is true, of course, that the technique of 'collapsing scale' combined with my own sense of not knowing, in any activist, academic or consultancy sense, any other part of the world in any depth, at least since 1993, mitigate against answering the question. At the same time, a literature on international interventions elsewhere, and, indeed, in general, has emerged, focusing on many of the same agencies who have had a trajectory of working in 'complex political emergencies' (Duffield, 1994), starting in B-H, Croatia and Kosovo before moving elsewhere.

Borrowing an insight from Chapter Two, I would suggest that South East Europe can only be understood in terms of 'the coming together of many contexts whose combinations generate the conditions of possibility for particular agents (individual and collective) to perform specific actions' (p 54). Among the multiple combinations that may be relevant to the issue of policy reform as translation in South East Europe, I would emphasise, at one level, the complex articulation of '(post-)conflict', 'post-socialism' and 'variegated capitalisms', often mistranslated as a linear notion of 'transition', and, in policy discourse terms, the de- and reassembling of linkages between social policy, security, refugee return and democratisation contingent upon that articulation. In addition, although this is far from unique, welfare is profoundly de-territorialised and informalised in many parts of the region in the context of diverse diaspora, cross-border claims and entitlements, multiple and asymmetric citizenships, enclave welfare, forced migration and return, inter-household transfers, clientelism, and the existence of 'parallel power networks' (Stubbs and Zrinščak, 2009, 2012). It is the emergence, or, perhaps, better, 'construction in performance', of the region as a socio-political space, largely ascribed from outside, in which political and institutional arrangements have been destabilised and sub-national, national and trans-border relations remain heavily contested, which is crucial here. In short, as Clarke (2008) has suggested, it is a region in which 'governance and the subject and objects of governing are in process of simultaneous and mutual invention or constitution'.

Marina Blagojević (2009) has argued that the region, which she terms 'the Balkans', is facing multiple transitions that can be elaborated, in part at least, as the contradictory 'modernisation' of the 'semi-periphery', which constructs a kind of 'semi-otherness' of the region in relation to an imagined West. The idea that the region is both different from and like the West, leads to 'the promotion of policy measures which should help those societies to "adjust" to the center and to speed up their "modernisation"' (Blagojević, 2009: 99). This occurs through an emphasis on 'formal adjustment' often judged by external actors as too slow. A template based on modernisation in conditions of deindustrialisation and re-traditionalisation, she argues, creates an internal ambivalence through 'simultaneous opposition and acceptance, imitation and rejection' (Blagojević, 2009: 99), so that two possibilities – 'catch-up' or 'further peripheralisation' – tend to coexist.

Her analysis helps to explain both the nature of most, externally driven, reform strategies and their multiple translations. She suggests that weak structural constraints allow for a kind of 'open space' for political and policy interventions 'while at the same time lack of "structureness" severely limits the scope of their effectiveness' (Blagojević, 2009: 101).

Even in its paradoxical formulation, such an approach may be too 'structural' and insufficiently sensitive to 'agentic' possibilities in a 'crowded playground' (Arandarenko and Goličin, 2007) of reform actors whose actions cannot be reduced to a single imperative or motivation, but have to be seen as themselves generating, occupying and transforming new and emergent spaces of power (Newman, 2012; Stubbs, 2013). These actors include 'traditional' international organisations, such as the World Bank, the European Union and United Nations (UN) agencies (notably, the United Nations Development Programme [UNDP] and UNICEF), but also a Regional Co-operation Council, specific governance structures (such as the Office of the High Representative in Bosnia-Herzegovina), numerous international non-governmental organisations (NGOs) and 'think tanks', and a range of other agencies that blur clear boundaries between 'international' and 'domestic' actors, creating a hybrid and flexible 'intermestic' sphere (Pugh, 2000). Interpreters, intermediaries and 'flex actors', skilled at blurring roles and juggling representations (Wedel, 2009; Stubbs, 2013), often offering their expertise across a range of unstable institutional sites and settings, hold particular power in translation in this context.

The work that these forms of transnational or intermestic actors perform is, of course, fluid and complex, often translating larger schemes of modernisation into implementable projects, programmes and schemes, relying on networks of trust and cooperation as much as, if not more than, contextually or sectorally based 'expertise'. It is through the production of a 'right to intervene' that new assemblages of governance emerge, often denying, or paying lip service to, earlier welfare assemblages in the pre-1991 socialist period, during which Yugoslavia developed social welfare policies often seen as 'between' those of an imagined 'West' and 'East' (see Deacon, 1997: ch 5).

Notwithstanding the profoundly transnational nature of both welfare and its reform, what is perhaps most interesting in the case studies that follow is the continued strong focus by international actors on particular nation-states, many of which only emerged relatively recently. International actors appear complicit in a kind of 'methodological nationalism' that '"normalises" the current post-Yugoslav situation, perceiving the newly generated and largely still incompletely consolidated nation-states as "natural" results of long-term historical processes' (Bilić, 2012: 44). At the same time, the categories of ethnicisation and nationalism are also naturalised, being both overplayed in the context of democratisation and state-building and underplayed in the context of social welfare reform. Of course, a focus on nationalisms as the principal explanatory framework for the wars of the Yugoslav succession served to both homogenise and even primordialise 'national groups' and limit discussion of class, gender and other divisions. At the same time, the failure of social welfare reform programmes to explicitly address nationalisms as part of the strategic repertoire of political elites furthered the 'technicisation' or reform.

In the first case study, it is clear that UNICEF's efforts were framed very much in terms of influencing national reform efforts and establishing possibilities of regional lesson-learning rather than focusing, directly, on transnational policy issues. In the second case study, although DFID developed a regional strategy for the Western Balkans, and clearly drew from experience in one country for work in others, there was little or no attempt to tap into issues of transnational concern. At the same time, shared language, history and cultural practices can lead to wider regional understandings among so-called 'local' reform actors, sometimes bolstered by programmes of regional networking. This has both created a new group of regional policy consultants, advocates and researchers, and opened a space for region-wide repertoires of recalcitrance.

The performance of reform in the region, then, involves a multiplication and reworking of diverse 'political imaginaries', often in profoundly surprising ways. An already-inscribed European Union–World Bank 'cooperation–contestation' binary is, in part at least, about where the region belongs – is it European or, like the Third World, 'in need of development assistance'? It is as much about 'constructing subjectivities and identities' (Lendvai, 2007: 27) as it is about policies. The 'projectisation' of the lifeworld, as a result of the 'mutual assimilation of donor and state power', seems to require the 'mobile sovereignty' (Pandolfi, 2003) of an expanding apparatus as a multi-mandated crystallisation of more diffuse transnational processes, constitutive of new identities in their work of translation between the universal and the particular, as well as between the political and the technical. In South East Europe, this apparatus multiplies and translates ideas of what is 'technical' and what is 'political', creating myriad new opportunity structures in a region in which informality, flexibility and trust in people you know who work in institutions is more important as a resource than trust in the institutions themselves. Many of these issues both impact the performance of reform and are retranslated as irrational 'blockages' or bracketed as 'outside the scope of the project to deal with'.

> *John Clarke (JC):* These terms deserve more attention! They perform critical work in the encounters of policy and politics. The category of the 'irrational' is one critical way in which the boundaries of both politics and policy are determined: both are expected to be 'rational', albeit in different ways (politics should be rational-deliberative; policy should be rational-technical). However, the 'irrational' is a way of naming disruptive or transgressive forces, discourses and practices – and irrationality is usually attached to particular sorts of subordinated people: women, minority groups and, in spatial terms, the 'local' contrasted to the global processes of reasonableness. 'Outside the scope' is a managerial device that is used to construct, revise and rebuild boundaries around the immediate task. It is also a way of defining what is 'reasonable' – and allows the ruling out of 'unreasonable' expectations, demands, aspirations or even observations. Both constitute vital discursive resources.

> *PS:* Definitely. I would even argue that precisely the labelling of some forces, events and persons in these ways should always alert us to the ways in which power operates and circulates within projects. It is a difficult discursive balancing act, though, because that which is labelled as 'irrational' or 'outside the scope' is now, sometimes, reinserted through the use of consultants, who are encouraged to help project staff 'think outside of the box' – a technocratic translation of that which is beyond the scope of the project in a sense.

The United Nations Children's Fund and childcare system reform in South East Europe: translating technicism and constructing consensus

The plight of children in residential institutions in parts of South East Europe, particularly in Romania and Bulgaria, was a source of international concern from the early 1990s, leading to a complex mix of transnational charitable and humanitarian interventions. The wars of the Yugoslav succession also saw UNICEF return to the region and itself engage in the coordination of relief and support for children in need, alongside its monitoring of the social impacts of economic transition in the wider region. By the end of the 1990s, the issue of state responses to vulnerable children became significant in the process of Bulgaria and Romania's accession to the European Union. Later, UNICEF scaled up its presence in the wider region (which it termed Central and Eastern Europe and the Commonwealth of Independent States [CEE/CIS]) and began to prioritise childcare system reform. UNICEF worked increasingly in partnership, particularly with the World Bank and the European Union, to build a common agenda for childcare reform among governments, key stakeholders (including NGOs) and donors. Over time, UNICEF advocated for a more integrated and holistic approach to childcare reform based on a systems framework.[7] As a part of this, UNICEF, with the financial support of the Swedish International Development Agency (SIDA), organised what were termed four sub-regional 'high-level consultations on the progress of child care reform in partnership with governments' within the project 'The reform of the child care system in CEE/CIS – taking stock and accelerating action'[8] between 2007 and 2009.

Here, I present a critical interrogation of the first of these consultations, for South East Europe, held in the Bulgarian capital, Sofia, between 3 and 6 July 2007.[9] Using material originally compiled for a conference paper written jointly with Reima Ana Maglajlić (Stubbs and Maglajlić, 2013), my concern here is to show how the conference performed the work of translating universalising logics into a set of narratives to 'fit' the region of South East Europe. These narratives, far from monolithic, constitute a kind of childcare system reform assemblage or field, tending to marginalise, but never completely silence, other, more critical, narratives. Three aspects, three stories in a sense, are crucial to this work of performance: a story of virtuous 'progress unbound'; a story of international collaboration and 'cosy consensus'; and a story of building a set of robust practical competences or 'practice makes perfect'. Taking each in turn, I explore how these narratives, based on

---

[7] A child protection system is defined as certain structures, functions and capacities that are assembled to prevent and respond to violence, abuse and exploitation of children. While the components and actors in the system may be common across countries, the specific nature of the system is dependent on the country context, its culture, beliefs, attitudes, and practices. It is dynamic and emerges from and adapts to the changing context, the perceived child protection risks and population demands. (Source: http://cpwg.net/capacity-building/cb-events/ [accessed 18 February 2014])

[8] Source: http://www.ceecis.org/ccc/xindex.html (accessed 18 February 2014).

[9] A UNICEF dedicated web page (http://www.unicef.org/ceecis/protection_7062. html [accessed 18 February 2014]) still exists and contains a near-complete collection of materials, including a number of background papers, conference presentations and a subsequent Consultation Report, written in May 2008. Subsequent quotes from documents found on this site are cited as notes with URLs.

'communicating, observing, comparing and acting' (Tag, 2012: 42), served to reproduce, in translation, many of the 'travelling orthodoxies' (Mosse, 2011: 7) of international development programmes.

Throughout the conference, a key message from UNICEF was one of progress being made, with the social welfare of vulnerable children increasingly a priority, and governments of the region 'embracing' reform. A consensus had supposedly been reached, 'agreeing that the old system of institutionalizing children was dehumanizing and counterproductive'. A 'paradigm shift' had occurred, moving from a system where the state 'assumed all responsibility' for children, 'stripping them of their independence and dignity … without losing their commitment to the vulnerable'. UNICEF staff stressed 'that the family is the most appropriate environment for children to grow up in' and should be 'the focus of our support'. The opening speech by the Bulgarian minister of labour and social policy emphasised the importance of 'responsible parenting' and that 'children must know that there is 'Mum, Dad and me. Nothing can replace a home.'[10]

In this assemblage, the idea of rights-based, child- and family-centred approaches, translating a particular, rather recent, and predominantly Western, view of childhood (Pupavac, 2011), is combined with ideas of 'responsibilising parents' and 'strengthening families', resonating with discourses about a limited role for the state (Yazici, 2011). An idealised view of children as autonomous individuals is combined with a more conservative romantic myth of children as vulnerable beings to be protected, within a frame of limiting state intervention. Diverse, complex, family forms in different conjunctures are, thus, reduced to a universal idealised model of childhood to be embraced by all. Complex material, intergenerational and gendered forms of social relations are collapsed into 'Mum, Dad and me'. Translating the importance of 'local ownership' of reforms, then, into specific practices, the dominant narrative praised governments for taking decisive action in the interests of children and placing responsibility back onto parents.

A different story can be found in a report commissioned by UNICEF as a background to the conference but largely ignored during the event,[11] arguing that reforms have tended to be 'top-down' and 'faced … instances of political opposition, artificial regional follow-up and

---

[10] Source: http://www.ceecis.org/child_protection/consultation_report.pdf (accessed 31 July 2013), p 8.

[11] A draft report, written by Reima Ana Maglajlić, is still available at: http://www.unicef.org/ceecis/SEE_CC_multicountry.pdf (accessed 18 February 2014).

local ignorance, delusion or fatigue'.[12] This report suggests that when translated into nationally owned sets of practices, the intentions of the reforms tended to be lost in a proliferation of new agencies and decision-making bodies, with unclear and competing mandates. While a number of presentations in working groups sought to show how and why 'past efforts did not achieve results',[13] much of this suggested the need only for better coordination and planning, failing to see the gap between a dominant story of progress and a consistent alternative story of limited results, failed initiatives and unintended consequences, which, in a semi-periphery context, became features of the reforms. It is as if 'the many and unpredictable ways in which development's "travelling rationalities" (and technologies) get translated (back) into local social and political arrangements ... with unanticipated, maybe even perverse, effects' (Mosse, 2011: 5–6), was not allowed to affect the optimism of the narrative of 'unbound progress'.

The second key element of the dominant story was the supposed strengthening of a consensus and complementarity of approach between key international organisations[14] ('the major international players', as they were termed by UNICEF) 'to support systems reform in the social welfare sector'. The three named were UNICEF (with 'a child rights perspective which puts the child at the centre of the response'), the World Bank ('through the prism of reducing poverty') and the European Union (which 'seeks to ensure that there is social inclusion'). The UNICEF presentation[15] noted, using World Bank poverty data, that 'children face a greater risk of poverty than other population groups'. At the same time, the UNICEF Child Protection Advisor presenting this was adamant that there should be no discussion of child poverty and, above all, cash transfers in the conference, presumably because this risked breaking the fragile consensus that the agencies should 'recognize our complementary roles and call upon each other for expertise in areas where we are stronger'.

---

[12] Source: http://www.unicef.org/ceecis/SEE_CC_multicountry.pdf (accessed 18 February 2014), p. 18.

[13] Source: http://www.unicef.org/ceecis/wg5t1_3.ppt (accessed 18 February 2014).

[14] Source: http://www.unicef.org/ceecis/16400_7080.html (accessed 18 February 2014).

[15] Source: http://www.unicef.org/ceecis/16400_7080.html (accessed 18 February 2014).

Noémi Lendvai (NL): 'There should be no discussion of child poverty', despite a dominant underlying reason for children ending up in institutional care being related to poverty. This is an important moment. But what moment? The absurdity in a Kafkaian sense: talking about 'things' without the 'things'. Or, the politics of silencing: removing, deliberately, an essential and systematic aspect of institutionalisation and the active work that is involved here in the crafting of the absences is the very fact that makes the consensus fragile, not one that sustains it. The wizardries of 'reforming', and 'changing', compelling as they are, silence, divert, displace, pacify and demobilise the very policy spaces that they aim to support.

PS: Yes, and this, of course, is always a risk for those seeking to 'manage' such consultation events. How to disallow discussion of 'the elephant in the room' without provoking a backlash among participants because it is, after all, an elephant and not just a mouse! However, I think it also relates to the way in which a strange division of labour emerges between and, indeed, within international organisations, in this case, between UNICEF and the World Bank, and, indeed, within UNICEF, between those focused on the domain of 'child protection' and those focused on 'social protection'. None of these are, of course, fixed, and they are constantly moving in ways that are not always expected.

The role of the World Bank, a joint organiser of the conference, is worthy of detailed examination. As is often the case in inter-agency collaboration (cf Deacon, 2013), the key UNICEF advisor and the main representative from the World Bank, together with a key consultant who had mainly worked for UNICEF during her career but had, also, recently, been engaged in a number of reform initiatives by the World Bank, shared a long history of collaboration, even friendship, and were all from the former Yugoslavia (Slovenia, Serbia and Croatia, respectively).

The key World Bank presentation[16] focused on a 'human capital' perspective in which 'investing in children' reduces social costs, contributes to the labour force participation of mothers and, above all, 'generates higher economic returns'. The World Bank is said to have learnt that 'champions of change' are needed in government, and that partnerships are needed based on a shared vision and 'speaking the same language'. The emphasis on clearly drawing out 'the human capital

---

[16] Source: http://www.unicef.org/ceecis/16400_7080.html (accessed 18 February 2014).

aspect of social welfare services' appeared, at one level, quite tangential to the core conference concerns. At the same time, understanding the World Bank as increasingly 'multi-mandated' so that it brings its own (neoliberal) economic logics into the domains of other agencies is important. In short, in the name of inter-agency collaboration, a rather strange assemblage was created, and discussed as if it was far more stable than it actually was.

The European Union presentation[17] was also much more closely linked to its own platform on 'social inclusion' than to the main themes of the conference. At the same time, it is quite significant that the presentation from the European Union representative emphasised the value of more universal approaches to cash transfers, in this case, child benefits, as well as focusing on marginalised and discriminated groups, including Roma. Indeed, throughout the conference, the representative sought to ensure that 'the voice of Roma', largely through one person from one Bulgarian NGO, was heard. The absence of a focus on 'the most vulnerable' by UNICEF, surprising in the context of the organisation's long-standing concern with 'equity' issues in childcare, reinforces a sense that a consensus was being constructed that focused on the lowest common denominator that international agencies and governments could agree upon.

My own draft report on international organisations, commissioned ahead of the consultation,[18] suggested that 'external assistance has at times contributed to a fragmented, inconsistent, badly sequenced, and short-term reform agenda'. An argument that 'other reforms fail to consider impacts on child care and/or have unintended negative consequences for child care system reform' relates, clearly, to the problems of the wider economic reform prescriptions of the World Bank and the International Monetary Fund, later to be of central importance in the context of the economic and financial crisis, but was not a central theme of the conference. Crucially, the critique that 'international organisations have tended to prioritise working with "champions of change" at the expense of ensuring wider buy in' anticipates and challenges the World Bank's positive view of such 'champions'. The critique of a 'passion for pilot programme' and the creation of new agencies that 'compete in a crowded arena for the

---

[17] Source: http://www.unicef.org/ceecis/p1_3_1.ppt (accessed 18 February 2014).

[18] 'Draft report on international organisations and child care system reform in South East Europe'. Available at: http://www.unicef.org/ceecis/IO_and_CCR_SEE.pdf (accessed 18 February 2014).

leadership role in reforms' resonated with other critical voices in the conference, but did not become a central theme. My report argued that international organisations are complexly politically situated and are themselves agents in the reform process, occupying diverse, contested and contentious roles, and, not infrequently, competing for leading positions. The consultation, as designed, however, translated this into the idea that these organisations and their practices are somehow external to the policy landscape, bringing somewhat neutrally a range of tools and techniques to improve coordination and, hence, practice.

It is in the story of implementation and practice that the issue of translation becomes most significant and problematic. A key aspect of the paradigm shift noted earlier is said to be the adoption of 'the individual case management approach', linked to a wider range of issues relating to 'a continuum of services from prevention to recovery, to gate keeping systems through to planning and budgets'. An extremely complex, but essentially technical, systems approach to reform, developed by UNICEF, was being presented as the only way forward, regardless of the understandings of what this meant among attendees who, to re-quote the World Bank presentation cited earlier, did not at all 'speak the same language'. Perhaps the most difficult concept to grasp was that of 'statutory services', not least because the concept proved extremely difficult to translate into the languages of the region,[19] most often being translated as 'state services'. Indeed, even in English, the distinction between the two concepts was not made clear during the consultation. In her first presentation, the Child Protection Advisor stated that 'decision making on individual cases ... is the mandate of statutory services who are responsible for management of each individual case'. This risks being tautological and, in any case, also requires understanding of the concept of 'case management' to be meaningful. A second crucial idea is that of 'the continuum of services' or a set of functions that the system needs to perform to safeguard the child's rights. These functions, in the order presented, are: preventing unwarranted separation; early identification of risks; assessment and registration; planning, referring and purchasing services; providing services; monitoring progress; reviewing cases; 'and deciding upon closure or redress'. The argument was that 'all these functions need to work in a flow' and are 'very relevant also for children currently in institutions'.

---

[19] To the best of my knowledge, the simultaneous translators utilised during the consultation were not given any special training or a list of key words.

In a consultation involving diverse participants from different countries with very different histories, traditions and practices of law, public administration and social work, this attempt at clarity was always likely to have the opposite effect. For the Yugoslav successor states, with professional social work and de-concentrated public social work services since the 1960s (Stubbs and Maglajlić, 2012), it created the impression that these 'Centres for Social Work' carried out statutory social work functions, which, given the fragmentation of responsibility for individual cases between different professions, and gaps in legal protection for children, is disputable. For those countries where social work has only developed very recently, often under donor-driven agendas, the definition described a possible future scenario rather more than current realities. Crucially, while presented as *the* central principle, technique and tool for reform, the consultation did not take into account the fact that understandings of 'statutory services' and 'case management' in the region were diverse, although everywhere rather undeveloped, or, indeed, that many participants in the consultation had been involved in diverse, often donor-driven, reforms, prior to this consultation, without these terms being used at all.

In a key presentation, there is a suggestion that change has to be managed, but no political dimension is discussed; instead, a whole batch of new concepts are introduced, largely impossible for most participants to decode and decipher, such as: levels, mandates, regulators, temporary arrangements and fiscal flows.[20] Apart from the depoliticisation and the ever-increasing complexity of the framework being presented, the idea that reform is a technical matter is, of course, extremely problematic. Above all, it fails to pay attention to issues of how different interests may align themselves in favour or against the reforms, and on what basis. What the complexity helped to reproduce was a division between those who saw themselves as a kind of vanguard, committed to the process and familiar with the language, and those who may have been willing to be persuaded but who found the jargon intimidating. In many reform situations, intermediaries or brokers play a key role, 'simplifying templates' (Mosse, 2011: 15) and translating terms and concepts between different groups. Here, the intermediaries rather added to the complexity. The move away from a kind of 'moral universalism' to a 'technical universalism' (Mosse, 2011: 17) may have been meant to ride roughshod over political objections and uncertainties. In fact, it produced confusion and, among some

---

[20] Source: http://www.unicef.org/ceecis/wg5t1_3.ppt (accessed 31 July 2013).

participants, a growing scepticism regarding both the meanings of the consultation and the likely impact on change.

The absence of a more reflexive understanding of translation is also notable. Participants did not share a common language or common conceptual mapping of key concepts, much less a common understanding of the relationship of these concepts to each other within complex systems. A shared commitment and general political will for reform was, also, more assumed than discussed. Disagreements within and between actors – in particular, in and between international organisations, but also between government and non-governmental actors, between government and opposition, and so on – were largely removed from view, and the connections between childcare reform, wider social welfare reform and broader socio-economic restructurings were judged as outside of the scope of the consultation.

In contesting the dominant framings of the consultation, the critique presented here resonates with many of the concerns that have been raised regarding development interventions in complex governance arenas (cf Ferguson, 1994; Mosse, 2005). The tendency to technicise what are deeply political issues is compounded by an aggregation of all children, regardless of disability, age, class, ethnicity, gender and location, across 10 countries with very different historical trajectories and current social, economic and political trends. The voices of the users of services were not heard at all; the voices of the front-line or street-level social workers, a profession or semi-profession with very different histories and trajectories in each of the countries, were also rather silenced. Interestingly, in contrast to some UNICEF-led events in which 'human stories' are, often highly problematically, presented to create emotional reactions, and certain individuals are nominated as 'the voice of children', this was a highly technical event largely attempting, if not always succeeding,[21] to be non-emotional. Models, schemes and projects were presented in a form supposedly lending them to 'lesson learning'. This separation of the technical from the emotional is surprising, reflecting, it seems, the dominance, in this event at least, of systems thinkers, increasingly influential in UNICEF's child and social protection frameworks (UNICEF, 2010, 2013).

---

[21] There was a growing 'backstory' throughout the conference, with a significant number of participants expressing, in the margins, their concern at the narrowness of focus and rather sugar-coated emphasis on 'success'. There were also complaints from the Montenegrin delegation that there was no translation into their language. In the context of Montenegro's declaration of independence and separation from Serbia in June 2006, this merely highlighted the continued political salience of language questions in the region.

Of course, a focus on stories alone is never enough, although it does convey the nature of the translation work performed by such consultations and the rhetorical nature of the 'success' ascribed to them. In part, the analysis presented here can be accused of merely using an 'academic' register to critique an event that works in a different, interventionist, register. Little of the interactions between participants, none of the backstage manoeuvrings and no sense of the way in which most participants saw this as 'just another conference' to be added to the calendar is conveyed here. Also in need of explanation is how a particular constellation of actors was able to ensure the dominance of such a systems approach at this particular time and place. In many ways, the very idea of a 'consultation' was translated into an exercise in performing a narrative that expressed one view of reform and marginalised any opposition to it. It is worth bearing in mind that a proposed 'centre of excellence' in the region never materialised, that the key Child Protection Advisor moved to a post elsewhere soon afterwards and her replacement seems less committed to a systems approach, and that, later, Bulgaria's practice in relation to deinstitutionalisation was subject to intense critical and media scrutiny (cf Ivanova and Bogdanov, 2013), all of which points to the somewhat transient nature of policymaking and the unstable nature of the reform assemblage that was developed.

Reforming social welfare systems in Bosnia-Herzegovina: consulting for the Department for International Development

Between 1999 and 2006, I was involved extensively, as a consultant, in designing, implementing and evaluating DFID's work on the reform of social welfare in B-H, discussed here, as well as in Croatia, Serbia and Kosovo. B-H is, as noted earlier, a highly fragmented, unstable and crowded space of governance, in which the consultancy mode, for a wide range of different actors, international, domestic and 'intermestic', represented a key mode of insertion 'into activities that mattered' (Wedel, 2009: 24). Initially, DFID's work was project-based, attempting to link local-level 'pilot' reforms with entity-level policy change. I was recruited to undertake a pre-design 'scoping mission' and then, as part of a larger team, to design a three-year project with a budget of £4 million on 'Reforming the Systems and Structures of Central and Local Social Policy Regimes in B-H'.[22]

The antecedents of this project can be traced along a number of interlinked, overlapping but, perhaps, separable trajectories, illustrating very clearly the nature of the blurring of organisational and interpersonal agendas, and the importance of particular circumstances in creating particular reform translation pathways and assemblages. Through a research connection with Helsinki, I had been involved in helping to design an earlier project funded by the government of Finland, which involved a Bosnia-based international NGO, the Independent Bureau for Humanitarian Issues (IBHI), and the UNDP, in a pilot project in two municipalities. The project was based on shared thinking that international donors should focus less on one-off humanitarian-type projects supporting 'vulnerable groups' and more on reforming the architecture of social welfare governance from the bottom up. I had already become familiar with the work of the IBHI and was impressed by the insights of its Bosnian director, who had returned to Sarajevo after being the Yugoslav ambassador to the Organisation for Economic Co-operation and Development (OECD) in Paris. The involvement of the IBHI provided, for me, as a foreign consultant, albeit one living in a neighbouring country, a plausible story that the project fitted 'Bosnian realities and specificities'.

At the same time, a new social policy advisor within DFID, who had previously worked for Save the Children, originally in Africa and later in B-H, on designing programmes of support to Ministries of Social Policy, was also keen to try to develop more sustainable social welfare reforms. My recruitment to undertake the scoping mission was accidental, with a DFID staffer who should have undertaken this task having to move at short notice to cover the crisis in Kosovo. Already, during the scoping stage, tensions between the supposedly more 'intellectual' ideas of myself and the advisor and the 'practical'

---

[22] As Maglajlić Holiček and Rašidagić (2008: 159–60) note:

> The goal of the programme was to 'strengthen the social policy regime in BiH at the central and local levels' and to 'promote an effective and efficient social policy at all levels, which is fiscally sustainable, demonstrates social innovation and contributes to the reduction of poverty, inequality and social exclusion' through:

- the strengthening of the municipal and cantonal social policy management and social service delivery;
- the fostering and enablement of Community-Level Partnerships and
- Community Action Projects between civil society actors in four pilot areas.

concerns of the British Embassy in B-H emerged. Part of the tension was resolved by pairing me, in the design phase, with a UK social work academic with much greater experience of project design, and who had worked closely with the advisor in the past. The academic was able to respond satisfactorily to the British ambassador's question 'How can I explain this project on the radio?'. My own flexible 'skills' were perhaps more important in securing cooperation from key local activists in sites that I had chosen.

In retrospect, the project as designed reinforced the 'semi-periphery' paradox in that all manner of project interventions are possible in a flexible 'open space' but these rarely achieve what they set out to, precisely because of the same lack of 'thick' structures in which they can be implemented. Indeed, although this particular project was of central importance for some of those directly involved, other projects on similar, or overlapping, themes were also being implemented with little or no dialogue or attempts at complementarity between them. Some aspects of project design illustrate the improvised and ad hoc nature of much of what passes for 'expertised' consultancy. For example, the way in which the budget was allocated between activities was hardly based on robust calculations; in one instance, I remember being advised that we needed to increase the analytical inputs of foreign consultants in the project design as 'this would help to use up the allocated budget'. The instrumentalisation of the project was also reproduced in terms of the involvement of key domestic actors. In an interesting translation from the idea of the importance of local 'buy-in', referring to the importance of ownership of the project by key Bosnian policy actors, these same actors were literally 'bought-in', with ministry officials and others paid to participate, in a personal capacity, in ad hoc governance structures, helping to formulate policy suggestions and recommendations that they felt under no obligation to implement in their official capacity (Maglajlić Holiček and Rašidagić, 2007, 2008).

Unlike the government of Finland project, in which the IBHI was chosen to be the main actor, the DFID project was subject to competitive tender, although it was made clear that the bidder most likely to receive the contract would be one that had secured the active involvement of the IBHI in the project. The contract was won by a UK-based for-profit consultancy company, Birks-Sinclair and Associates Ltd (BSAL), who mirrored and amplified, in many ways, the IBHI's flexibility on a wider stage. BSAL had previously been a framework contractor for the European Union's CONSENSUS programme, where they had been described as knowing 'the requirements for making good technical and financial proposals, but once awarded the contract, were not particularly interested in the project' (de la Porte and Deacon, 2002: 57). I was recruited into the project to undertake analytical work in two municipalities in one entity (*Republika Srpska*) and, in a highly emotionally charged set of disagreements, I became openly critical of aspects of BSAL's work, including: their valuing of international, at the expense of local, expertise; their denial of the sensitivity and particularity of the B-H context, with many of their consultants seeing the programme as 'just like one we implemented in Bulgaria'; and their tendency to adhere strictly to the wording of the project terms of reference rather than to take risks, which meant that their written reports, while extensive and glossy, rarely addressed what I considered the most important issues in the project as designed. Again, in retrospect, these disagreements, while apparently about substance and content, can also be seen in terms of my not sharing networks with BSAL, who, themselves, preferred to bring in people they trusted.

These disagreements[23] meant that I had no further direct involvement in the project. However, after the project ended, I was surprised to be asked, by DFID, to take part in an 'independent' social policy impact assessment. The focus was not on direct project evaluation, but on assessing the contribution of this and another project to social policy change, organised according to a number of key development 'keywords': stakeholder ownership, programme sustainability, partnership-working, dissemination of best practice, the impact of governance structures and issues of transparency, accountability and public participation. The summary report (Maglajlić and Stubbs, 2006), presented at a conference held in Sarajevo in 2006, suggested that longer time frames may be needed to 'create long-lasting, efficient, and effective policy changes' and that:

> such long-term, flexible, multi-level projects ... require a 'new generation' of implementers willing to be flexible, to go beyond the Terms of Reference, identify agents and coalitions for change, and continually reflect upon the implications of an analysis of local political economies. (Maglajlić and Stubbs, 2006: 8, 7)

---

[23] One particularly clumsy 'transgression' occurred when, prior to a 'stakeholder workshop' in Trebinje in *Republika Srpska*, I complained in an email about the heavy presence of foreigners in what was a rather complex political environment, suggesting sarcastically that if we all decided not to claim our daily allowances, a more substantial social protection system could be established.

In many ways, this was a translation of a more critical research perspective into a supposedly 'progressive' request for international actors to try to understand, and work with, 'drivers of change', failing to address the key point that, however well-conceived one 'project' might be in this arena, its capacity to create meaningful change remained limited. In addition, of course, it left unanswered the question of the legitimacy, and, indeed, efficacy, of externally funded projects engaging in exercises of social engineering.

Other commentators, including some also directly involved in the project, have reached radically divergent conclusions as to its value. Maglajlić Holiček and Rašidagić (2008) see the project as typical of a new phase, from 1999 onwards, of supporting international NGO and NGO-driven projects with some pretence towards a more 'strategic' focus. In reality, they argue, the translation term 'mixed model of welfare' became, in their words, 'a mantra to be repeated endlessly by the persons represented in the meetings sponsored by these projects' (Maglajlić Holiček and Rašidagić, 2008: 160). They go on to suggest that:

> The state per se was never made a part of the whole pilot reform exercise. The donor governments and their local implementing partners, after signing formal agreements with the state authorities, recruited representatives of key government ministries and institutions in an individual capacity, through their participation in informal, ad hoc, project bodies. Here they paid lip service to the implementation of project goals, while continuing their everyday work in the government. Project activities brought handsome rewards, but did not create obligations for state agencies or these individuals. (Maglajlić Holiček and Rašidagić, 2008: 161)

In fact, this instrumentalisation could have been predicted from even a cursory examination of the effects of 'projectisation'[24] in

---

[24] 'Projectisation', as the compartmentalisation of the life-world into ever-shorter, time-limited, separable, sequences of action, has been seen as one characteristic of the linked process of 'NGOisation', referring to:

the influence of donors' agendas on topics covered and on type of organisational structures preferred; the rise of short-term 'project cultures' or *projectisation*; the emphasis on professionalization and technical skills at the expense of broader social goals; the empowerment of a young, urban, highly educated English

B-H and beyond. In a semi-periphery context, the multiplication and fragmentation of governable spaces created the conditions for instrumentalised partnerships between a wide range of different actors operating on the border between the formal and the informal, the public and the private, and creating uneven, contradictory and unsustainable localised practices (Lendvai and Stubbs, 2009b: 684).

Those within the IBHI have also reflected on their role as a key 'local intermediary', arguing that this ensured 'the acceptance of the project by local stakeholders and greatly increased the efficiency of the foreign consultants, in turn strengthening partnership with local stakeholders, as well as local ownership and sustainability' (Ninković and Papić, 2007: 8). Quoting from a participatory evaluation undertaken within the project itself, but no longer available online, they note the sustainability of 'knowledge; experience; the ethos of partnership; and an awareness of the needs of marginalised people' (Ninković and Papić, 2007: 13). The equal involvement of BSAL and the IBHI is seen as a prime example of 'local demand-driven' project implementation, and is even suggested as a model for other South East European countries.

In his response to an earlier iteration of this text, DFID's former social policy advisor suggested that a focus on the project as deriving from DFID as a donor was too simplistic since this narrowed down:

> the range, scope and intent of the actors – thus for the UK (and in B-H in particular) it was often the case that the policy emerged from dialogue between the FCO [Foreign and Commonwealth Office], the MOD [Ministry of Defence], Treasury, and DFID. Thus the policy and subsequent action (which may or may not involve consultants) was nested within national and multilateral policy discussions.[25]

In addition, he pointed out that the linkage with the World Bank's work in B-H, particularly on pensions, veterans' benefits and social assistance reforms, was also a central project component, although not realised in practice, in part, as a result of the '"clientelism" between political parties and war veterans which continues'.

In the aftermath of this work, DFID continued to work in B-H, moving from projects to programmes and strategies, with new

---

speaking elite; the need to focus on project 'success' in very narrow terms; and the increasing distancing of elite NGOs from grassroots activism. (Stubbs, 2007: 221, emphasis in original)

[25.] Email correspondence, November 2011.

advisors strongly supporting the strengthening of analytical capacity at the central state level, largely through the Directorate of Economic Planning (DEP), creating a prototypical flexible agency responsible for drafting, with DFID and World Bank support, a Medium Term Development Strategy (MTDS), including a Social Protection Strategy. Long after the DEP lost influence, in part, because of changed political conditions but also, crucially, when one of its leading local initiators moved elsewhere, it remained the site of rather chaotic 'capacity building' by a number of international organisations keen to see strategies developed that are even more 'fictional' than those Lendvai (Chapter Five, this volume) describes. In a critical and reflexive text, Esref Kenan Rašidagić (2012) traces his own work on the MTDS and the importance of the establishment of the DEP, at the time known as the Economic Policy Planning Unit (EPPU), and its later demise as it lost political support from *Republika Srspka* but where political actors from the federation and donors continued to act as if it was functional. He concludes:

> Nowadays, DEP is in ruins, run by an incompetent political appointee and staffed by a few demoralized staff, its best and brightest having left for more intellectually and professionally rewarding institutions. The MTDS expired in 2007, and few seriously bothered to draft a new national strategy (with the RS [Republika Srpska] adopting its own development strategies in its place). The DEP web page currently (October 2012) sports a *proposal* for the new Country Development Strategy (CDS) 2008–2013, itself posted in 2010, the same situation is with the Social Inclusion Strategy, but few clues are given as to their expected implementation. (Rašidagić, 2012, emphasis in original)

In some contrast, the IBHI, as a key flexible actor, remains a crucial intermediary in social policy reform in B-H, being able to juggle multiple and shifting identities, roles, mandates and representations. Its resident director continues to combine the intellectual capital of being a critical independent thinker with the skills of a successful flexion networker. The IBHI's latest report[26] lists five current projects, from March 2011 to March 2014, with a value of some USD2.1 million, and

---

[26] Available at: http://ibhi.ba/Documents/Publikacije/2014/IBHI%20Review%20 SEPTEMBER%202014.pdf (accessed 19 February 2014).

48 implemented projects, dating from January 1996 to January 2012, with a total value of USD19.1 million. It is probably not a coincidence that, within the project noted earlier, the resident director's title was 'B-H Social Policy Co-ordinator', showing, in a sense, the ways in which non-state actors fill the spaces of governance and power. In many ways, the ability to switch between a political register of anti-nationalism and a technical register of managing effective, well-run projects, as well as organising conferences and producing timely and well-written publications, has been matched by the ability to mobilise connections, domestic and international, to get things done. The IBHI and its director, then, demonstrate multiple and shifting identities, roles, mandates and representations.

Crucially, involvement in social welfare reform, probably the largest source of the IBHI's revenue, not unlike BSAL on a wider stage, has always involved an awareness of the next big discursive shift – from poverty reduction, to social protection, to social inclusion – each bringing new opportunities and no fundamental difficulties in moving between World Bank, DFID and European Union policy discourses and frames. In perhaps the most blatant example of a translation device, the IBHI changed its name, recently, to the Initiative for Better and More Humane Inclusion, and is the founder of the Social Inclusion Foundation, receiving significant sums from the Swiss government.

This critical focus on the IBHI, given its important position as an intermediary in social welfare reform, should not distract from the central point, which is the proliferation of actors and agencies, and their multiple roles, implicated in defining and developing new spaces of governance and rule. It is not just the B-H state that 'has been improvised among a variety of actors operating across a range of spatial scales' (Jeffrey, 2013: 6). Governance is, quite literally, 'performed' through diverse forms of agency, consisting of multiple claims that may compete but, often, can coexist within a fractured public sphere, with a variable geometry of multiple practices and imaginaries.

Unsettling thoughts

A number of issues can be taken from the reform scenarios discussed here, marked as they are by front-stage performances and backstage manoeuvrings in front of multiple, active, audiences. Interestingly, the performance of reform is less often judged by results than by the quality of the performance. This privileging of form over content can be seen in the managed consensus of the UNICEF consultation and in many of the performative dimensions of the B-H reform projects. In the end, it is the assembling of rather contradictory elements and the use of often competing 'logics in translation' that define the encounters discussed here. Clearly, in addition, the binary between 'local' and 'foreign' is both central to the cases and impossible to maintain, in any meaningful sense, within the 'black box' of everyday encounters. It is the asymmetric relations of power that stand out, however, as well as the silencing or fetishisation of both service users and front-line welfare workers in the face of consultants and policymakers. In reality, of course, these actors develop their own translations, subversions and resistances to whatever reforms are suggested. The variety of projects, programmes, strategies and reforms noted here are all somehow already 'foreign' to the body that they are being introduced into, and never only, or mainly, rooted in local experience, but rather always already routed through a mobile, and highly unpredictable, process of translation.

> *JC:* The movement between silencing and fetishisation is an important one. Both are ways in which the 'asymmetric relations of power' are enacted. Silencing, we understand well; it is, after all, the normal position allocated to the subordinated (the place occupied, even if differently, by both users and front-line workers). However, fetishisation – the performative representation of the subordinated – is a different practice. It is a response to the critique of voicelessness and ensures that a voice (or a body that might have a voice) is present, but typically held in a bounded space in the performance of policy. Voice (in the sense of demands and desires rather than individual testimony) is to be performed, but its subjects are still spoken for in the policy practices that surround it.

> *PS:* Yes, indeed. There is 'voice' and 'voice', of course, and the fetishisation of voice can be opposed to a 'consultation otherwise', which would, presumably, strive to ensure that complex and varied demands and desires gain unmediated, dare I say, untranslated, access to the processes being discussed here and are able, perhaps within a process of translation, to alter them. Again, this is far away from a 'managed' consultation. It is not, however, impossible to conceptualise, although the attention to reflexivity, critical dialogue, translation and trust in the process would be both demanding and risky for those in positions of power.

The importance of emotions within such reform encounters has been rather played down in their representation here. In fact, in all cases, the emotional aspects of encounters, expressions of trust and mistrust, and simply 'getting on' with some people and not others were of immense importance. The struggle to articulate a position that breaks down a binary distinction between emotion and cognition, on the one hand, while also combining emotional or interpretational accounts with more material forms of analysis (cf Newman, 2012: 466) is clearly needed.

As noted earlier, auto-ethnography may offer a lens into relationships and practices, and their assemblage in translation, but it tends to reduce discussion of the multi-sitedness of inquiry, or the nature of flows across time and space, to that which the auto-ethnographer observed, participated in, heard about and/or speculated upon. While auto-ethnographic methods are well-suited to understanding how different forces, relationships and dynamics are condensed in particular locations, they are less useful in terms of articulating 'the ways in which different sites, scales and spaces ... are articulated to one another' (Clarke and Stubbs, 2010). There are always 'elsewheres' that appear to operate as propellants or, as usually in the case of taking social policy seriously, constraints, but to which the auto-ethnographer does not have access. Analytical insights need to address these elsewheres and, above all, provide an appreciative and nuanced understanding of the practices and discourses of both front-line workers and service users. Tracing flows of ideas, practices and people through reflexive case studies is crucial in order to address the technicisation of social policy and the need for re-politicisation in local, national and transnational spaces.

A translation lens is necessary both for analytical purposes and in prefiguring any possible emerging critical praxis. There is an urgent need to shift attention 'to the local and particular settings in which ideas are received, translated, mediated and adapted into new practices' (Newman, 2012: 473). Perhaps the key scepticism in the chapter is of externally driven, top-down social engineering, which so often leads to an instrumentalisation of social change. Reforms as performance so often neglect political struggle, historical awareness and, for want of a better term, cultural competence and sensitivity, which are so necessary for their implementation. With this in mind, the long-standing nature of resistance to external projects can be grasped by an extended quote from Ivo Andrić's (1995) novel describing local responses to Austrian rule, replacing that of the Turks, in 19th-century Višegrad in B-H:

> The newcomers were never at peace; they allowed no one else to live in peace. It seemed that they were resolved with their impalpable but ever more noticeable web of laws, regulations and orders to embrace all forms of life, men, beasts and things, and to change and alter everything, both the outward appearance of the town and the customs and

habits of men from the cradle to the grave.... Naturally, here as always and everywhere in similar circumstances, the new life meant in actual fact a mingling of the old and the new. Old ideas and old values clashed with the new ones, merged with them or existed side by side, as if waiting to see which would outlive which.... By a natural law the people resisted every innovation but did not go to extremes, for to most of them life was always more important and more urgent than the forms by which they lived. (Andrić, 1995: 135)

FOUR

The managerialised university: translating and assembling the right to manage

John Clarke

Introduction

> A young woman stares at the computer screen in her office. The screen displays a set of categories of how academic time might be spent in her university, with columns for 'Actuals' (for the past year) and 'Projected' (for the coming year). She must allocate her 230 working days to these categories. She puzzles about how to complete this 'Academic Workload Management' form. She seeks advice from her Head of Department (aka line manager) and her mentor. One says 'just make sure the days add up to 230', the other says 'it looks more plausible if you don't put round numbers in'. She finds the advice both reassuring and not at all helpful.[1]

In this chapter, I explore some of the conditions that make this vignette possible. How does academic time come to be calculable and manageable in these ways? How do heads of department come to be imagined as line managers? How do such management technologies and practices engender dismay and cynicism? In order to do this, I need to consider management as a travelling idea and assemblage that is translated into different spaces and settings. This places the chapter

---

[1] Like the other vignettes in this chapter, this story derives from my working life at the Open University. These vignettes report events, encounters and conversations in the manner of participant observation. I was, indeed, a participant (as a managed subject and a managerial subject) and was observant in my own and other universities. This chapter also draws on an earlier exploration of the managerialisation and modernisation of universities written for a special issue of *Learning and Teaching in the Social Sciences* (Clarke, 2010b). I am grateful to Susan Hyatt, Boone Sheare and Sue Wright for making me think – and think better – about these issues.

in a distinctive relationship to our collective interest in translation, as established in Chapters One and Two: the processes of translation explored here all take place within English, rather than involving translation between languages. Nevertheless, the analysis is rooted in the idea that there is more than one English. Management is articulated as a distinctive way of thinking, calculating and ordering the world that has complicated relations with other ways of thinking, calculating and ordering. Thus, what are at stake are practices of translation, even if the apparently common language conceals the extent to which translation is in play. The chapter also explores the ways in which power is a central coordinate of the work of assemblage; indeed, it suggests that in the process of translation, the forms and sites of power and authority are reassembled. In this way, the chapter fills out one key aspect of our efforts to use the concept of assemblage. However, the opening vignette is not just about management in general, nor even the more specific form sometimes called the New Public Management (NPM); it also requires attention to higher education (HE) as a sector and the university as an organisational formation in which management has come to be embedded. More particularly still, it means attention to British/English universities as the site of *managerialisation*: a process of reshaping organisations around managerial logics, techniques and prerogatives. This process began – in British public services – in the 1980s and has continued (driven by waves of managerial innovation) to the present (2014, as I write). As I hope to make clear, this narrowing focus does not mean that the wider processes and dynamics are irrelevant; rather, they form the necessary conditions of possibility for the specific reassembling of power in and through management in the university.

What is the problem?

Management has been a productive area for studies of both the transfer and translation of ideas and practices (eg Czarniawska and Sevon, 1996; Sahlin-Andersson and Engwall, 2002; Morris and Lancaster, 2005). In contrast, the NPM has been less of a focal concern for such approaches, perhaps because of a problem of defining the NPM itself (see, eg, Pollitt and Sorin, 2012). Here, though, I will argue that looking at managerialisation through the lens of translation and assemblage makes issues of power and authority more visible.[2]

---

[2] I will sidestep the 'substantial branch industry in defining how NPM should be conceptualised and how NPM has changed' (Dunleavy et al, 2006: 96), though it

I share Meaghan Morris's (2006: 5) sense of the value of a 'translative (rather than narrowly trans-national) practice of cultural work that can attend to institutional differences, moving, when need be, from one institution and/or speech situation to another'. In this chapter, however, I will be tracing the movement of policy not from one language to another, but between 'epistemic communities' in a different sense. Contemporary approaches to managing have certainly moved between different spaces and sites, but they tend to take place in English following their rise to dominance in the US in the 1980s, when they promised to free corporate management from organisational shackles (Clarke and Newman, 1993). Although their travels take place in English, they are nevertheless translated between different settings (from capitalist corporations to public sector organisations; from the US to other locations, including Britain). They also involve the larger sense of translation that we have been developing here: as a practice of articulating particular ways of thinking and acting. Discourses of new management certainly speak English, but they speak a distinctive 'managerial English', offering ways of imagining organisations, their inner lives and how they are to be coordinated. They also attempt to establish that language and its ways of thinking and acting as necessary, normal and natural. In the process, other ways of thinking, acting, calculating and organising are displaced.

At the same time, a number of studies have recently taken up the idea of assemblage as a way of thinking about objects of analysis that are not necessarily coherent, integrated or unitary, but that may perform or be enacted as if they are (Ong and Collier, 2005; Li, 2007a; Newman and Clarke, 2009). Increasingly, such mobile assemblages take the form of global phenomena that, as Ong and Collier (2005: 11) suggest, 'have a distinctive capacity for decontextualisation and recontextualisation, abstractability and movement, across diverse social and cultural situations and spheres of life'. For Ong and Collier (2005: 12, emphasis in original), such phenomena take particular forms in assemblages, where they are combined with other situational properties and forces:

> An assemblage is the product of multiple determinations
> that are not reducible to a single logic. The temporality of

is worth noting that, drawing on Dunleavy et al, Pollitt and Sorin argue that 'NPM is a two-level phenomenon. At the higher level it is a general theory or doctrine that the public sector can be improved by the importation of business concepts, techniques and values.... Then, at the more mundane level, NPM is a bundle of specific concepts and practices' (Pollitt and Sorin, 2012: 5).

an assemblage is emergent. It does not always involve new forms, but forms that are shifting, in formation or at stake. As a composite concept, the term '*global* assemblage' suggests inherent tensions: global implies broadly encompassing, seamless and mobile: assemblage implies heterogeneous, contingent, unstable, partial and situated.

For now, I want to suggest that the modern version of management (dating from what Clarke and Newman [1993] called the 'second managerial revolution') can be understood as both 'global' (a travelling and would-be 'universal' object of desire or necessity) and always being materialised in very particular assemblages.

So, we might revisit the NPM as just such a *mobile assemblage*, in which the 'core' is itself never fixed or final, but made up of 'mixed messages' that change over time as new 'discoveries' are added to its sacred texts and tenets.[3] This implies treating management as a global phenomenon, but one that always takes place in particular assemblages. It claims: a certain sort of universality (all organisations need to be well-managed); an abstracted and technical character (with ways of thinking and acting that transcend specific interests, or local politics); and a capacity to bring about improvement (well-managed organisations do better than badly managed ones). At this level of abstraction, management is also an ideology – *managerialism* – which proclaims the value and necessity of management for organisational, economic and social progress, and establishes the foundational claim that to be effective, managers must have 'the right to manage' (Clarke and Newman, 1997). The translation of the global conception of management into particular settings involves the production of managerialised assemblages, which are articulated around empowering management (enabling them to exercise forms of power and authority in specific organisational and social settings). The global phenomenon of management is also made up of repertoires – of discourses and devices, texts and techniques, roles and resources – that provide the material from which specific managerialising assemblages may be composed. These repertoires include:

- a litany of *imperatives and injunctions* ('set managers free to manage'; 'do the right things, not do things right');

---

[3] At the same time, it should be remembered that the NPM is itself the *academic abstraction* used to name the complex drive towards reforming public administration, governance, management and services, rather than a thing itself. This has implications for debates about what constitutes the NPM.

- a vocabulary of *conceptual and discursive resources* (producing an enormous and still-expanding lexicon of strange yet strangely familiar terminology – strategy, customer-facing orientations, values, missions, going forward, culture change, becoming businesslike, etc – that are now often parodied as 'management-speak');[4]
- a songbook of *analytical and empirical justifications* (from public choice theory, to lists of excellent organisations, to 'success stories' of managerial transformation);
- a catalogue of *transformative devices* that may be put into place (contracts; choices; incentives; targets);
- a tool box of *techniques and technologies* that can be deployed as ways of ordering the internal world and external relations of particular organisations (budgetary consciousness; performance appraisal; tools of measurement; governing through data (Ozga et al, 2011); shared values; visions and missions; etc);
- a cast list of *identities and identifications* that characterise people and places in the realm of the organisation or service (types and layers of managers; executives; leaders; teams; external-facing or customer-facing staff; project teams and managers; real and imagined customers; stakeholders; etc); and
- a set of *scripts* for preferred types of relationships and dispositions among the cast. Scripts establish the type of encounters and interactions that should take place (in which X is enabled or empowered, or incited to behave responsibly, or expected to display enthusiasm).[5]

Here, we can see one of the dimensions that working through 'assemblage' adds to the view of policy as translation. It enriches the careful attention to language and discursive practice in translation approaches by drawing attention to the banal or prosaic 'stuff' through which policy comes to life – the places (eg different sorts of offices or meeting rooms), the forms (from student assessment to workload management), the handbooks and guidelines (through which strategic visions, statements and objectives are translated into injunctions, instructions and guidance), and the face-to-face or online architectures

---

[4] The parodying and critique of 'management-speak' is now widespread, with lists of most-hated phrases, translation guides and varieties of 'bureaucratic bingo' (where participants score on hearing key phrases used in meetings).

[5] This list deliberately makes use of a variety of categories that suggest the performative character of managerialism (scripts, cast lists, songbooks, litanies, etc) and combines them with others that speak to the ways in which managerial authority is embedded in techniques, technologies and devices.

in which encounters between different sorts of agents are enacted. Assemblages are the concatenation of very different sorts of things – including, but not limited to, people and language. They combine the material, the affective and the discursive elements of organisational (and social) life in both dramatic and banal ways.

Any particular instantiation of management will borrow elements from across these repertoires. The particular instance will involve translation – borrowings, adaptations, inflections, re-articulations – as well as selective omissions, refusals and, importantly, the recoding of established positions and practices in newly managerialised framings. So, the managerialisation of universities creates new managerial positions and practices. It re-imagines existing administrative and academic hierarchies as if they were managerial (eg grasping them as 'line management' hierarchies). It attempts to dismantle existing identifications, affiliations and subjectivities and inculcate new ones more in-keeping with a managerialised system.

The repertoires of managerialisation are held in – and mobilised from – a variety of forms and settings: guidance from transnational organisations like the Organisation for Economic Co-operation and Development (OECD); handbooks and textbooks for managers (and those who would become managers); educational programmes (MPAs/MBAs, etc); international, national and local events about public service change; internal training and development programmes; and the catechism of individual appraisal and development.[6] In such

---

[6] The author had a final 'career development and staff appraisal' encounter with his head of department that was organised around two recent managerialising framings: the 'Leadership Competency Framework' and 'Valued Ways of Working'. An extract from the second of these explains the 'order of things' in a managerialised Open University:

What is Valued Ways of Working?

The Open University mission statement, open to people, places, methods and ideas is well known by staff and students alike. This mission shapes the way we do things and the decisions we make that ultimately result in the high quality experience our students, peers and customers know us for. Presented in a simple-to-use framework, the Valued Ways of Working tool is a helpful prompt for reflecting on how we contribute to the success of the University. Taking good practice examples from across the University, it showcases the behaviours that help us perform at our best. Units, teams, managers and individuals use the framework to support them in recruitment decisions, coaching, personal reflection, one-to-one line manager meetings, CDSA [Career Development and Staff Appraisal] preparation, and team development. (Taken from the Open University Human Resources Development Intranet, November 2013)

settings, managerialisation is discursively constituted as a necessary condition to be achieved. It is normatively extremely difficult to resist explicit or implicit pressures to be 'businesslike', 'modern', 'efficient' or 'excellent'. Such terms are simultaneously banal and managerially colonised: excellence acts as an abstract aspiration yet is concretely specified in managerially calculable forms. Outdated administrative systems, processes and relationships are multiply condemned: public service reform – and the associated reform of public service governance – is recurrently demanded as an economic, social, political and ethical necessity. Nevertheless, such translations of management reveal complicated and shifting ways of inhabiting these injunctions to be modern and businesslike: hospitals turn out to be different from local authority social services and from universities – the mixtures of market-like devices, forms of management and competitive evaluation/measurement vary from site to site (see, eg, Newman and Clarke, 2009; Wright and Boden, 2011).

It is precisely this complex mixture of the universal/global and particularity that makes managerialism such a potent force – and that indicated why the combination of translation and assemblage provides a critical way of understanding its significance. Translation alerts us to its capacity to move – to connect places and settings as if they were the same (all capable of being improved by the application of managerial wisdom and authority). It also draws our attention to the ways in which managerialism enters particular places, being actively appropriated to their peculiar qualities, processes and relationships and yet transforming (or promising to transform) them in the same moment. At the same time, I want to suggest that the core of these particular translations of managerialism involves assemblages of power. Despite the many uses of the concept of assemblage (and, indeed, the many frustrations that the concept can evoke), for me, its productive value lies in the way that it combines attention to the ways in which the making (and remaking) of relationships between people and things is also a process in which forms of power and modes of authority are reworked and realigned.

Managerialisation as reassembling power

Assemblage provides a way of thinking about how travelling policies and practices are articulated with power or, more precisely, are implicated in the re-articulation of power in different forms and settings (although this is not a concern shared by all approaches that use assemblage). From the outset, the *managerialisation* of public services travelled on the promise of reorganising established formations of power and authority. As Clarke and Newman (1997) argued, managerialism promised to displace and subordinate the existing forms of authority and decision-making logics of public services: representative politics; professional expertise and its associated discretionary judgement; and bureaucratic norms of conduct. Managerialism promised innovation, dynamism and efficiency in place of the cumbersome, sclerotic, interest-driven 'old ways'. In their place, managerialism promised to construct or empower alternative forms of authority, most obviously, in demanding that managers be given 'the freedom to manage' (see Clarke and Newman, 1993).

Managerialisation is associated with the articulation of new forms of authority, for example, the salience of 'strategic management' or, subsequently, 'inspirational leadership' (on 'leaderism' in public service management, see O'Reilly and Reed, 2011). Some variants of the NPM promise to take account of the diverse 'stakeholders' who populate the internal and external worlds of the organisation. Most variants contain a promise to 'empower' the consumer/customer by creating capacities for choice or making organisations responsive. More occasionally, there are promises to empower 'staff'. Such varieties of empowerment involve shifting the calculating frameworks and the decision-making logics that are at work in the organisational fields being managerialised as older forms of power (and the knowledge/ judgement/decision-making systems with which they are articulated) are displaced or subordinated.

Such promises of transformation produce highly uneven effects in practice. The articulation of managerial logics into new spaces occasionally replaces existing organisational orderings of bureaucracy and professionalism, but more typically subordinates them in complex mixed-mode organisational forms. The resulting organisational spaces then contain multiple calculating frameworks and decision-making logics jostling for position (on contested combinations of managerial/customer and administrative justice logics, see Clarke et al, 2010). Managerialisation can rarely 'clear the field' of other forms of knowledge, power and logic entirely; this is often lost sight of in accounts of neoliberal or managerial hegemony within the transformed university (accounts that are often accompanied by a strangely nostalgic view of academic authority or the fantasy of an academic community; see, eg, Ginsberg, 2011). However, what is consistent is the way in which the assemblage of management rearranges the field of agency and power: valorising some types of knowledge and judgement; celebrating some types of action and orientations (eg a 'can-do' mindset); and privileging some kinds of agent or forms of agency. Here, established forms of power, knowledge and agency are reworked, with some forms of agent and agency becoming dominant while others are displaced or accommodated in subordinated positions (Clarke and Newman, 1997).

Reinventing the university

The contemporary forms of management have emerged through many travels: the journey from corporate managerialism to public governance; from anglophone innovation to more or less willing adopters elsewhere; and from central government strategies of transformation and modernisation to more specific sectoral and organisational experiences of reform or 'transformation'. In this context, I explore the encounter between British/English universities and the mobile assemblage of management.[7] This involves distinguishing the specific geopolitical space (England), the sector (higher education) and the site (the university, understanding that what constitutes a university has been changed in the process).

Like all public institutions in the UK, from the 1980s onwards, universities were expected to make themselves more modern, to become more efficient and businesslike, and to transform their systems of administration and governance. The 2011 White Paper on higher education, *Students at the heart of the system*, was announced on the government information website as follows:

> The White Paper comes as part of the wider government agenda to put more power in the hands of the consumer. The Government has launched a major programme for public sector modernisation by cutting waste and bringing choice, encouraging competition and opening the market up to new providers. For higher education, this means that in future funding will follow the choices of the student.[8]

Here is a familiar set of public service reform tropes – freedom of choice, consumers, increasing efficiency, opening the market to

---

[7] The designation British/English denotes the complicated constitutional field of action that is produced by a UK that contains distinct and different constitutional entities. Education in Scotland has always been a separate political and administrative domain, a separation increased by the partial devolution of governmental powers to Scotland in 1998. Education policy in England is made by the British Parliament for the English education system.

[8] Source: https://www.gov.uk/government/news/putting-students-at-the-heart-of-higher-education

new providers – all bundled as 'modernisation' (now in its second decade as a keyword linked to managerialisation). However, in what follows, I want to suggest that the familiarity of these tropes tends to conceal a strangely heterogeneous set of conditions, conjunctions and consequences. That is to say, they embody and enact different forces, different imperatives and different orientations that are made to appear as parts of a coherent direction (modernisation). I address these conditions through an approach that might (generously) be described as a sort of participant observation, drawing on the experience of working in, and writing and talking about, the HE sector in the UK during these 30 years. The evidence I offer is, then, necessarily, localised, specific, fragmentary and unreliable. However, in reflecting on my experiences of being reformed, modernised, managed and led, it is possible to tease out some consistent tendencies and recurrent tensions. Conversations with friends, colleagues, collaborators and even managers (who are sometimes the same people) have tended to reinforce my sense of these changes. In what follows, I have tried to bring out their diverse, possibly divergent and even contradictory character, instead of treating them as expressing or emanating from a singular and coherent political project. They cannot be reduced to larger tendencies in capitalism (despite Roggero's [2011] compelling account of the contradictions of knowledge as labour). Nor are they merely the bastard offspring of a globalising neoliberalism.

> *Noémi Lendvai (NL):* What if, for a moment, I would argue that there is nothing wrong with the 'bastard offspring of globalising neoliberalism' argument. I know it is deeply unfashionable, because we are now in a post-neoliberalism debate, in which 'neoliberalism' (not with 'N') is one of many processes. However, what if, for a moment, I would argue that the managerialisation of HE in the UK is a deeply colonising process, a new one, no doubt, producing thousands of students keen to 'learn about public management'.

> *John Clarke (JC):* I would accept the point, but also insist that most offspring have more than one parent – and we need to know that other forces, pressures and discourses are in play in this process. That, I hope, is the significance of arguing that they are not 'merely' the offspring of a globalising neoliberalism. I am sceptical of attempts to explain a complex particular situation by referring to a singular cause. Neoliberalism is not a single parent; nor are its offspring miraculous.

I will argue instead that their heterogeneity is better understood as a site of what the French Marxist philosopher Louis Althusser called 'contradiction and overdetermination' (1969). Overdetermination identifies precisely this sense of multiple forces, pressures and dynamics that are at work in a particular moment of time and space. In the case of universities, the diverse processes, strategies and practices of reform have become condensed and compounded in institutional and organisational sites, producing particular combinations of tensions and antagonisms.

The long struggle to transform universities in the UK emerged in the Thatcherite project of transforming public institutions, striving to subordinate them to market-centric and managerial modes of coordination – both as systems and as individual organisations. As Randy Martin (2011) has argued, it is important not to equate the arrival of managerial authority with the necessary social labour of organisational or institutional coordination. Universities before the 1980s were not merely a setting for academic genius, the pursuit of knowledge for its own sake or the site of a happily self-regulating academic community. They required a form of coordination – professional, administrative, collegial and hierarchical – that maintained the conditions for forms of intellectual production and reproduction that were (lest we forget) elitist, exclusionary, discriminatory and hierarchical.

The transatlantic New Right – embodied first in the figures of Thatcher and Reagan – combined a variety of contradictory political tendencies, not least the articulation of neoliberal approaches to deregulation, anti-unionism and state reform, with profoundly conservative and authoritarian social, moral and cultural orientations. Despite the relatively narrow and elitist character of university recruitment and practice in the UK, universities found themselves arraigned alongside other public organisations as a key element in the social democratic/progressive/liberal 'consensus' that had to be unlocked so that enterprise and enterprising individuals could be liberated. The attack on the 'social' sciences became a characteristic focal point for those concerns (including the charge of 'Marxist bias' levelled against the Open University by a Conservative minister of education in 1984).[9] A series of key institutional innovations changed the landscape of HE, most notably, the dissolution of the binary division between universities and polytechnics, the abolition of academic tenure, the expansion of the range of organisations that could call themselves universities, and the creation of a quasi-market in students between 'competing providers'. The 1980s were also marked by a commitment

---

[9] See: http://www.open.ac.uk/blogs/History-of-the-OU/?p=20

to subject the HE system and individual universities to the pursuit of 'economy, efficiency and effectiveness' and 'value for money'. This was conditioned by tight central control of funding regimes, and was articulated in the expectation that universities would make 'efficiency savings' through more effective internal management processes. Such changes were common across the range of public services and it could be argued that other sectors experienced more dramatic and sustained dislocation and transformation through marketising and managerialising processes, including extensive changes driven by 'purchaser–provider' splits or contracting-out processes (eg compulsory competitive tendering). Nevertheless, these innovations of the 1980s constructed a different landscape for HE (see Wright, 2004; Wright and Boden, 2011). These features were built upon by subsequent governments, not least in the introduction of full-cost fees for university students in England.

There have been a number of consistent, if not coherent, tendencies in government approaches to HE. A continuing invention of market-like or market-making mechanisms that treat students as choice-makers or consumers and universities (or Higher Education Institutions [HEIs]) as service providers has remained a core conception of how the sector should be organised. It is, though, important to hold on to notions of markets *being made*, as a series of devices and mechanisms that can be situationally deployed, particularly in the face of what Thomas Frank (2001) calls 'market populism' – a universalising discourse of the market's capacity to solve all problems. As Julia Elyachar (2005: 15, 24) has argued:

> The notion of the market is so familiar that we tend to take it for granted, we really don't know what it is. 'The market' functions as a folk concept more than a scientific term....
>
> Rather than the market, we need to think about a multiplicity of markets that are the outcomes of specific forms of labor, culture, technological mixes, and modes of organisation specific to time and place.

This marketising dynamic is often represented as a process of enabling the entry of 'diverse providers', as in the current Coalition government's commitment to 'creating a more diverse, competitive higher education sector by reviewing the way alternative providers can access funding'.[10]

---

[10] Source: https://www.gov.uk/government/policies/making-the-higher-education-system-more-efficient-and-diverse (accessed 13 August 2103).

A second recurrent tendency has been the policy of 'widening participation' in HE, moving towards a 'mass' rather than 'elite' system. Not surprisingly, progress has been neither smooth nor simple, particularly given the disputed impact of a tuition fee and loan system of student finance. In 2013, the so-called 'student Tsar' claimed that financially risk-averse universities were likely to favour 'reliable' middle-class students:[11]

> Professor Les Ebdon, head of the Office for Fair Access (Offa), said that universities seeking to maximise their income were encouraged to admit 'good middle-class' applicants rather than take a risk on disadvantaged students who were more likely to drop out.[12]

The current UK Coalition government has identified HE as part of its global strategy:

> This strategy sets out how the government and the whole education sector will work together to take advantage of new opportunities around the globe. It aims to build on our strengths in higher and further education, in our schools overseas, in our educational technology and products and services, and in delivering English language training.

This strategy includes:

- 'our warm welcome for international students';
- 'supporting transnational education';
- 'leading the world in education technology';
- 'actively encouraging development of Massive Open Online Courses (MOOCs)';
- 'a new relationship with emerging powers'; and

---

[11] The simultaneous rise of the NPM and a governmental enthusiasm for 'Tsars' is an interesting coincidence.

[12] Source: *The Observer*, 10 August 2013. Available at: http://www.theguardian. com/education/2013/aug/10/university-middle-class-bias-hits-poorer-students (accessed 13 August 2013).

- 'building the UK brand and seizing opportunities', which 'will ensure we grow both our economy and our wider links with partners around the world'.[13]

Here, we can see the reframing of universities in both a national and global matrix. It deploys a characteristic set of contemporary managerial discourses and devices in the elaboration of a strategy: branding (the UK brand); new education technologies; and the commitment to developing and exploiting relationships and partnerships. It also celebrates the figure of the international student – to be given a 'warm welcome' (this was a deeply controversial issue given the fall in international student applications consequent upon the government's anti-immigration rhetoric and practice).

Finally, governments have been consistently enthusiastic about 'improving' the governance, administration and management of universities, including a will to enhance the capacity for 'leadership' at senior levels (Deem and Parker, 2008). In the Open University context, leadership is understood as being composed of the following capacities:

- Leading Others to Achievement
- Strategic and Analytical Thinking
- Planning and Organising
- Influencing and Relationship Building
- Driving and Embracing Change
- Student and Customer Focus[14]

This Open University list is not particularly distinctive, but it does nicely capture the will to manage (and the will to managerialise). The list translates two different sets of dynamics (the rising discourse of leadership itself and the current imperatives of HE) into a series of organisational priorities and the dispositions that are required to realise them (note the recurrent use of the gerund form to underline *practical* dispositions: leading, driving, embracing, building, etc). Managerialisation has been the connective practice that translates multiple priorities, pressures and problems from the 'external environment' into an apparently coherent *organisational* project (Clarke and Newman, 1997).

---

[13] Source: https://www.gov.uk/government/publications/international-education-strategy-global-growth-and-prosperity (accessed 13 August 2013).

[14] Source: Human Resources Development Intranet (accessed 13 August 2013).

Making the university manageable

Writing about universities in the US, Randy Martin (2011: 107) explores an important paradox of the process of managerialisation:[15]

> The shift in value of higher education from a public to a private good centers power and authority on senior administrators, who are taken to be responsible to delimit a particular brand of excellence that will maintain the health of the enterprise. At the same time, faculty governance under the sign of the proletarianisation of the professions is transcribed into ever more time-consuming administrative duties. The tensions between a centripetal management manifest in an increasingly centralised administration and a centrifugal managerialism – evident in the diffusion of accountability protocols among faculty and staff – generates all manner of fault lines as to which kinds of decisions belong to whom and what conditions of partnership advance the university's purpose. The simultaneous centering and dispersion of management speaks to a more general blurring of the boundary between what is inside and outside the university as an organisation. The result is a series of mixed metaphors and messages.

This doubling of centralisation and dispersion captures a very peculiar dynamic of managerialisation. It both empowers the senior/strategic management or leadership while enrolling all staff into its logics, and also, as Martin, suggests, produces tensions, mixed messages and antagonisms. Managerialism disperses 'responsibility' across all layers of the organisation while concentrating the power to create and disseminate visions, strategies and objectives in a central core. It also enables the recruitment of external forms of managerial expertise in the guise of consultants who will 'enhance' the organisation's capacities. In the process, the quasi-collegial, quasi-democratic decision-making processes that existed unevenly in universities have been displaced or rendered vestigial parodies (talking about decisions already made

---

[15] The US is a different social formation, with a different system of HE and a different version of the 'mobile assemblage' of managerialism. Nevertheless, Martin's observations about the arrival of new forms of management and their reordering of the internal world of the university are suggestive precisely because they are recognisable as a different form of this mobile assemblage.

elsewhere). In part, this shift arises from a thoroughly managerial frustration with the unpredictable and time-consuming 'inefficiency' of such academic decision-making forums. However, the shift also marks a redefinition of the relationship between academic staff and the university. They are certainly 'valued human resources' (in the favoured mode of address of Human Resources [HR] departments) but they are certainly not 'partners' in strategic decision-making (except for those who come to occupy 'leadership' roles).

> **Paul Stubbs (PS)**: To misquote Shakespeare's *Twelfth Night*, can it be said that 'some are born leaders, some achieve leadership positions and some have leadership thrust upon them'? Is it possible and perhaps even relevant to distinguish between those academics who take on leadership functions, somewhat reluctantly, because it is their turn, and those who embrace leadership positions without qualms? This is, perhaps, important only in terms of the relationship between particular assemblages of the NPM and real agency in specific settings, in this case, UK universities. It may, also, of course, be important in terms of understanding diverse repertoires of resistance and recalcitrance.

> **JC:** I agree – it matters both for understanding the different means of enrolment into managerial positions and for the organisational and psychic conflicts that take place. The issue also speaks to the ways in which managerialism borrows and bends other discourses (student-centred approaches, quality, leadership, etc).

This dynamic is at the core of transforming the university into a manageable organisation precisely because it redefines questions of 'ownership and control' in decisive ways. Where universities previously operated as a form of professional bureaucracy (a hybrid that combined – more or less comfortably – professional decision-making and bureaucratic administration; see Mintzberg, 1992), they increasingly attempt to mimic the corporate line-management form, in which staff (of various types) are simultaneously a resource, a cost and a problem to be managed in pursuit of the organisation's strategic objectives. We should remember that both professionalism and bureaucracy are themselves shifting and mobile assemblages (and that the professional bureaucracy is a hybrid of these forms). Perhaps the result of these transformations might best be described as a managerial professional bureaucracy (or managerialised professional bureaucracy) because what emerges is a combination of modes of authority and power, rather than a singular entity. However, the relationship between these different modes is certainly 'structured in dominance', articulated around – and subordinate to – managerial power. Martin's point about the dispersal of accountability and responsibility indicates something important about the way that this process incorporates 'modern' managerial lessons about how 'excellent' organisations 'empower' staff (Clarke and Newman, 1993). Staff are enrolled into processes that combine line management (including intensified forms of performance management) and forms of self-management – being budgetary conscious, knowing how one contributes to the 'mission', practising 'valued ways of working', listening carefully to the 'cascade' of organisational news, and, above all, 'embracing change' (no matter how ill-advised or wrongheaded it might appear, since change is incontrovertibly virtuous).

> I sit in a workshop to which I have been invited at the Open University under the title 21st Century Academic. Along with around 30 other academics from across the university, I listen to introductions from three members of the university's senior management team about the importance of recognising and embracing the need for change. Sent off to discuss the issue confronting us (and the university) in small groups, we were expected to report back. The group to which I have been allocated has an astonishingly bitter and bad-tempered discussion about the perceived mode of address by senior managers ('the world has changed, the sector has changed, the university needs to change – and only you are stopping it') before delivering a report back centred on a drawing of a dinosaur on a piece of flip-chart paper. 'That is who you think we are' is the brief accompanying statement – denied (albeit not very convincingly) by the members of the senior team receiving the report back.

For the senior management, this workshop represented one tactic for bringing a recalcitrant workforce 'up to speed' – a way in which they could be brought to understand the problems and challenges facing the university and how they could adapt or develop in ways that would help the university to overcome these problems and face these challenges. The 'dinosaur' image captured the perceived positioning of academic staff in this managerial discourse: self-obsessed, out of touch, intransigent and backward-looking. This 'staff development' process sought to both conscientise and responsibilise academic staff as actors in a managerialised university. It was not wholly successful, but nevertheless marks a critical moment in the reassembling of the order of the university such that staff could be 'enabled' to contribute to its mission. Leadership, in this sense, involves both defining the mission and enrolling people into its achievement.

We might understand this repositioning of academic staff as a transition from one form of self-management to another. The older model of professional bureaucracy assumed that professionals were largely self-governing and self-directing (supported, if also sometimes constrained, by administrative bureaucracies). This model of professional autonomy assumed a relatively powerful norm- and ethos-setting authority of the profession that would be embodied by the professionals and enacted in the judgements they made in practice. In the emerging managerial university, the 'professionals' are increasingly viewed with suspicion as people who cannot be trusted to pursue the best interests of the (specific) organisation. Their loyalties and criteria for judgement lie elsewhere (in professional orientations), thus requiring management that can define objectives, priorities and criteria for judgement – including the expectation that performance rewards should be calculated in relation to the individual's contribution to the university's strategic objectives (alongside, or even instead of, some more abstract criteria of academic excellence). This is not to romanticise the older model (and its undoubted problems of collective ordering), but to note how power and judgement have been remade in the pursuit of an incorporated model of organisational success.

This corporatising version of management is itself framed by the relocation of individual universities within a 'system' whose elements are articulated by competitive-evaluative devices that aim to define and measure 'success'. 'System' works as a particular sort of representation: it represents the assemblage of actors, actants, sites, relationships, resources and so on that are mobilised and directed to achieve policy objectives. Systems – as a practical concept – provide a key element in managerial discourse, in part, because systems are imagined as manageable objects. They are manageable because they can be mapped, measured, rearranged and directed by the exercise of managerial techniques (see Stan, 2007). Such systems are, in principle, rendered transparent by the array of audit, evaluation and performance management techniques that have been developed during the last 20 years or so. HE is grasped as a national system, one that can be ordered and directed by central government policy, funding and forms of regulation. It is a multi-national system within the devolved UK, and is – in some uneven and contradictory ways – an international system (in terms of collaboration, competition and the attraction of students and other valued resources). However, its framing as a national system is founded upon the governing logics of competition and evaluation in which each corporate entity is a subsystem or element defined by its relationships to the system as a whole and to its competitors (on the 'competitive–evaluative nexus', see Clarke, 2005a).

Universities are enmeshed in multiple logics of competition: to attract (and retain) students; to win research funds; and to achieve 'success' in various performance evaluation systems (teaching quality, research quality, student evaluations, etc). While some of these logics of competition take market-like forms (eg attracting students), these are better seen as market-making devices (in which the value of students is partly established by the government). As Janet Newman and John Clarke have argued (2009), in the remaking of public services, a variety of such market-making devices have been deployed that act to encourage a range of actors (organisations, managers, staff, users) to think of themselves as economic/entrepreneurial agents engaged in market-like relations, practices and calculations. In such moves, we can see the practices of translation: as particular identities or positions are recoded, the relationships between them reworked, and an imaginary of the whole is presented as both what is and what will be (when glitches have been overcome).

Such market-making devices are certainly critical forms of ordering the 'system', but they are accompanied by other competitive logics. Competition for research funds, for example, is organised through research councils in which 'peer evaluation' combines with central imperatives about topics, modes of working and the forms and uses of knowledge that are desired. It is supplemented by the national processes of research evaluation (the Research Assessment Exercise, succeeded by the current Research Excellence Framework) through which the work of all academic departments that are identified as research-active is compared and evaluated – with rankings attributed at the end of the process. In this competition around research, central imperatives, such as the controversial valorising of 'impact', are articulated with forms of peer review to establish 'quality' criteria for evaluation (see Pain et al, 2011).

Teaching (albeit now construed as teaching and learning, or learning and teaching) has equally been subjected to a variety of evaluative devices – inspections and audits – that produce benchmarks, quality marks and rankings (Strathern, 2000). Such technologies are combined with internal and external surveys of student opinion (to gauge 'customer satisfaction') about the quality of both the university experience and of teaching in specific subjects.[16] In these processes, we see mixed modes and technologies of governance – inspection, audit, customer surveys, peer review – that contribute to a system organised around competition. In the resulting HE system, 'success' becomes an inescapable organisational priority, though the form and calculation of success may vary. The Russell Group of Universities announces its value in terms of 'world-class research': 'Russell Group universities are global leaders in research. Between them, the 24 members of the Russell Group undertake over two thirds of the research undertaken by UK universities and two thirds of the very best research deemed "world leading"'.[17] In contrast, Loughborough University announces itself as providing the 'best student experience': 'Loughborough is the only university to have been voted England's Best Student Experience for six consecutive years in the Times Higher Education league table'.[18] It is impossible to avoid pursuing success (in some form or another) because success is the route to survival, to resources, to expansion and, of course, to further success. Such competitive logics, especially those embodied in the devices of performance evaluation and resource allocation, demand that each university understands itself as a competing enterprise, striving for success.

This model of a system to be coordinated by market and managerial logics is not unique to HE (in the UK, it has been applied in some form to most public services), but it is a powerful way of framing the internal worlds of universities, demanding their adaptation to compelling external imperatives. So, universities, though nominally autonomous, are required to conform to a number of strategic demands: promoting national competitiveness; creating a 'knowledge economy'; producing 'useful knowledge'; enlarging 'access' to HE; or delivering 'enterprising selves'. They are simultaneously subjected to the obsessions of performance management: the requirements of efficiency, economy and effectiveness that have been attached to public funds. In addition, universities are expected to perform as 'well-managed organisations', displaying the forms of transparency, accountability and effective internal processes that are announced as the necessary forms of 'good governance' (on policy technologies, see

---

[16] See the Quality Assurance Agency website. Available at: www.qaa.ac.uk

[17] Source: http://www.russellgroup.ac.uk/world-class-research.aspx (accessed 14 August 2013).

[18] Source: http://www.lboro.ac.uk/about/achievements/best-student-experience. html (accessed 14 August 2013).

Ball, 2008: 41–5). As Newman and Clarke (2009: 102) have argued, contemporary models of 'good governance':

> establish norms, ways of seeing and thinking, ways of calculating and acting that both create the conditions for specific governance innovations and infuse the practices of governance that ensue. Good governance – whether on the part of public sector bodies, businesses, NGOs [non-governmental organisations] or many of the 'flex' organisations discussed earlier – is, then, both a normative discourse and a set of technologies. The latter renders areas of potential political conflict, or struggles over different kinds of 'public' interest, into more neutral decisional spaces.... Political judgements and calculations are displaced away from the formal – and cumbersome – mechanisms of representative democracy to a plethora of governing bodies, boards, consultative committees and trustees.

This model of a system articulated by competition and evaluation forms a set of relationships that distributes 'relative autonomy'. Each university must imagine itself as a corporate entity, geared to competitive success, and needing to develop its own unique 'strategy'. As the following invitation indicates, this is a turbulent and troublesome system in which to be competitive:

Modernising Higher Education: delivering value in a global market
24 September 2013, The Barbican, London

- Are you interested in the future of the UK higher education sector and its position in the international marketplace?
- Do you want to know how the sector can modernise itself, becoming more efficient and effective?
- Look at the latest efficiency and productivity strategies and inspirational improvements to student experience
- Learn from high-profile keynote speakers and practical case studies, as well as sharing your own experiences

Confirmed Speakers Include
Paul Clark
Director of Policy, Universities UK

Katelyn Donnelly
Executive Director, Pearson and Author, IPPR 'An
Avalanche is Coming' Report
Dr Shaun Curtis
Director, International Exeter, University of Exeter
Geoff Stoakes
Academic Lead for Research, Higher Education Academy

Topics to be Discussed
Competing in a global market
Strategies for change
Delivering value in a global market
Better use of estates and assets
Future challenges and opportunities

**Modernising Higher Education: delivering value
in a global market** will consider the future of the UK
higher education sector and its position in the international
marketplace.

Covering the latest efficiency and productivity strategies,
inspirational improvements to student experience, and
teaching and learning innovations, the conference presents
an ideal opportunity for professionals from right across
the higher education sector to learn from high profile
keynote speakers and practical case studies, as well as
sharing their own experiences with contemporaries in the
busy networking session. (Modernising Higher Education
Conference, 2013: Public Sector Events)

This invitation frames the field of HE in terms of competition within
a global market as the terrain of 'modernisation', summoning potential
participants on a 'need to know' principle (are you interested, do you
want to know, look and learn, network …). It links the identification
of key topics (What needs to be managed?) and the latest techniques
(the latest innovations to help manage them). It performs the
characteristic managerial translation of the 'threats and opportunities'
of the external environment into the internal world of the university
as things to be managed. Its promised speakers occupy distinctively
'modern' positions in the new system: a Director of Policy from
Universities UK, self-described as 'Universities UK is the definitive
voice for universities in the UK. We provide high quality leadership

and support to our members, to promote a successful and diverse higher education sector';[19] an Executive Director from Pearson (the education publishing company); and a Director of International Exeter – a mode of naming that conflates a strategy (internationalisation) and an entity (International Exeter). The cast list is completed by the Academic Lead for Research (another neologism from a word that used to be attached to dogs) at the Higher Education Academy:

> The Higher Education Academy champions excellent learning and teaching in higher education....
>
> Our mission, as stated in our Strategic Plan 2012–2016, is to use our expertise and resources to support the higher education community in order to enhance the quality and impact of learning and teaching. We do this by recognising and rewarding excellent teaching, bringing together people and resources to research and share best practice, and by helping to influence, shape and implement policy.[20]

Both the naming of positions and the conflation of desires and achievements in strategies, missions and visions is reminiscent of Marilyn Strathern's (2006) commentary on the mode of communication by bullet points adopted in university strategy documents. Alongside this by-now entirely normalised communicative style, we should also note the landscape of organisations, relationships and collaborations implied in the conference invitation. Universities are surrounded by and interpenetrate with a variety of other entities that are university/education/HE supports, advisors, consultants and companies that form the 'HE sector' and think about its 'position in the international marketplace'. As an attendee, you could participate in the 'busy networking session'.

The systemic framing of competition that is visible in this invitation – and many other forms – incites universities to think of themselves as corporate entities: as businesses, or at least as 'businesslike' organisations. As Martin (2011) suggests, the need to achieve success (or even survival) requires the managerialisation of each institution. The organisation must have effective strategic direction (or 'leadership') to identify a course through the array of emergent possibilities, problems and pitfalls that constitute its environment. However, it must also have rigorous internal management systems to achieve the purposive and effective

---

[19] Source: http://www.universitiesuk.ac.uk/aboutus/Pages/default.aspx

[20] Source: http://www.heacademy.ac.uk/about

deployment of all of its internal resources in pursuit of the corporate strategy. So, universities must learn to be – or at least present themselves as – well-managed organisations.

Finding things to manage

Once installed, managerial coordination is marked by a colonising desire to find new things to manage, enrolling them into the managerial assemblage. In the university, people/human resources are the key object, given the proportion of the costs of being a university that they constitute (although it should be noted that, according to the Higher Education Statistics Agency [HESA],[21] during the past decade, administrative staff have formed more than 50% of university employees). (In this data, no distinction is made between managerial and administrative posts – a reflection of the problems of naming things – including people – in a mixed-mode organisational form.) The repertoire of techniques and technologies for 'managing people' has expanded considerably, mirrored in the growth of the HR function in most universities. Elaborate recruitment and retention policies have been developed (which also condense and translate a series of political struggles over equality into recruitment and career monitoring, in diversity in the workplace policies, and more). New forms of contracting have developed, with over one third of academic posts being held on short-term contracts.[22] Such contracts reflect a corporate concern with 'flexibility': the ability to manage, move and mobilise resources (including historically intractable academic staff – and their costs) in a more 'dynamic' and 'efficient' way, more effectively geared to the organisation's 'emerging strategy'.

At the same time, an elaborate apparatus of workload management, personal appraisal and career development policies and practices has been developed, mostly embedded in forms and reporting systems to ensure compliance and accountability. In the midst of such processes, it is often difficult to distinguish between support and surveillance as the bureaucratised process appears to substitute for organisational interest and attention. There is no doubt that such systems – and their attempt to produce compliance – respond to formerly widespread non-existent and/or bad practice in academic recruitment, career development and

---

[21] Data from HESA. Available at: http://www.hesa.ac.uk/index.php?option=com_content&task=view&id=1898&Itemid=706

[22] Data from HESA. Available at: http://www.hesa.ac.uk/index.php?option=com_content&task=view&id=1898&Itemid=706

more. Whether they resolve such problems is a more difficult question. As with so many other forms of 'tick-box' performance management, ticking the box becomes the organisational and individual imperative (see Clarke, 2005a; Travers, 2007).

As people – the 'valued human resources' of the organisation – become more visible as an object to be managed, so more aspects of the self come to be areas of organisational concern. While an interest in health and wellbeing – and the provision of health and counselling services – might be welcomed (in the face of uncaring organisations), the unstable cocktail of support and surveillance is visible here too. Some universities have adopted the 'Bradford Factor' approach to managing staff absence. As the Organisation for Responsible Business describes it:

> The Bradford Factor is a method of calculating absence in order to put a 'weighting' on the absence. For example; a Company will probably be more concerned (and experience more disruption) from frequent odd days sickness, [than] an employee who has one period of absence for a week.[23]

This system has induced people (especially support staff, whose presence/absence is more visible and monitored than that of academic staff) to take annual leave days to be sick or to deal with personal/family emergencies in order to avoid their "Bradford' score making them visible as someone to be managed. The management of sickness may be a particularly dramatic example, but many managerial techniques and technologies produce this 'gaming' effect: they themselves become environmental problems for people to cope with, individually or collectively.[24]

---

[23] Source: http://www.orbuk.org.uk/article/the-bradford-factor

[24] NL has suggested that there is a further issue that can be glimpsed through this example: the way in which time and temporality have also become the objects of management. I cannot pursue it here, but it would include questions of: the different ways in which time is quantified, measured and managed (see the first vignette); the time horizons imagined in strategy (When did the 'Five Year Plan' lose its Stalinist connotations?); the reformatting of the academic year to fit national and international 'markets'; the calculation of time as a valuable resource; the computerisation of timetabling and scheduling; and, not least, the ways in which different demands make some types of time more flexible – information and communication technologies (ICTs) enabling working at a distance, student finances making study time coexist with paid employment time and so on.

One further contradictory example of the expansive management of people is the growing interest in what might be called emotion management, including the expectation that people will be 'enthusiasts' – living the mission (on the corrosive effects of enthusiasm, see Du Gay, 2000). Academics are not immune to appeals to ethics and values, and, in particular, tend to be enthusiastic about perceived conjunctions between their own personal, professional and political values and those of the university. However, they are also prone to what might be called professional scepticism or cynicism and those reluctant to commit to what appear to be changing corporate enthusiasms. This is an unstable mixture, and often becomes visible in attempts to realign the relationship between staff and the mission:

> I sit as a member of a strategic committee discussing the university's (then) current mission statement. Some members of the management team think that the time has come to change ('renew') it. One justification for doing so is that it would give staff a sense of progress, implying that we had achieved the aims of the existing mission. A more doubtful set of voices suggest that such a view would be misleading (we had not achieved all of the aims) and, anyway, people had only just come to terms with knowing the existing mission. To change it would be premature. A third view claims that, in practice, very few people know what the current mission is, so that changing it would fail to address the main problem – the detachment of the mission from the bulk of its intended audience. In the end, the meeting decides to stick with the existing mission and give people a chance to get to know it.

Such deliberations speak to the difficulties of enrolling staff into a managerial assemblage – the flickering visibility of affective distance, cynicism and scepticism that are always potential companions of efforts at 'culture management'. Since Peters and Waterman (1982) announced the importance of managing culture as a route to organisational excellence, managers in all sorts of settings have pursued this ideal with enthusiasm. It identifies the peculiar realm of meanings, emotions, norms and dispositions as something that can be laid bare and made available for 'improvement'.

In the following section, I will come back to the experiences of living in a managerialised world, but, first, I want to pursue the inexorable expansion of manageable things a little further. There are tangible things to be managed: the built environment, physical assets and financial resources and reserves (to say nothing of the intricate practices of budgetary devolution, modelling financial flows and the invention of 'cost centres'). Increasingly, the future to be managed is entangled with new technologies that allow new modes of teaching and learning, but also point to the possibilities and problems of converting MOOCs into viable apparatuses for enrolling, retaining and monetising dispersed students.

> *Dave Bainton (DB):* The language of assemblage draws attention to the various embodied components of the broader university assemblage – not only the academic staff, but, critically, students. Students are no doubt afforded a range of responses to their management but there remains the question of how a managerialised university reassembles the student body. Translation adds a nuance here of how the performance of 'student' becomes differently enacted – not only which people might become students, but how they become differently through their enrolment.

> *JC:* This is a critically important issue as the conditions, relationships and practices of 'being a student' are remade, not least by the managerialised construction of 'being a customer' (and its enactment in changing economic relationships).

Students – who, from time to time, flicker into and out of a parallel identity as customers – also require managing: their recruitment and retention involve strategies and tactics that link the financial health of the university to its image and reputation, and to the practices and sites through which the 'student experience' is produced (lectures and seminars, libraries, residences, the local environment, etc). Here, too, management is simultaneously internally directed and other-oriented – at least in terms of monitoring and contrasting the more or less immediate competition. However, students are diverse, not least in terms of the different values that mark domestic and international students. Universities take their place in the larger flows of migration and the borders and barriers of national immigration policies. Universities were among the loudest complainants when the UK Coalition government announced targets to reduce immigration, resulting in a sharp fall-off in 'international student' applications. This gives a special significance to the 'warm welcome' promised to international students in the government's 'global strategy' quoted earlier. However, the enrolment of international students brings other issues to be managed in its wake, not least the involvement of universities in monitoring and reporting on 'Tier 4' students (the UK Border Agency [UKBA] designation for non-EU individuals). For example, Newcastle University warns such students that:

> It is now compulsory for Newcastle University to report to the UKBA on Tier 4 students who fail to register with the University, who do not attend regularly or who staff suspect of breaking the conditions of their student visa (e.g. by working more hours than they are allowed to). If this happens, your visa may be curtailed and/or you may be removed from the UK.[25]

Management systems have been introduced to make such reporting regular and continuous. They implicate academic and administrative staff not only in monitoring, but also in being open to having suspicions about a particular group of students. Hartwich (2011: 15) argues that the contradictory identification of international students by UK governments has produced perverse consequences for universities, beginning from the fears about international students which mean that:

> legitimate international students become reconceived as potential abusers or burdens to the system by policy-makers, and their numbers must be capped.
>
> This mentality is particularly damaging to academia, where students are traditionally seen as serious and responsible adults to be trusted by their institutions. The fact that universities themselves have capitulated in monitoring their students has already chipped away at this relationship of trust. It has turned international students into people to be watched and possibly reported to the authorities, which transforms the dynamic between staff and students. Pastoral duties of monitoring student attendance and progress became over-ridden by surveillance. With the proposed cap, it is sensible to assume the UKBA will expect universities to carry out even more monitoring duties, making the situation worse.

Perhaps the most significant field of managerial expansion has been in relation to intangibles: the strange symbolic realm of communication,

---

[25] Source: http://www.ncl.ac.uk/students/progress/visa/Compliance/

value statements, corporate image and ethos, the brand, and, above all, reputation. Reputation is a critical resource to be managed, naming the distinctiveness of the particular university (its world class-ness, excellence, best at … qualities). Reputation is what may be translated into practical outcomes: attracting students, recruiting high-quality staff, enrolling partners into collaborations and more. Most universities encourage – and report – public appearances or statements by academic staff as adding to the collective reputation of the organisation and emphasising the value attached to being outward-facing, or being engaged in public engagement (Mahony, 2013). Reputation is a critical element of the symbolic realm of management – being, above all, about 'success' – but it is accompanied by a variety of other managerial concerns, including the improved coordination of internal and external communication processes, for example, the Open University's preoccupation with 'cascading' messages down its imagined line-management system.

Managerial metaphors are, as Randy Martin suggests, often mixed – so what is in play in the image of cascading communications? Clearly, senior management imagine a hierarchical map of the university – not unlike Mintzberg's image of the divisional organisation, which combines functional division and a clear line hierarchy of control in each division brought together at the top in the executive (individual or collective). I might suggest that this apparently clear organisational map is both a fantasy and a piece of inaccurate mapping. More importantly, perhaps, it embodies a non-dialogic model of communication, with authoritative pronouncements being conveyed to a more or less grateful audience. Finally, the image of the cascade incites alternative imaginings among its recipients. I have heard two particularly striking ones: the first understands the cascade as a waterfall and likens the experience of being cascaded upon to the fate of rocks being worn away over time at the bottom of a waterfall; the second – and cruder – version likens the cascade to being urinated on in a steady stream. Both of these hint at the uncontrollable quality of metaphors – and at the limits of managerial fantasies.

Living in a managerialised world

The issue of managerial fantasies – and their limits – is a critical starting point for thinking about how a managerialised world is inhabited.[26] In

---

[26] My interest in 'fantasies' here has some significant overlaps with the idea of fictions developed in NL's chapter. I like the idea of fantasies because of the quality of

this section, I will link the issue of fantasy to questions of performance, not in the sense of performance management, but rather in terms of management being something to be performed (see Chapters Two and Three, this volume; on the concept of performance management, see also Clarke, 2005a). Although questions about power and privilege are certainly significant for understanding managerial careers in HE, it would be wrong (and overly cynical) to neglect other seductions that may be in play when contemplating how people become managers. Nevertheless, as vice chancellor salaries increase (and become a source of controversy in 'austere times'; see, eg, Morgan, 2011) and an alternative career trajectory opens up for academics in academic management (with training and development programmes, as well as reward systems), it is important to note the material qualities of the seductions of the managerialised world. At the same time, we should recognise the cultural dynamics that are in play in enrolling people into such posts and careers: the desire to 'make a difference'; the recognition of management as part of 'public service'; and the better coordination of the academy (Martin, 2011). Whatever the conditions of entry, the process of becoming a manager implies a significant performative dimension, not least learning how to behave 'like a real manager'. The 'real manager' is an ambivalent figure in the popular imagination, both desired (embodying power, status and effectivity, possessing the *capacity* to make a difference) and despised (brutally insensitive, out of touch, self-regarding and careerist). Attempts to perform like a real manager are thus likely to stress the 'transformative', 'can-do' and 'heroic' forms of leadership (rather than the collegial, distributed or stewardship versions), in part, because they look and sound managerial. However, fantasies about doing management often run aground on the grim realities of the messy organisational space of the university as 'can-do' becomes 'can't quite do'. Reactions to the ensuing frustrations vary. I have seen members of senior management teams shout and swear at subordinates as cherished plans do not materialise. I have seen them insist 'but I'm just like you' when accused of behaving too managerially, forgetting the hierarchical model of the university to which they were otherwise apparently committed. One former vice chancellor expressed

projection that it implies – the imagined and desired future state. It also carries some Freudian echoes that point to the potentially disruptive and dangerous effects of fantasies – both about mistaking them for reality, and in what happens when such fantasies are frustrated. These dangers were identified at the level of individual psychology, but there is a growing interest in collective and organisational psychodynamics that may be important for thinking through the conditions and consequences of such fantasies 'in translation'.

intense frustration about the fact that some academics knew that vice chancellors were on fixed-term contracts and were prepared to simply 'wait me out'. This is a contradictory and often uncomfortable space in which the capacity of the organisation and its members to frustrate, delay or undermine grand plans and visions is a significant force (even if it is not coherent and rarely capable of generating alternative visions and missions). Nevertheless, people are enrolled or enticed into becoming managers through diverse means and have to find ways of inhabiting those positions and the relationships in which they are enmeshed.

However, as Martin suggested, the managerialisation of the university is not confined to those who are named as the senior management team, or whose job titles encompass 'management'. The process reaches down into all tiers and terrains of the organisation, where people are invited/required to think of themselves as line managers or responsible for the management of people or things. We might all be or become managers. Indeed, the most fascinating invitation to management development that came my way recently was for a course entitled 'Discover the Manager in You'. The promise on offer was simultaneously fascinating and alarming: on the one hand, the idea that any of us could be managerial material was seductive; on the other, it did evoke *Alien*-like images of the manager in me bursting out of my body and laying waste to all around.

Three powerful forces are in play in enrolling people into this process of dispersed managerialisation. One is the not-to-be-underestimated appeal of working in and contributing to a 'well-managed organisation'. The second is the persistent desire to 'make a difference', to contribute to the common project or even to minimise the adverse impact of some changes. The third force, and perhaps the most profound and far-reaching, is the Thatcherite claim that 'there is no alternative' (TINA). In this view, universities are stuck in the competitive–evaluative nexus and have no alternative but to compete. Equally, the model of the organisation necessary to survive or succeed in that environment is a matter of 'being businesslike' and pursuing corporate objectives in a well-managed way.

Perversely, of course, TINA is not a force that generates enthusiasm or attachment. Rather, it creates conditions of more or less grudging compliance – what Benson and Kirsch (2010) have called a 'politics of resignation'. The resulting organisational cultures are somewhat contradictory, centred on grumbling passivity, or what Jeremy Gilbert (2009) nicely captures as the paradox of 'disaffected consent'. Such responses are grounded in a mode of cynical distance from missions and visions, supplemented by a strange delight in the surreal qualities of the latest management device: the online leave management system; the enthusiasm for digestible 'gobbets' of online learning resource; or the inspirational incitement to become a champion. Such disaffected consent crystallised in one dramatic event in the faculty of social sciences some years ago.

> The (then) vice chancellor is aiming to develop a model of scenario planning as a strategic device for the university and as a process to engage staff in planning the future. As a consequence, an event is set up in the faculty to enable us to engage in a scenario planning exercise. It does not start well: various members of the group of academics challenge the four scenarios with which we are being asked to work (scenarios generated earlier in the process by external consultants). A range of social science evidence and argument is deployed to demonstrate the scenarios' lack of realism, plausibility and applicability to the university. The workshop facilitators insist that these scenarios are what we have to work with (and are common to similar events across the university). Grudging acquiescence is eventually followed by a more devastating attack on the methodology of scenario planning itself when an economist (interested in corporate strategy) points out that corporations abandoned this approach to strategy a decade ago, and enumerates the reasons for their choice. The facilitators are not equipped to address these meta-level questions and the whole event grinds to an unsatisfactory halt, much earlier than intended. As a result, the social sciences faculty's reputation drops a few notches further among senior managers.

For me, these exchanges, like the dinosaur example, exemplify the managerialised landscape of contradictions, tensions and frustrations. Disempowered academics fight back by deploying their conventional professional weapons: being smart, while also being difficult and recalcitrant. Such behaviours exemplify the difficulties of constructing the 'right to manage' in this sort of setting. However, they also speak of how far-reaching the rearrangement of power and authority has been: these are the symbolic vestiges of professional power, expressed in what might elsewhere be called the 'weapons of the weak' (Scott, 1985, 1990). The increasing resort to what Scott calls 'hidden transcripts', in which subordination is reflected upon outside the public domain, manifests itself in conversations, *sotto voce* mutterings, petty acts of mutiny and occasional public outbursts (including writing books and articles about the state of the university). There are still forms of collective refusal and negotiation as unions (both staff and student) try to contest or at least constrain the spread of managerial authority. However, it is also important to grasp the ways in which the search for solutions to surviving this environment have been individualised, creating what Ros Gill (2009: 32) has called 'a panoply of privatised responses for managing the unmanageable'. Individuals 'keep their heads down', get on with their own research or teaching, and plan careers that do not rely on collaboration with others. Overall, though, I am most struck by the varieties of 'disaffected consent' that inhabit this landscape: consent to the contingent necessity or inevitability of a mode of being governed to which 'there is no alternative'; but disaffection from the mode and its manifestations in techniques and technologies; disdain for heroic models of leadership; and a sort of foot-dragging or grudging compliance to organisational transformation. Perhaps this is nothing more than the conventional relationship to managerial power, wherever it appears. Certainly, industrial sociology reveals a long history of resistance, refusal and recalcitrance to managerial authority that parallels Scott's studies of peasant societies (see, eg, Ackroyd and Thompson, 1999).

Conclusion: the unstable assemblage of managerial authority

Managerialisation exists in a complex relation to the other trends and tendencies that have remade universities over the last 30 years. It is a process that accompanies, but is not identical to, marketisation, competition and evaluation, consumerism, personalisation, changes in funding regimes, or the drive to widen participation. In that sense, the transformation of universities is 'overdetermined' – the effect of multiple forces and processes. Managerialisation is certainly a process that gains momentum from each of these other developments, being represented as the only available means of creating the 'businesslike' organisation that can cope with, adapt to and survive these multiple pressures. Partly because of the universalising drive of managerialism in the same period, 'management' looks like the obvious and natural answer to these pressures. 'More and better management' has been the necessary corollary of the demand for organisations of all sorts to become more businesslike.

The promise of managerialism is that it can contain and reconcile these pressures in the pursuit of organisational survival and success. This is a powerful force in generating consent (even disaffected consent), especially when combined with the absence of compelling alternative promises and possibilities. Nevertheless, this is not an unproblematic or unconditional promise. It is problematic because it makes managerialisation the means by which the larger tendencies are translated into the operating logics of the university – managerialisation domesticates them as the unavoidable conditions of the university's survival: they are the environment to which it must adapt. Managerialisation, as a result, evokes scepticism both for its own logics and for being the bearer of those external forces that it deploys as the 'new realism'.

This returns me to our wider interest in translation and assemblage. Management, in its contemporary incarnation, involves a double movement of translation. It is translated into universities from its many elsewheres: the management handbooks, the MBA courses, the agencies of support and advice, the management or leadership training programmes, government policies, and the universalising presumption that 'more and better management' is the key to organisational survival and success. In this process of translation, management travels, is (sometimes) enthusiastically adopted and is bent to existing organisational logics and forms of power, even in the process of transforming them by its arrival. The work of translation is ongoing – it requires continuing effort to normalise and naturalise these ways of thinking, being and acting. As I noted at the beginning, the fact that this translation takes place within an apparently common language tends to conceal the practices of translation taking place. However, it certainly involves what managers themselves like to call 'a change in culture': the establishment and inculcation of new ways of thinking, calculating, ordering and mapping the internal and external domains and dynamics of the organisation, expressed in new dispositions and modes of conduct. For me, then, the idea of translation is productive as a way of highlighting this process of reworking organisational landscapes. However, it can also draw attention to a second dynamic of translation.

The translation of management into the internal ordering of things in the university (and the external sets of relationships in which the single university is enmeshed) is enabled by the other dynamics that surround it: the wider establishment of the NPM in theory and practice; the ideological drive towards installing the logics of competition, markets and entrepreneurial selves in the relationships, techniques and technologies in which organisations like universities are inserted; and the associated corporatisation of the university – incited to imagine itself as a business and to be businesslike. These are the conditions that underpin managerialism, but they are also the dynamics and forces that management then translates into the interior life of the university. Management (and managerial conceptions and practices) translates them as the normal, natural and necessary conditions with which organisations must engage. This is a critical second movement in the dynamic of translation – management, in this view, appears both as an object and subject of translation. It is translated into the internal order of the university and acts as the medium through which powerful external forces are themselves translated into the world of the organisation.

Managerialism – and its promise to drive improvement – rests on the claim to power: management can only provide solutions if managers are given the right to manage. This has meant the transformation of the internal architecture of university governance and decision-making towards a managerial model. These transformations certainly vary from place to place, partly as an effect of the types of architecture that they encounter at the outset, but also because of the forms of refusal and resistance that have been put in their way. Nevertheless, the dominant tendency has been to transform varieties of professional bureaucracy into managerialised formations, requiring the reworking of both professional and administrative logics, forms of judgement, and types of power and authority. It is in this sense that viewing management as what Ong and Collier (2005) call a 'mobile assemblage' is vital for me – the repertoire of elements from which managerialisation imagines a 'well-managed organisation' carry logics, modes of calculating, modes of coordinating and modes of subjection that articulate managerial authority as the normal condition. This means that older forms of power/knowledge and authority have been variously displaced, co-opted and subordinated. Such re-articulations have had contradictory effects, not least because managerialisation finds it both relatively easy and useful to co-opt bureaucratic systems, practices and technologies to managerial purposes (as a result, academic complaints are as much about the excesses of the 'new bureaucracy', the emergence of a 'tick-box culture' and so on as about explicitly managerial forms).

I have tried to show how managerialisation has affected universities in multiple ways – especially in the double movement of enhancing the power of 'strategic' leadership and dispersing managerial norms, practices and consciousness throughout the organisation's landscape. This is exacerbated by the expansive colonising tendency of managerialisation as it seeks to identify and control all the factors that may make a difference to the accomplishment of organisational success. Nevertheless, the centralising (centripetal) tendency of managerial power produces a strained and contradictory terrain as it engages (and tries to displace or contain) the forms of communal authority and coordination previously practised in many universities. The double movement (the centralisation of managerial power and the dispersal of managerial techniques and technologies) has created varieties of resistance and recalcitrance – what, following Jeremy Gilbert, I have called disaffected consent. While these usually lack formal articulations, their persistence as 'hidden transcripts' (Scott, 1990) should not be ignored. Managerial power has been successfully assembled, coming to act as the dominant mode of authority in most universities. However, it remains the site of cynicism, scepticism and disaffection. It is this unstable and unfinished condition that is too readily omitted from accounts that overstate the domination of powerful forces (neoliberalism, globalisation, managerialism, etc) and from overly romantic accounts of 'resistance' that overstate the capacities of the subaltern. Attention to the dynamics of translation and the practices of assemblage offer a way of avoiding these two extremes and give analytic purchase on the unstable and unfinished.

FIVE

Soft governance, policy fictions and translation zones: European policy spaces and their making

Noémi Lendvai

Introduction

Translation offers immensely rich repertoires for tracing policies as they move, travel and morph. However, while many different things move (ideas, templates, policy toolkits, actors, actants, artefacts, lessons, best practices), we know remarkably little about how policies travel across languages, or how policies are produced through translation practices. This chapter aims to interrogate the European Union's (EU's) Open Method of Coordination (OMC) for social inclusion and its complex and unexpected translations into Hungarian. For this chapter, translation offers an alternative to the 'epistemic modernism' that dominates mainstream policy studies and its understanding of policy transfer, policy diffusion and policy learning. Despite the insistence of both policy and academic discourses, this chapter will not look for evidence of policy 'learning', 'lesson-drawing' or 'convergence'; quite the opposite, it questions rationalistic assumptions of policy transfers, it argues for unlearning rather than learning, it brings into sharper focus traces of fictions rather than traces of evidence, and it argues for understanding the OMC not as a techno-zone, but rather as a translation zone. These are, of course, not binary oppositions: fiction is not the opposite of reality, fiction makes reality; unlearning is a particular form of learning; and the techno-zone as a representation is crucial in the making of the translation zone. What a translation perspective does in this chapter is to make an alternative academic inquiry possible: an inquiry that asks new questions and allows for radically different representations of policy, as well academic discourses on 'Europeanisation'. This chapter cannot, on its own, answer to this call, but what it aims to achieve is to offer some initial, provisional and tentative steps towards that agenda.

Policy in translation: four shreds

In order to explore a translation perspective, this chapter builds on four shreds of translation: the performative, the relational, the multiple and the political. Each of the shreds plays an important role in trying to capture the complex 'translations' of social inclusion through the EU's OMC.

The performative, which has long been neglected by mainstream policy studies (Gottweis, 2007), works with a notion of a 'lived and embodied conception of "doing" rather than interpreting or implementing policy' (Newman, 2013b: 526). It also implies that 'the political process is not merely a matter of interests and/or arguments, politics constantly needs to be *enacted* and a policy process understood as a multiplicity of staged performances' (Hajer, 2005: 446, emphasis in original). As policy worlds are performed, policies 'are mediated and translated, refused, inhabited or reworked by those they summoned' (Newman, 2013b: 527). The performative also implies a simultaneous dynamics of creativity and constraints, activism and incorporation, retreat and proliferation. It is also a world with 'multiple spaces of power and resistance with which actors engage – pragmatically as well as politically' (Newman, 2013b: 527). The performative is important because it reconfigures some of the taken-for-granted notions of policies, such as intentionality, rationality, consequentialism and directionality. As Hajer (2005: 449) asserts: 'performing not only co-determines which rules are followed in the process. It also co-determines which definition of reality is followed, what temporal-spatial frame is seen as "appropriate", and what constitutes a "legitimate intervention"'. The performative also cross-cuts 'illusions of order' and an assumed consensus of policies, what I will call later 'the consensus on consensus'. This performative element will be used to show the fiction-writing and fiction-making of inclusion policies in Hungary, a central argument in this chapter throughout.

The relational shred emphasises that translation is 'a political act where translation works across different cultures and unequal, always negotiated relationships' (Palmary, 2011: 101). For the linguist Monti (2009), translation implies an intercultural and interlingual negotiation. For the post-colonial scholar Pratt (1992: 4), this negotiation condenses in contact zones, that is, in 'social spaces where disparate cultures meet, clash, and grapple with each other, often in highly asymmetrical relations of domination and subordination'. For Pratt (1992: 7), the relational is interactive and improvisational, as well as asymmetrical:

contact zone is an attempt to invoke the spatial and temporary co-presence of subjects previously separated by geographical and historical disjunctures, and whose trajectories now intersect. By using the term 'contact', I aim to foreground the interactive, improvisational dimensions of colonial encounters so easily ignored or suppressed by diffusionist accounts of conquest and domination.

For Pratt, the relationality of contact zones is also performative, where the encounters are often improvisational and unexpected. Apter (2006) captures relationality and sites of in-translation as a 'translation zone'. She argues that:

> [i]n fastening on the term 'zone' as a theoretical mainstay, the intention has been a broad intellectual topography that is neither the property of a single nation, nor an amorphous condition associated with postnationalism, but rather a zone of critical engagement that connects the 'l' and the 'n' of transLation and transNation. (Apter, 2006: 5)

I will argue that rather than seeing the OMC as soft governance and as a form of techno-zone, capturing it as a translation zone enables us to draw on forms of relationality and encounters that shed light on the politics of translation as well. The relational shred also enables me to reconfigure a diffusionist account of policy transfer (Lendvai and Stubbs, 2007), where, within the epistemic modernism of mainstream policy studies, it is assumed that 'A' is the original, 'B' the copy and policy transfer takes place from A *to* B. Here, policy transfer is one-directional; the task of 'B' is to mimic, emulate and copy 'A'. 'A' is often considered to be the 'leader', and, importantly, institutional isomorphism is assumed (for an overview of policy transfer literature, see Dobbin et al, 2007). In contrast, a relational notion of policy translation collapses the distinction and directionality between 'A' and 'B'. Rather than policies travelling from 'A' to 'B' – 'A' being the original, preformed and readable, and 'B' being the reader and the downloader – as policies travel, policy translation takes place between A *and* B, with multiple lines of influence, as a negotiated, uneven, unequal and improvisational encounter. The relationship between A and B is also articulated in and through connections with other nodes, creating complex assemblages of policy dynamics.

My third shred emphasises multiplicity. Influenced by the mobility turn, globalisation studies had produced a wealth of insights into the immense velocity, force and depth of global interconnectedness. Nowadays, it is a common argument to envisage 'fast policy transfers' (Brenner et al, 2010; McCann and Ward, 2013), the 'proliferation of portable, technocratic policy tools' (ibid) carried through 'global knowledge networks', and 'key knowledge institutions' (Diane Stone, 2002; 2012). Policies, institutions and ideas, and above all policy paradigms, are seen as immensely 'mobile' and 'moveable' from one context to another, and universally applicable in their international 'diffusion'. For Mosse (2008), globalisation has fostered the rise of global policy agendas centred on the adoption of a particular set of 'travelling rationalities', such as the general applicability of technicalised knowledge. These rationalities have claimed important currencies that have enabled them to travel internationally between countries and contexts, and to 'flow'. The powers of fast policies and policy mobilities have mostly been assigned to their portability, structured disciplinarity and associated networks of powerful agents. Importantly, mainstream policy transfer literature has relied heavily on new sociological institutionalism, which has emphasised institutional isomorphism and homogenisation as a result of diffusion (for a critical overview, see Beckert, 2010). What we might call the 'illusion of similarities' had an important role in driving institutionalism in assuming, discovering and reinforcing isomorphism. The 'illusion of similarities' is also coupled with a widespread belief among International Relations (IR) scholars that policy diffusion rests upon 'norms', yet norms are undefined and unexplored, both conceptually and empirically (Towns, 2012). Critical for my third shred is the unpacking of the assumed singularity of the underlying norms, content, effect and work of moving policies, not least because translation implies a multiplicity of policies: as policy travels across languages, sites and scales, it is produced, assembled and populated differently. Originally, in the sociology of translation, developed by Bruno Latour (1987), the notion of 'immutable mobiles' aimed to capture the processes by which objects transferred from one practice to another have profoundly transformative effects. For the IR scholar Barry (2013: 2, 3), 'translation implied both movement in space and the transformation of space', where 'translation gives new life to a text in other times and places'. Law and Urry (2004) argue that social scientists need to re-imagine themselves, their methods and their 'worlds', in which the multiplicity, 'more than one, but less than many', is produced through diverse and contested social and material relations. In translation studies, conceptualising the anisomorphism of languages has been a key driver of critical scholarly debates (Tymoczko, 2006a). Monti (2009), for example, looking at the translatability of

Lakoff and Johnson's (1980) *Metaphors we live by*, finds that languages differ considerably in terms of their metaphoric expressions and associations, which implies an asymmetric relationship between linguistic systems. Translation, then, directs us towards the 'unfit to fit', in which assumed similarities and commonalities are questioned. Best (2012: 90) puts it nicely:

> devices and techniques work to reduce messiness, contain overflowing, create common meanings and practices and thus reduce ambiguity. Yet, despite these clever mechanisms for reducing the ambiguities of social interaction, they tend to persist ... moreover, our very efforts to constrain such ambiguities may create others. The kind of forms that we fill out on a regular basis would appear to be one of the least ambiguous kinds of inscription. They take potentially ambiguous inputs and translate them into something standardized and calculable. Yet, this kind of translation always misses something: a form will tend to assume a standard respondent and create boxes and categories accordingly, forcing those who do not fit ... to squeeze themselves into the existing boxes. The form appears to be unambiguous – all the boxes neatly filled out and capable of tabulation and analysis – but actually produces all sorts of ambiguities when anyone tries to interpret the actual relationship of the form's contents to the world beyond it.

It is in this process that singularity and the 'common' breaks down, and Escobar's (2011) 'pluriverse' becomes meaningful and alive. The call by De Sousa Santos (2005: 16) to work with the multiplicity and variety of social practices is also an important challenge for policy studies:

> Translation is the procedure that allows for mutual intelligibility among the experiences of the world, both available and possible, as revealed by the sociology of absences and the sociology of emergences, without jeopardizing their identity and autonomy, without, in other words, reducing them to homogeneous entities.

My fourth and final shred is translation as political. It is this shred that departs from the notion that translation is a simple matter of communication and transfer in a singular epistemological and ontological world. The political is important because both the relational and the multiple imply unequal, uneven relations and negotiations as policies move. The political is also attentive to both translation and non-translation – that is, the production of voices as well as silences (Tymoczko, 2006b), thus visibility. The political is also the interrogation of what Tymoczko (2006a) calls the epistemic dimension of translation, that is, how translation not merely reflects existing knowledge, but rather is a form of knowledge production itself, where translation is a text about text, a form of 'metatext' (Tymoczko, 2006a: 447). Translation is also political as it is 'a significant medium of subject re-formulation and political change' (Apter, 2006: 6), or, as Tymoczko (2006a: 459) reminds us, 'translation has a potentially radical and activist edge, that is driven by ethical and ideological concerns, that it participates in shaping societies, nations, and global culture in primary and central ways. Translation can change the world.'

Governing social inclusion: the European 'common space'

> European institutions have contributed to promoting a cognitive and normative harmonisation of social security reforms in Europe through the enforcement of a *common* language, a *common* vision of reforms and *common* objectives. (Cerami, 2008, emphasis added)

By the time of the EU's eastern enlargement in 2004 and 2007, the OMC had become an influential new mode of governance, seen as 'innovative' (Buchs, 2008a), 'deliberative' (De la Porte, 2007) and 'experimental' (Zeitlin, 2005). The OMC has also been seen as 'soft governance', with novel methods compared to more classical, regulatory or redistributive modes of EU governance (Buchs, 2008b; Barbier and Colomb, 2011). This new governance method was based on 'regular exchange of information, deliberation, policy evaluation and "naming and shaming" between the Member States' (Buchs, 2008a: 765) as a way of facilitating best practices and achieving greater convergence towards EU goals. Theorisation of soft forms of governance has varied, but has concentrated around 'policy learning, policy transfer, deliberation, participation, peer pressure, shaming, diffusion and mimicking' (Buchs, 2008b: 23), with the expectations that through 'the sharing of experience and good practices, all the countries can learn from one another and are therefore all in a position to improve their policies' (Frazer and Marlier, 2010: 226). Here, the European 'common space' becomes a highly technicalised policy space, what

Lewis and Mosse (2006) calls a 'techno-managerial order', crowded by best practices, common indicators, policy targets and guidelines, the transposition of strategic priorities, and peer reviewing, leading to 'the deepening of knowledge' (Frazer and Marlier, 2010). The 'common space' includes 'developing a common understanding of concepts (e.g., multidimensionality, mainstreaming, evidence-based strategies and quantified objectives, partnership between actors, participation, policy impact assessments) and to ... identifying and agreeing on key policy priorities in relation to social inclusion' (Frazer and Marlier, 2010: 231). Importantly, diffusion, adaptation and learning are thought to be the key mechanisms of 'identifying and promoting the most effective social policies' (European Commission, 2008), and, as such, the OMC has also been seen as the engine for catch-up convergence:

> The EU influence on social protection agenda setting, institution building and policy formation is especially pronounced in countries with Southern or Central and Eastern European welfare regimes and with a dismal record of competitiveness. In these countries EU funds have probably helped reform processes. If social protection reforms have led to changes of the national welfare regimes and competitiveness, the results may be some socio-economic catch-up convergence. (Kvist and Saari, 2007: 241)

By 2004, when Hungary became a member of the EU, the OMC had become an extensive framework: assembling a very particular policy space of objects, texts, ideas, groups and events, data sets; promoting 'modernisation', 'institution-building' and 'capacity-building'; and 'mobilising relevant actors'.

For critical scholars, the assumption that the OMC is a technical, highly formalised and horizontal governance tool has been problematic. For example, for Ashiagbor (2005), the OMC represents a policy agenda that promotes very specific policies aimed at market-enhancing financial sustainability and welfare-to-work policies. For Borghi (2011), the OMC is not just a set of formal rules, but, rather, a device of governmentality: a regime of justification that enacts the social in a particular way. More precisely, the OMC is used to mobilise and enact an individualised notion of the social as a normative foundation of welfare capitalism. For Borghi (2011: 334), the social OMC is part of a broader political project of individualisation, with a:

growing, shifting and weakening of the meaning of publicness that, in the frame of network capitalism, is increasingly substituted by devices and models of social regulation based on direct ... horizontal interaction among individuals (according to the network mode of coordination), at great risk of asymmetrical and de-politicized disequilibrium.

Kroger (2009) argues that the OMC as a governance mode has been systematically under-conceptualised, overdetermined and depoliticised, where policy learning has been taken for granted, participatory democracy has been assumed to foster legitimacy and, finally, policy, perceived as a set of neutral policy instruments, has been assumed to make politics.

What critical scholarship offers here is a reminder that 'policies travel over space not as harbingers of objectively proven truth, but as political-economic technologies of power' (Peet, 2003: 11, quoted in Brenner et al, 2010: 349). In order to look at this process, and consider how the social, cultural, political and ethical gets translated into the technical, there is a need to deconstruct the 'techno-zone' of the OMC without an imposed theoretical framework. Moving beyond the 'illusion of order' (Lewis and Mosse, 2006), and beyond the 'consensus on consensus' on what the 'OMC' or 'social inclusion' is about, is when translation becomes an open-ended endeavour.

Translation: travelling across languages and policy spaces

One of the most important types of work that translation does is to strip away the taken for granted. Every time we translate, we have to stop and pause. To be meaningful, we have to ask the most basic of questions. For Spivak (2000: 313), translation is 'where meaning hops into the spacy emptiness between two named historical languages'. This 'spacy emptiness' seems a very meaningful metaphor for understanding translation. For Spivak (2000: 320), translation is the work of agency, where 'there is also that special relationship to the staging of language as the production of agency that one must attend to'. Here, for Spivak, translation is an immense cultural work involving both an 'act of intimate reading' and surrendering to the text and responding to its special call. For Spivak (2000: 321), the act of translation is also deeply political, as it:

remains dependent upon the language skills of the majority.... What one overlooks is the sheer authority ascribed to the original. The status of a language in the world is what one must consider when teasing out the politics of translation.

As such, translation is not an act of equals, 'it is only in the hegemonic languages that the benevolent do not take the limits of their own often uninstructed good will into account' (Spivak, 2000: 321). It is through this spacy emptiness, which is both productive and constraining, that the deeply political nature of translation can be captured.

At a first glance, the space between Hungarian social policy and the EU's social inclusion agenda does not look that empty. In fact, the 'Europeanisation of social inclusion' has been portrayed as a dense policy space crowded by numerous policy tools, discursive frames, various governance arrangements and institutionalised forms of cooperation. Radaelli (2003) argues that the OMC is a 'master discourse', which provides policymakers with a common vocabulary and with a tool to legitimise a set of policy objectives setting out new tasks across different policy domains. For Radaelli (2003: 9), the OMC, 'where knowledge and learning are created and diffused across countries ... may work like radar searching for solutions and new usable knowledge'. Within this new mode of governance, 'ideational convergence', 'norm diffusion' and 'cognitive Europeanisation' all point to the expectation 'that policy-makers converge in their assessment of causal mechanisms at work in policy areas, definitions of desirable and unacceptable policies, and beliefs about how policies work' (Radaelli, 2003: 10). 'Cognitive Europeanisation' has been a particularly popular concept among social policy scholars, both in the 'West' (Guillen and Alvarez, 2004) and the 'East' (Kusa and Gerbery, 2007; Lendvai, 2009), pointing to the common cognitive and ideational framing of social policy. Yet, as Spivak reminds us, no matter how much of the institutionalised commonness we take for granted, translation implies an inevitable space and distance, as well as a particular emptiness and spaciness, between the 'original', 'majority', 'powerful' and the 'shadow', or the 'newcomer'.

To make matters even more complex, the 'Europeanisation of social inclusion' is not a translation between two historical, 'earthy' languages, as Spivak claims. Rather, it is a translation of and in between at least three languages: Hungarian, Eastern European English (Salakhyan, 2012), or, perhaps more precisely, Hungarian English, and EU English (Clarke, 2005b), with all their distinctiveness. The hegemony of 'policy English', 'global English' or 'EU English' has long been recognised

(Pennycook, 2003; Phillipson, 2008). Much less work has been done on the microscopic interplay between linguistic representations and their policy implications. A refreshing exception is Koskinen's (2008) work, which argues that EU English has very particular features, where the so-called Euro-jargon can be characterised by excessive buzzwords, fuzziness, abstract style, neologisms, a specialised bureaucratic vocabulary and complex sentence structure. However, as Koskinen asserts, translation is not simply a technical matter, it has rather important implications for policy; first of all, the ways in which linguistic resources are employed, mobilised or discarded affect the relationship between the reader and the writer (in this chapter, the EU as well as the member state [Hungarian government] are both writers and readers). For Koskinen, however, the politics of translation is in the nuanced ways in which the text directs and tells the readers how and what to do. As she argues, the common formulation is telling:

> The Commission will
> Member States should
> The social partners are invited to ... (Koskinen, 2008: 142)

Crucially, the implications are that translation not just conveys policies, but silently crafts hierarchies, constructs relationalities and hides assumptions. Translation, as such, does not transmit, but makes, policies. Further to this, it is important to tease out the way in which the presence of these three policy languages implies that the 'common space' is not that common. The OMC might define, describe or ascribe in EU English; however, its presence remains multiple once we break up the monolithic assumptions of monolingualism. As Barbier (2013: 111) argues:

> [w]hile national elites can perfectly well speak to each other (in English) in European Commission meetings and understand each other in a functional (and superficial) way, they cannot do so when they compete in their respective electoral arenas, where the tone, language, substance and political culture change radically.

From techno-zone to translation zone

The empirical work presented in this chapter is ethnographic work carried out in Hungary in 2003 and 2013. In 2003, as part of my PhD fieldwork, I spent a year carrying out policy ethnography, tracing traces of Hungary's accession to the EU and its implications on social policymaking. Influenced by anthropology of policy and disillusioned by the mainstream policy literature, I was taken by ethnographic work 'as a way out of overdetermined paradigms, as theoretically sophisticated antidotes to the excesses of theory' (Riles, 2006: 1). In 2013, inspired by the collaboration of this book, I revisited some of the sites of my previous research, looked at the trajectories of flagship documents and strategic reports, and reinterviewed some of my informants. What I end up with in this process is a series of reflections on my initial research, which prompted a complete reconceptualisation and rereading of my 2003 work, as well as conducting follow-on research with faint, fragmented but revealing traces 10 years on. Finally, to allow for different and multiple voices, I put direct quotations from my interviewees in italics.[1]

The puzzles around the most basic aspects of languages and translation were present throughout my initial fieldwork. The Joint Inclusion Memorandum, which was prepared in 2003 as a first step towards participating in the OMC/inclusion, was perceived as:

> *"building a communication bridge between the EU and us. And it that sense we had to find a common language. We had a huge number of issues, which needed detailed explanations, because when we translated the text into English, it turned out the Commission did not understand it, or misunderstood it. I don't mean the English, but things that are evident for us, was not evident for them at all."*

Similarly, as another policymaker argued:

> *"we did not understand each other [Hungarian policymakers and EU officials], I felt that they did not understand our problems and issues, and here I don't mean it in a linguistic sense, but in a substantive and cultural sense. We can express ourselves in English, and everything can be said in English too, but still all the underlying contents, which we share in the region, is simply not there in the Commission."*

---

[1]   The interviews were conducted in Hungarian. In my own translation practice, I gave priority to the original metaphoric language rather than the Englishness of the text. As such, the English translation might appear strange in places.

The struggle for the 'common language', the self-evidence of one's own policy framework, the need for precision and access to the underlying contents when one translates makes the bridging efforts hard work. The 'reading' of each other's documents has been tainted with difficulties throughout. These quotes highlight the important spaces beneath the surfaces of the 'common', the 'shared', the 'same' language and the breakdown of the supposed linear assembly-line process of policy transfer and policy learning. The distance between the 'author', or the 'original', and the reader always requires complex, and messy, conceptual, cultural and political work. To 'blackbox' this process and label it as 'imitation' or policy 'learning' misses crucial questions around who learns here and what. What sort of work goes into translation and what implications does it have for forms and practices of social inclusion policies across spaces and places? How are tensions around authorship handled, silenced or managed? Before I proceed to thinking about these questions, let me stay with language a little bit longer and look at some linguistic difficulties in translating 'social inclusion' from EU English into Hungarian and Hungarian English.

As a native Hungarian researcher, the position that is afforded to me by being located across two languages is a unique opportunity that warrants some responsibility. All too often, research on the Europeanisation of social inclusion is rather mono- or unilingual. Consequently, linguistic diversity, matters of translation and their implications for policymaking are erased from theoretical and empirical discussions. As Barbier (2013: 120–1) asserts:

> The situation in sociology and political science is paradoxical: while it is generally recognised that language (and hence languages) is essential in political activity, these disciplines seldom talk about it. They implicitly postulate that language is a secondary aspect and any problems it raises will eventually be solved through translation – into English. Few comparative researchers assign explicit importance to languages, even though linguistic questions constantly arise in ethnographic observation, statistical categories and the history of political action.

In the following sections, I will try to demonstrate in what ways translation matters, not just as a matter of language, but as a broader process of policy production and assemblage.

From 'social inclusion' to 'societal togetherness' and back

Concepts such as 'social inclusion', 'social exclusion', 'gender mainstreaming', 'streamlining' or 'flexicurity' do not lend themselves to easy translation into Hungarian. None of these words has a straightforward translation. When, in 2003, the European Commission asked Hungary to prepare and sign a Joint Inclusion Memorandum (JIM), the task was not just to prepare a policy package, a 'strategic vision', on the fight against social exclusion, a much more fundamental work had to be done first, that is, to create and negotiate indigenous words for terms such as 'exclusion' and 'inclusion', and to pacify the unbearable foreignness of EU English. Both 'exclusion' and 'inclusion' have thrown some important problems at policymakers. 'Social exclusion' has two possible translations in the Hungarian language: one that is a passive verb (*tarsadalmi kirekesztettseg*), where somebody happens to get excluded; and the other one is an active verb (*tarsadalmi kirekesztes*), where there is an active initiation of exclusion by somebody, and, as such, the agent of exclusion is linguistically present. The active verb translation is a lot sharper translation. It draws on more urgent critical edges, and issues of agency and responsibility are a lot more pronounced; in moments of reflexive translation, we could even translate it back into English as 'active exclusion' (with an ironic twist and diagonally opposite connotations to activation and 'active inclusion'). The first Hungarian National Action Plan for Social Inclusion 2004–2006 (hereafter, NAP/inclusion) uses the passive version 11 times, while the active version is used 40 times. In the process of tracing the newer and newer versions of the same strategic reports, it is noteworthy that the activism clearly declines and the active verbs slowly disappear as we move ahead in time.

The translation of 'social inclusion' into Hungarian has been even more difficult and troubling for the policy community. The literary translation of 'social inclusion' is '*tarsadalmi befogadas*'. '*Befogadas*' is not a term that was used before, it has an everyday use of to welcome or to accept somebody in; however, it has never been a policy term, and, as such, Hungary never had an 'inclusion policy'. It is its alien scaffolding that makes this term so interesting. While, during the JIM process, the Commission has asserted considerable pressure to use the literary translation, the first NAP offered a more independent space for considering alternative translations. As a result, something remarkable happened; the Hungarian version of the first NAP/ inclusion became the National Action Plan for Societal Togetherness (*tarsadalmi osszetartozas*). As a result of a process of 'deliberation' and 'participation', 'social inclusion' traversed into 'societal togetherness': the social became societal, and inclusion became togetherness. The translation was suggested by the biggest and most influential association of Alliances of Social Professionals (3SZ), who argued that 'social togetherness' has a strong association with solidarity, social integration and a horizontal rather than a vertical notion of inclusion. Again, there is no such thing as 'togetherness policy'; yet, the term has a strong association to symbolic politics, the need for new forms of social solidarity and, as Ferge (2005: 38) put it, the need for a 'political vision on an integrative societal policy'.

An important moment in this process of 'back-translation' is that '*tarsadalmi osszetartozas*' ('societal togetherness') has been translated back as 'social inclusion' in the English version of the NAP (the European Commission insisting on the term 'social inclusion'). As such, 'social togetherness' gets erased, disappears from the eye of the English version of the policy documents and becomes invisible. Erasures take place in multiple sites: it erases a Hungarian contribution, or 'talking back', to the EU's OMC/inclusion about how member states might understand 'social inclusion'; it erases diversity; and, above all, it erases dialogue about what social inclusion might be in different spaces. This important shift becomes unavailable for researchers, who conduct a discourse analysis of key policy documents based on the English version. The work that is done in a process of "*finding a shared language and voice around social exclusion and inclusion, which hasn't existed before*", the work of needing "*to rethink all of our basic axioms about social policy*", and the transformation of " '*socialist*' to '*social*' let alone '*societal*' policy" becomes invisible in the English version. My point here is not just that we need to attend to languages, but also that processes of translation multiply policies. As policies travel across languages, scales and spaces, they become something different. The Hungarian NAP in Hungary and in the Hungarian language represents different sets of discourses, connotations and notions of agency compared to the 'official' English-language Hungarian NAP. By looking at the English version only, we would miss the detour of 'social togetherness', with all its cultural and political work. Interestingly, 'societal togetherness' as a Hungarian translation survives several rounds of OMC and its reform: the National Strategy Report on Social Protection and Social Inclusion 2008–2010 still uses the term 'societal togetherness'.

The multiplicity of policies is assertive not just across languages, but also across scales and sites. For the European Commission, the political activism that the Hungarian-language NAP is trying to achieve seemed to be less relevant. It is through translation that the 'common space' of social inclusion becomes not one, but many. No matter how common the EU's indicators, targets and priority areas appear, social inclusion policies always have different presences, voices and assertions. Insisting on the back-translation as 'social inclusion' (rather than 'societal togetherness') not only erases the process of translation from 'deliberative governance', but also implies a disengagement from key policy concerns of the member states. What is also very noticeable is that there is a major fault line between Hungarian- and English-speaking academic discourses: while language and translation problems appear in all major Hungarian academic discussions (see Szalai, 2002; Sziklai et al, 2010), there is a total silence around translation issues within the English-speaking academic discussions.

Policy translation as fiction-writing

While the theoretical focus on 'cognitive Europeanisation' has drawn scholars to look at discursive practices, with a special focus on policy texts, my ethnographic research remained puzzled by the question: what happens when 'social inclusion governance' is 'summoned'? What happens to 'governance', and to 'policy' without vocabulary, without taken-for-granted terminologies, without matching 'policy'? What happens, when "*we have no consensual words to describe what we are doing for the EU*"? In aiming at answering these questions, I draw on interviews, as well as 'documents' (strategic reports, action plans, etc). However, rather than approaching key policy documents via discourse analysis and interrogating their presumed discursive power, I have taken a more ethnographic approach, with an emphasis on documents rather than text, where documents are conceptualised as paradigmatic artefacts of modern knowledge practices (Riles, 2006). Importantly, documents, then, can and do just as much 'anti-meaning' as they do meaning-making, and can and do produce and assert unanalysable nonsense (Strathern, 2006).

In many ways, the JIM and the NAPs/inclusion, both as policy texts and strategic policy frameworks, are 'fictions'. They do not exist; they are intangible and weightless. It is very noticeable that even several attempts at reading these documents leave us clueless as to their content. As a ministerial advisor commented on the first NAP/inclusion "*this draft is a dream. It really is a dream.... We are talking fiction here*". As I am going to argue, fiction-writing is, then, a particular practice and form of policy translation. In the early years, the OMC/inclusion has been fiction of all kinds: the fiction of language; the fiction of strategic planning; the fiction of public administration; and the fiction of political commitments. The fiction, here, is productive and agentive, as well as disciplinary at the same time. My argument here is that while scholarship on ideational and discursive Europeanisation assume that ideas and discourses will inevitably lead to the 'common', and consolidate 'shared ideas' into particular institutional forms, underneath the surface, both the policy process and the associated institutionalisation will remain uncertain, fragmented, contradictory and multiple.

The fiction of OMC/inclusion has not just been the fiction of language, although the 'unbearable foreignness' (Barbier and Colomb, 2011) of words such as 'flexicurity', 'mainstreaming', 'streamlining' and 'feeding in, feeding out' is an important aspect of the fiction – these buzzwords do not mean anything, so they can mean anything. It is also the fiction of institutional practices: the fiction of new committees; the fiction of stakeholder engagement; and the fiction of best practices. The fiction of a 'National Action Plan' for 'Societal Togetherness' 2004–2006 has also produced a fiction of strategic planning. The fiction of strategic planning was an important one. While a new department for strategic planning was set up in 2004 in the Ministry for Social Affairs to coordinate this work, and a new inter-ministerial body was established responsible for negotiating and drafting the NAP, many questions remained: how to produce a strategy with no multi-year budgeting at hand; how to secure financial and political commitments to social inclusion targets; how to set strategic directions in areas with cross-cutting institutional competences of the ministries (such as taxation, the minimum wage, increases in welfare benefits); how to write a strategy that does not pose any extra financial commitment on the government; and how to write a social inclusion strategy that does not cost anything. Strategic planning might be more like wondering:

> "We have three general problems. First, that the existing programmes are very fragmented, they are not cross-referenced, they are unclear about exact aims and objectives, and they are overly general and unspecific. Our second problem is that we do not have any financial tables for 2004–2006. And finally, we only have targets if the programme is run by the EU, where such targets are part of the programme itself." (Head of Strategic Planning Department, Ministry for Social Affairs)

> "We have lots of strategies, yet, we do not have a united governmental strategy on certain issues. A good example is the activation of elderly. If somebody would look at government policy,

they would get immediately confused. It is completely contradictory, some policies encouraging retirements, while yet others encourage employment. There is no one policy in this issue." (Ministerial advisor)

"The big systems can only think about themselves and within their own jurisdiction. What is outside of their competences, be it crucial for achieving their substantive aims, does not interest them whatsoever. So, who will give textual proposal about lowering or abolishing the taxation of the minimum income to be included into the NAP/inclusion?" (Ministerial advisor)

"The NAP has provided a synthesis, which the public administration has never seen before. Nobody before put together different programmes in a united and comprehensive framework. It is great, but as a result scares emerge, they get frightened of the density of programmes and most importantly, by the commitment they imply." (Head of drafting team)

The fiction has been promoted in a number of 'institutionalised' ways. No evaluation or monitoring system was put in place. Documents were drafted, coordinated, produced, circulated, submitted and reviewed by the EU, yet they were not followed up. Non-governmental organisations (NGOs) were sidelined altogether during the writing phase, as it was considered a government document and nobody knew how NGOs could possibly contribute here. The majority of targets have been removed from the final version. As a comment from the Ministry of Finance on a draft NAP/inclusion demonstrates:

"Although the EU everywhere possible recommends setting concrete and accountable targets, we should be careful not to present unfounded promises, especially in sensitive fields, where the government only has limited capacity to have direct impact anyway. In line with that principle, we recommend not to include the target to increase life expectancy, despite, of course that we agree with the aim." (Ministry of Finance)

With no multi-year planning, no financial commitment and missing targets, *"the scale of change is missing from all the strategies and programmes"* (policy advisor). The fiction is that while a text, an NAP, has to be produced, presented and organised, all looking plausible, and we can subject this text to a discourse analysis looking for ways in which new discourses emerge and offer structured domination of policy ideas, subject positions or particular forms of institutionalised practices, the Hungarian NAP for societal togetherness shows that we cannot assume the power of the text without considering the actual practices along, beyond and parallel with these textual productions. We should not assume the 'illusion of order', or the 'consensus on consensus'. It is all too easy to start research from a point where a large number of issues have already been taken for granted. For example, assuming that 'social inclusion' is neatly and precisely defined and framed, and then looking for policy transfers with a bundled-up and pre-packed understanding of what we mean by social inclusion, not only misses out on a crucial aspect of the construction of order, but also fails to challenge the 'consensus on consensus', and what is assumed to be 'common'. Treating such texts as fiction calls for questioning the apparent coherence of the techno-zone of soft governance; decouples policy texts and policy practices; and dives into the complex, contradictory and contested spaces of translation zones.

Policy translation as script-writing: traces of fictions

Ironically, fiction-writing is, of course, something deeply familiar in a post-communist context. The 'Five Year Plans' have been central to the fiction-writing of public policy in communist Hungary. Writing fiction, while 'impelling people to seek out ways to circumvent discipline' (Dunn, 2005: 175), has been an important coping strategy during the uncertain times of communism. As Kovacs (2002: 200) argues insightfully:

> Ambiguity mobilises routine coping strategies on the part of governments in ex-communist countries. Paying lip-service to a foreign dominant ideology while trying to do what they had anyway wanted/had to do (at home) – this is exactly what the governments in the region were trained for under Soviet rule. Their response is, therefore, pre-programmed: it is an amalgam of avoiding making spectacular mistakes on the surface and the pursuit of autonomous policies, as far as in-depth reforms (or the lack of these reforms) are concerned.

The uncertainty of EU accession and EU membership has also mobilised strategies of script-writing, that is, holding on to the familiar, the known. As a Hungarian social policy expert put it poetically: "*we*

do what we [can] know, we measure what we can know, and we love our own".
Reverting back to what is known, what is safe, mobilising coping
mechanisms have resulted in a NAP/inclusion 2004–2006 that the
head of the drafting team saw as follows:

> "*I am crying over the minimalism of the document. We have taken
> out everything that was shaky and problematic. What we have
> left is not much. In fact, what we have left with is a catalogue of
> EU-funded projects.*"

Fiction-writing is also a space where the tension between the 'old'
and the 'new' is disciplined. Reading Hungarian academic literature
around 'Europeanisation of social inclusion' reveals the immense
tensions in policymaking and social policy 'reforms' aiming to promote
'social inclusion'. Sziklai and his colleagues (2010) tell a story of
deinstitutionalisation of residential care for people living with disability
and care homes for people with mental health or psychiatric problems.
Deinstitutionalisation of large residential homes, community-based
social care and care promoting inclusion and access to mainstream
society for such vulnerable social groups have been on the policy
agenda ever since the late 1990s. As Sziklai argues, in the NAP/
inclusion 2004–2006, priorities of improving day-care facilities and
providing community-based services have been emphasised, alongside
a legislative commitment of dismantling large residential homes. Yet,
while community-based social care has been a priority in the NAP/
inclusion, between 2004 and 2006, the government continued to spend
around 8 billion Hungarian Forint on improving existing large-capacity
residential care homes for people living with disability and people
with mental or psychiatric problems, or, in fact, building new ones.
From the point of view of policymaking, this points to the fiction-
writing of the NAP. Paying lip service to the EU's social inclusion
agenda, declaring strategic objectives in the NAP, while, in practice,
financially supporting the exact opposite is one example of how policy
is performed and enacted. However, as Verdes (2009) asserts, there is
one important element here that sheds light onto the appropriation of
discourses. What happened, he argues, is that the EU's discourses on
'modernisation' of social policy, 'social inclusion of vulnerable groups',
the 'fight against social exclusion', 'respect' and 'human dignity' got
appropriated by the institutional establishment, which then used them
to legitimise its own existence, authority and institutional practices
'within the fences'. The result is not the dismantling of large-scale
residential, institutionalised, totalitarian care, but the opposite: the

emergence of a discursively modernised, re-institutionalised care in the same physical confines (Verdes, 2009), in its new totality. 'Discursive Europeanisation', then, does not necessarily imply institutional 'change', or 'policy convergence', as is all too often assumed. In my 2013 interviews, deinstitutionalisation has appeared again:

> *"Let's say that the story starts by a large residential home needing to find money for their leaking roof. Of course, they have no money to repair, but what they know is that they could apply for the EU's Structural Funds under the heading of social inclusion as promoting deinstitutionalisation/community-based care, and carry out a loft conversion, where they build independent living quarters for some of their residents. The roof is fixed, Structural Funds money spent, yet community-based care is nowhere to be found."* (Social policy advisor)

What is interesting here is that fiction is not just a discursive, linguistic strategy, or a strategy for report-writing; fiction is, indeed, real. The new loft, with a new name tag on it, is *both* fiction and reality at the same time. It is a fiction of community-based care, it is also a fiction of deinstitutionalisation by the very institutions themselves. At the same time, the fiction takes on new material realities: new spaces and new names. As such, no matter how fictional discursive strategies are, they are also always embedded in material relations and do inform fundamental policy debates across different policy spaces in terms of how inclusion is understood, performed, enacted, enforced, resisted or colonised. As Dunn (2005: 190) argues insightfully:

> In Europe, the process of installing normative governmentality is referred to as 'harmonisation' and 'integration'. But rather than accepting these words with their positive overtones, it is important to also see the ways that the power of standards excludes certain groups, disarticulates them from the European order, and leads to patterned and structured inequalities. Standards can create barriers to both market and political participation, and catalyze new forms of conflict, both open and covert. Ironically, in its drive to govern the ungovernable spaces of postsocialism, the European Union may find that the products and people it wants to regulate become less regulated than ever before.

John Clarke (JC): Is there a risk that the 'real', here, becomes an example of a sort of 'dirty realism'? That is, the story could be read as demonstrating the cynical or calculating exploitation of fictions by 'vested interests', embedded in politics, agencies and institutions. As a result, it suggests that we should concentrate our analysis on 'what really happens' rather than the circulation of fictions.

Noémi Lendvai (NL): I agree. This dirty realism is evident even in some of the 'critical policy studies' literatures, where, for example, discourses are understood as manipulative devices behind which stand powerful interests. I am interested in fiction more in terms of its productive and performative aspects. Fiction, here, is not something that is put to a particular use in a strategic sense; rather, fiction is many things – coping, survival, playfulness, irony, nostalgia, memory or hope. Above all, it is the messiness of policy.

Dave Bainton (DB): I am interested in the issue of genre in these fictions, and how this relates to their potential for policy otherwise. We can take these fictions not simply as one side of a policy encounter, but rather that there is an attempt to transpose the ground of this encounter from one that is technicised to one that is fictional. At stake is a translation of the nature of policy, where policy as fiction opens possibilities of irony, dissonance, recalcitrance, uncertainty, multiplicity and paradox. Might we therefore see policy as fictions as being potentially productive of policy otherwise?

Fictions: 10 years on

What happens to fictions over time? How do they settle, embed and mould in the policy landscape? How, if at all, do they open up counter-hegemonic possibilities? How do they institutionalise? Returning to the site of my ethnographic fieldwork in 2013, 10 years on, gave an insight into how fiction travels over time. Reflecting on their experiences, my interviewees asserted:

> *"What was really new in 2003 was the idea that poverty is not just a static condition, but a dynamic process, a problem of inclusion. Somebody is either doing something or not, so a sense of state responsibility emerged. If you look at recent policy documents on exclusion, you notice that we shifted overwhelmingly towards the passive verb. Togetherness did not help either. The connotation has been that we are all one nation, together in one big room,*

and the door has been locked on us. The sharpness and the edge of the activism of active exclusion and inclusion were lost. You do need to work on including somebody, but you do not need to do anything to be together. Unfortunately, the status quo of non-action has been reinforced." (Social policy advisor)

"For me, the story of social inclusion in the last 10 years is that of non-translation and non-embeddedness. 'Inclusion' stubbornly remained an external communication strategy of the government. There is a lot of window-dressing, there are lots of coats being put on, but underneath the surface there is a disjointed relationship between policy and politics, between new professional values and political directions, between declared goals and actual implementations, between money and rhetoric, between the OMC and the Structural Funds."

"It seems to me that there is also a deliberate non-translation. There are numerous good inclusion indicators (such as child poverty), yet, there is no political commitment to use them to gear policies. We have the Structural Funds, which are the sources of 90% of development funds and new investments in the field of social policy, yet, nobody links them to social inclusion priorities set by the OMC process. There is also a non-translation between administrative levels. Nobody talks about regional or local inclusion strategies. The Structural Funds have in 2008 accepted deinstitutionalisation as a social inclusion priority for spending; can you see a reference in the National Strategies on social protection and social inclusion about deinstitutionalisation? No, there is none. The shreds are running on separate paths, and inclusion policy remains fragmented, disjointed and un-embedded in the EU's inclusion discourse." (Social policy advisor)

In terms of my documents, and their traces, the last trace of 'societal togetherness' can be found in the 'National strategy report on social protection and social inclusion 2008–2010'. From 2010 onwards, the term 'societal togetherness' disappears from reports, as it at first traverses back into 'social inclusion' (*tarsadalmi befogadas*), and from 2011 onwards, becomes 'societal catch-up' or 'societal closed-up' (*tarsadalmi felzarkozas*). Yet again, 'societal closed-up' is translated back into English-speaking reports as 'social inclusion'. The linguistic re-engineering of both the 'social' and 'inclusion' is well under way. In a consultation paper, the Hungarian Member of the European Women's Lobby (Hungarian Women's Lobby 2013: 5–6) argues:

> the phrasing of the fourth priority of the proposed National Development Plan for 2014–2020 '*Societal closed-up, addressing challenges of demography, and the Good State*', we find problematic. Why do we address challenges rather than reduce inequalities? Why do we use the term societal close-up and not social inclusion? This latter one is particularly problematic since societal close-up is translated into the English version of the document as social inclusion, which is a very misleading translation.... We are also very disappointed to see the terminology of the 'Good State' (particularly with the rather awkward capital letters). Again, in the English version it translates as good governance, but that is deeply misleading.... Using the term 'state' rather than governance, erases the principles of partnership and participation.

Paul Stubbs (PS): Is there more that can be said about the implications of what you write based on ethnographies carried out 10 years apart? In the quotes from civil servants and others from 2013, there appears to be a greater reflexivity, perhaps even disillusionment, regarding the nature of the 'fiction-writing': perhaps, instead of becoming better at fiction-writing, they have become more conscious of it as a process of fiction-writing. Would you agree? Can this, in any way, be related to the changing contexts of both Hungary's position within the EU and the changing nature and positioning of 'social inclusion' vis-à-vis some of the 'elsewheres' of EU policymaking, particularly those related to fiscal austerity?

NL: Disillusionment, tiredness and greater consciousness of fiction-writing (as opposed to 'dreaming') are definitely tangible. At times, it manifests itself more in terms of referring to the fiction or collapse of 'Social Europe', as well as to the failed imaginaries of a more inclusive Hungary, as well as EU. Indeed, behind the discursive activism of social inclusion at the EU level lie the many spaces of 'policy elsewheres' – fiscal austerity, economic competitiveness and the marginality of Social Europe at EU level – while a particular form of authoritarian neoliberalism of the Hungarian policy spaces presents equally marginal notions of the 'social'. There are multiple fictions being enacted here, which might be worth thinking about more, particularly in relation to the fiction of Social Europe.

Conclusion: reflections on the politics of translation

The puzzle of this work started somewhere very similar to Koskinen (2008), who, while working for the European Commission as a Finnish translator, was puzzled by the difficulty of making (common) sense of both Finnish and English texts produced by the EU or by the Finnish translators' team. My puzzle started similarly in 2003, reading the Hungarian and English versions of the JIM and not being able to make sense of the document. The long, monotonous sentences, along with the buzzing of new words, was a rather strange read. I was further puzzled by the fact that many academic scholars would take such policy documents and subject them to 'discourse analysis' to learn about 'discursive Europeanisation' and 'ideational convergence'.

This chapter was not looking at conceptualising social inclusion policies as a form of discourse understood as a speech act, a communicative act, a form of domination or hegemony (Howarth, 2010), or as a coordinative discourse (Smith, 2011). Nor was it aiming at providing a textual analysis of policies, within the tradition of critical discourse analysis. Rather, it was an attempt to move away from the taken-for-granted terrain of norms, commons and techno-zones of the EU's soft governance, and trace more fine-grained processes of fiction, appropriation, (non-)embedding and resistance to the supposed 'master discourse'. Translation is an immensely important process here, where translating across languages not only transmits, transfers and transplants, but also makes, crafts and alters, policies. Importantly, it points to Muller's (2007: 207) assertion that '[i]n ignoring the politics of translation, we de-politicize the antagonisms and struggles for meaning that take place in a foreign language'. This chapter shall not be a unique, or exotic, example of the particularities of Hungarian language, culture and politics. The cross-cultural productivity of travelling policies always implies a need for many more stories to be written to open up the 'black box', to make visible forms and practices of translations, and the plurality, diversity and multiplicity of social inclusion in the EU. Translation offers an open-ended endeavour, where we do not yet know what is coming. Translation is more about how we shift direction, how we capture shifts in translation, how we pause and think differently and how we attend 'to what slips out, does not fit or gets lost in translation' (Best, 2012: 86). Translation might also help us to untangle the equation in which to 'Europeanise' is to 'modernise', unlearning the common and the taken-for-granted ideas that policies are supposed to converge towards. As Kapoor (2004: 642) puts it:

> unlearning means stopping oneself from always wanting to correct, teach, theorise, develop, colonise, appropriate, use, record, inscribe, enlighten: the impetus to always be the speaker and speak in all situations must be seen for what it is: a desire for mastery and domination.

As Scott (2002: 152) argues, the project of EU integration and 'the construction of a European space of meaning' is where new 'symbolism is needed to guide collective action by creating a sense of common understanding and provide a "language" that promotes consensus-building'. I am taking three problems from this process: the problem of EU language and its translations; the problem of consensus and the common; and the problem of collective action.

From the point of view of translation, the language of the EU is an 'unearthly' and imagined language that is both fictitious and enabling (Diez, 1999). Pennycook (2003: 523) proposes to talk about linguascapes to 'capture the relationship between the ways in which some languages are no longer tied to locality or community but rather operate globally'. EU English has been characterised by:

> textual uniformity, whatever the topic or readership, based on approximations that are immediately recognizable as impairing good communication. The words are clear enough, the syntax not structurally complex, and apart from a few new foreign borrowings, there are no obvious discrepancies with ordinary language. Yet, lexical vagueness and weak logical connections spread the sense of mechanistic virtuality that makes the voice of Europe sound awkward, abstract and completely distant from any languages spoken in everyday life. (Tosi, 2005: 385)

It would be a different research project to look at the policy implications of EU English. Nevertheless, the awkward buzziness and vagueness of key policy terms, such as 'mainstreaming', 'streamlining' and 'flexicurity', will end up in an inevitable contact zone when they get translated. The Hungarian translation of 'inclusion' as 'togetherness', or 'closed-up', is the result of the awkward encounter, the fiction of the language of EU inclusion policy, the fiction of the Hungarian translation and the fiction of policy texts produced in the process of 'deliberative governance'. Consensus-building, referred to by Scott, is then based on this performative encounter with many fictitious elements. Discursive Europeanisation may lead to not ideational convergence, but rather a series of policy fictions, and performative policies, which just as much undermine the 'common' as converge towards it. It may well be that both in terms of policy frameworks and academic scholarship on the EU, too much emphasis is placed on an assumed consensus. The 'consensus on consensus' is reinforced and reproduced by both policy discourses within the EU circuits and by academic discourses, which take for granted what we mean by the buzzwords and aim for the 'common'. Here, Diez's (1999: 599) long-standing, yet ever so contemporary, warning remains important:

> the various attempts to capture the Union's nature are not mere description of an unknown polity, but take part in the construction of the polity itself. To that extent, they are not politically innocent, and may themselves become subject of analysis along with articulations from other actors.

Finally, translation highlights that aligning to a particular set of policies is just one set of dynamics among the many. Many diverse sets of strategies are mobilised in this process (non-embedding, window-dressing, resisting, appropriating, reaffirming), and, as such, concepts such as 'catch-up convergence' may be of little help to capture this complex set of translation practices. This chapter is asserting a point made by Lewis and Mosse (2006: 4), who argue that policy texts are a particular representation of policy practices, one that often 'hides the actual contingencies and network of practices'. At the end, translation sits in the crossfire 'between the "monotheistic privilege" of dominant policy models and the polytheism of scattered practices surviving below' (Mosse, 2004: 645). In translation zones, where multiple speakers speak multiple languages, multiple regimes of inclusion cannot be collapsed into a modernist vision of policy learning and policy transfer. We need to open up new spaces of contestation and resistance, and sites of policy production, that enable us to capture the complexities of travelling policies. We also need to rescue 'policy' from its techno-zone and epistemic modernism.

SIX

Translating education: assembling ways of knowing otherwise

Dave Bainton

Introduction

This chapter explores puzzles around 'translation', 'global educational agendas' and 'policy transfers' through a dialogue between theoretical considerations on translation and policy transfer, with ethnographic work carried out in rural communities in Ladakh, India. In an attempt to offer a critical voice to processes of global epistemic reorganisation, 'translation' is used as an approach that has the potential to break out of the straitjacket of the disciplinary boundaries of policy studies, thereby contributing to a new way of imagining what policy might be (Yanow, 2011). Translation, I argue, by being sensitive to mechanisms of silencing and social rupture that accompany such transnational transfers, makes visible how global policy reassembles the social.

However, as I ultimately go on to argue, a translation approach offers not only a way to analyse hegemonic dimensions and articulations of global policy transfer processes, but also a way to expand counter-hegemonic possibilities. This demands an enriched conceptualisation of translation as far more than a fragile linguistic and conceptual process in which 'unintended consequences' can be attributed to how the original authentic (Western) policy may have been 'lost in translation'. Rather, policy translation is more critically, and more positively, understood as an active, creative process that has the potential to bring new educational worlds into being.

From policy transfer to policy translation

Globalisation has been associated with the emergence of a 'global policy space' – a space that has increasingly become crowded with a growing number of policy domains subjected to global policy production. This process of privileging the global as a scale for 'policy' has hugely expanded the scope and range of policies pursued by international organisations, such as the United Nations (UN), the World Bank or the International Monetary Fund (IMF) (Best, 2012). Among the many reasons contributing to this expansion and accumulation is the currency and logic of 'policy transfer', which Diane Stone (2002: 5) defines as the 'emulation or synthesis of policies, institutions, ideologies and ideas across time, place or policy domains'. Within this rationale, policies, institutions and ideas are seen as immensely mobile and moveable from one context to another, insofar as they are understood to be universally applicable in their international 'diffusion'.

International organisations all rely on policy agendas that are based on a 'floating institutional architecture'; they are floating because they are assumed to travel and move easily from one context to another, and they are institutional because they focus on institutional designs, such as 'good governance', while 'best practices' collapse the 'social' and the 'political' into matters of technical, administrative and managerial competences and 'calculative practices' of standards, benchmarks and forms of (ac)counting (Higgins and Larner, 2010).

As Mosse (2008) argues, globalisation has fostered the rise of global policy agendas centred around the adoption of a particular set of 'travelling rationalities', such as the general applicability of technicalised knowledge, which produces erasures of history and its relevance. These rationalities have claimed important currency that has enabled them to travel internationally between countries and contexts, and to 'flow', thereby populating the global policy space. For Mosse (2008), actors in the global policy arena affirm the power of ideas and the status of 'thought work' and 'knowledge banks' in the world system, and, in so doing, a particular form of global policy space is assembled.

In this chapter, 'translation' is deployed as a set of theoretical tools to offer a critical response to this global policy space and to question the naturalisation of such a 'global policy'. I agree with Escobar (2012: xxxii) when he argues that we must question not only its existence, but its formulation:

> something similar happened with globalisation discourses of all kinds. In these discourses, whether mainstream or Left, an alleged 'global space' is seen as naturally and fully occupied by forms of socionatural life that are in fact an extension of Western-style modernity. No matter how qualified, globalization in these discourses always amounts to a deepening and a universalization of capitalist modernity. There is something terribly wrong with this imaginary.

I argue that the process of international policy transfer is actually better understood as a process of *translation* across this global policy space of a set of concepts, instruments, logics, outputs, lines of influence, ambitions and so on. Emerging out of a set of (usually Western) linguistic and institutional configurations, policy is then translated into another language, political context and institutional and legal framework.

In troubling global policy, this chapter takes 'translation' as a useful and deconstructive term that is deployed to think about globalisation and global policy production. In attempting to denaturalise the rise of such a global policy space, this chapter argues that the epistemic territorialisation and policy rationalities that accompany global policy should be seen not as spontaneously emergent, but rather as actively produced through power-laden policy translation practices. The saliency of a translation metaphor in understanding global policy production rests upon a critical interrogation of 'mobilities' as the displacement and dislocation of knowledge, truth and power relations; it is the process of global policy and knowledge production that this chapter seeks to reflect upon.

Critically, this policy translation process is problematic as it takes place within a global policy space that is inscribed by particular rationalities of development. As Mosse (2007) puts it: '[n]ew processes of aid "harmonisation" align internationalized policy and its technical instruments into "travelling rationalities" that appear to erase (or conceal) the regional, institutional, agency or sector specificity of the development process'. These processes are doubly problematic, in that these travelling rationalities:

> are never free from social context ... they begin in social relations, in institutions and expert communities, travel with undisclosed baggage, get unravelled as they are unpacked into other socio-institutional worlds – perhaps through the interests of local collaborators, official counterparts, or brokers – and are recolonized by politics in ways that generate complex and unintended effects. (Mosse, 2008: 121)

As Iveković (2002: 2) so aptly notes, in processes of translation, 'What is to be translated is not texts, but contexts'. Such a translation of contexts makes problematic Mosse's easy distinction between the intended and unintended, where the reshaping of people's lives might be disregarded as a thoughtless other of a policy enmeshed in epistemic modernism's intentionality. Rather, translation draws attention to the dynamic and complex ways in which all policy is assembled. While the language of unintended consequences serves to focus concern upon fracture lines that policy might create, it also maintains the concept of the intended. A transition lens serves to remind us how translations are dynamic and unfolding, where the consequences are not so easily predicted, and that we might, instead, be better to give attention to the creative moment where alternatives become possible.

Assembling education policy

In searching for a way to conceptualise policy that allows for the full implications of a translation perspective to be made visible, we use the term 'assemblage' (taken from Deleuze and Guattari, 1988). A term that is gaining increasing popularity, 'assemblage refers to "the process of arranging, organizing fitting together … [where] an assemblage is a whole of some sort that expresses some identity and claims a territory" (Wise, 2005: 92). As McCann and Ward (2013: 8) note: 'thinking about policy as a constructed whole in this way avoids the tendency to assume that policies emerge in full form from a specific place or that they circulate unchanged'.

The concept of policy assemblage is used here, first, as an act of inclusion, in order to expand from a narrow focus on discursive aspects of social life to trace the ways that education policy is a heterogeneous assemblage of objects, narratives, practices, families, gods, places, ancestors, ghosts, technologies, ambitions, temporalities and institutions. Indeed, what assemblage offers here is analytic sensitivity not only to the multiple and multiformed elements of policy, but also to the processes and politics of inclusion and exclusion that govern what elements an education policy assemblage might include, and how they are articulated. Deleuze (2006: 176–9) refers to an assemblage as:

> first and foremost what keeps very heterogeneous elements together: e.g. a sound, a gesture, a position, etc., both natural and artificial elements. The problem is one of 'consistency' or 'coherence,' and it is prior to the problem of behavior. How do things take on consistency? How do they cohere?

Such a perspective does not understand policy as a text, however empowered, or as a set of intentions, however formulated, nor as a set of meanings generated or as a form of social organisation. Rather, here, education policy consists of those aspects of life that are found to be coherently linked to it – be they textual, virtual, intentional or material. Such an expanded view of policy, as we shall see, allows for an analysis of how policies work to reconfigure the lived realities of the people they affect.

I use the term 'assemblage' for a second reason too: because it alludes to a dynamic process of formation. The policy in its broadest sense (its meaning, actors, practices, texts, desires, subject positions and biographies) is assembled even as it is translated – and such assembly comes as a consequence of sustained effort and the conjuncture of multiple forms of influence, whose effects can be traced. There is no denying that the state world poverty is something that demands a response. One of the core policies that has leveraged action has been the agreement of the Millennium Development Goals (MDGs), including Goal 2: 'Ensure that, by 2015, children everywhere, boys and girls alike, will be able to complete a full course of primary schooling'. A second allied global policy instrument has been the Education for All (EFA) movement. This movement, which pre-dates the MDGs, was launched at the World Conference on Education for All in Jomtien in 1990, by the UN Educational, Scientific, and Cultural Organization (UNESCO), the UN Development Programme (UNDP), the UN Fund for Population Activities (UNFPA), the UN Children's Fund (UNICEF) and the World Bank. Reiterated at the world education forum in Dakar in 2000, this movement has pledged to meet the learning needs of all children, youth and adults by 2015. It is possible to identify a broad policy alignment among those working in the field of educational development that takes a rights-based approach (drawing on the UN Convention of the Rights of a Child 1989, and calling for educational provision as a right) as a way to mobilise efforts towards achieving EFA.

The global aspiration of EFA leads to processes where education is translated for ever-'harder to reach' groups, and children are appropriated into their complex assemblages. To explore the impacts of such social and cultural reorganisation, I now turn to a case study of how an EFA policy agenda 'translates' into educational practices for Tibetan communities in Ladakh, Northern India – in the form of a school for Tibetan nomads. In many ways, this case study exemplifies the very purpose of such global assemblage of education policy: the promotion of educational opportunities to marginalised communities. Yet, as we shall see, how this policy is translated creates community and cultural ruptures, and shines a light on the ways that education plays a strong role in the future life trajectories of individuals and their communities.

Stanzin's story in the following is offered here as a 'placeholder'[1] for all of the 'interesting, and sometimes even surprising disturbances [that] can occur in the spaces between the "creation", the "transmission" and the "interpretation" or "reception" of policy meanings' (Lendvai and Stubbs, 2007: 175). It is offered to help us locate our thinking about how education policies are translated into new contexts and the reassemblage of lives and possible livelihoods that takes place through this process – a reassemblage that involves, among other things, displacement, social rupture, erasures and paradoxes.

Education, displacement and ways of knowing[2]

At the age of five, Stanzin was one of the oldest children in the boarding school. She was just starting her third year there, and she was well used to the routines of the school. Soon, it would be time to go down to the river to take a quick wash and clean her teeth before the sun went down. It was midsummer, yet the wind sweeping down off the higher mountain plateau was still cold. She faced into the wind, trying to imagine where, amid the mountains, her family might be now.

Last week, she had been playing with her elder brother and baby sister at the summer huts. They are not far away – a day's walk past the hot springs, where the grazing was good for their Pashmina goats that her family lived off – but the memories of the two-week summer holiday had faded, together with her father's retreating figure, back into the landscape.

Stanzin looked down at Tashi next to her, playing with stones like the other little ones. He looked up and then turned his face away as she distractedly wiped his runny nose on her sleeve. She looked more closely at him: "And don't forget to wash your eyes, you're starting

---

[1]   Although the term 'placeholder' is used to mean a symbolic example, it is intended to disrupt any possible reification of the analytic here – that these might be thought of as (simple) examples. Rather, the directionality is opposite: that this is one context where the meaning of this analytic can emerge; other contexts, with other meanings, are there.

[2]   This section draws upon fieldwork experiences in Ladakh during 2008–09, and draws them into an ethnography that uses narrative devices. The purpose of this is to attempt to bring to attention those aspects of lived experiences that are always at stake in policy assemblage, but are often not represented – the affective, the felt, the embodied – to reveal their role in the processes of accommodation, rupture and displacement as education policies are reassembled.

to get redeye", she said. Stanzin tried to look out for him – she remembered her own first year here. It was tough for some of them, not understanding why their parents had left them here in this windy place, having to wash and look after themselves. They soon learnt, soon made friends, as she had, had begun to understand why their families thought that education was so important, and had begun to learn to read and write. She knew the Tibetan letters now, and she could sing plenty of the Tibetan songs that made her family laugh so much. She smiled to herself, took Tashi's hand in hers and headed down to the river.

Next year, most likely, Stanzin will no longer be here, at the point of this camera. For this boarding school, with its 40 or so children, three teachers, single dormitory and nearby river, testament as it is to the human capacity to bring into being schools in the most unlikely of places, teaches only children aged three to six. If Stanzin is to continue her education, she must travel, not up the valley to her family, but further away, down the valley into more distant and warmer lands, away from the Tibetan plateau where her family roam.

As I set off to climb the pass, I am surprised to see smoke rising from the low stone huts that mark the '*pulu*', the summer grazing grounds at the top of each valley, where, as if reluctant to give up its duty of refuge to those who live within it, the valley offers one last open, sheltered place before the path must wind its way upwards more steeply. Every other *pulu* I have passed through has been empty, but, here, two men are still following the traditional summer habit of going up with the animals for grazing. As I approach, they point us towards a large cloth on the floor upon which are laid a selection of bronze spoons and cups that they have made for passers-by – mostly trekking tourists and their entourages – to buy should they wish. I buy a spoon, and it is not by chance that this spoon is located here. This metal-working knowledge is not only embodied in these old men. It can be traced back to the 17th century and is also located – quite literally – in the valleys and mountains where the ore that is used to make these spoons is found.

Later, I am staying for a week in another village with a friend. I have heard a lot about the ceramics that it is famous for. The clay that can be used for making pots is found nearby. While I am here, I try to meet with the three men who are most famous for doing ceramics – I do not manage to – one is acting as a guide for a trekking group, one is working in construction and one is in Leh. "No one is doing ceramics now", Gyatso says. This is a different way of thinking about indigenous knowledge, not only practised, not only embodied, but also located – located in particular places, places that are affected by the dislocations that are caused by education. Later again, back in town, there are giggles as I pass two young schoolchildren, maybe six or seven years old, in the street in Leh,

"Where are you from?"

"I am from England. Where are you from?"

"I am from Zanskar."

"Why are you in Leh?"

"To go to school."

"There are no schools in Zanskar?"

"There are no good[3] schools in Zanskar."

"Where are you from?"

---

[3] The concept of a 'good' school was one that emerged as a category during fieldwork. This distinction was one that, as this quote shows, was prevalent even among early primary-age children. The distinction mobilised resources for parents to find one for their children, with displacement and family rupture as one consequence.

"Lamayuru."

"Why are you in Leh?"

"To go to school."

"There are no schools in Lamayuru?"

"No good schools in Lamayuru."

Crapanzano (2004: 103), in an essay on hope, quotes Minkowski as writing '[w]e are charmed by hope, because it opens the future broadly before'. It is perhaps not a surprise, therefore, that Lewis and Mosse (2006), in offering a typology of approaches to development policy, offer 'development as hope' as one formulation. While desire presupposes human agency, hope is desire's passive counterpart, dependent upon some other for its agency. It is apt. Educational success cannot be desired here, these students do not have sufficient agency for that. The possibility of these students educationally achieving is not in their hands: they have no money to go to a better school, have no teacher to teach them. The agency that they possess to study is insufficient alone, there is a resignation. Here, in this school, hope is all that is possible.

For Crapanzano, his interest in hope is as part of the elucidation of the concept of an 'imaginative horizon', searching to understand the role of that which we are able to imagine in creating our experience, which, in many ways, therefore, emphasises the productive nature of hope. It is not that I do not concur; rather, it is that I would wish to be critical, deconstructive and seek to reconfigure the role of hope as that which maintains particular assemblages of education. Hope also offers a softer reading of how hegemony is maintained – not only through manufactured consent or the institutionalised power of the school system, but also through the very human need to hope.

> The mobilizing metaphors of 'hope' have to be transformed into institutionalised incentives and interests in order to have an effect; but equally, a professionalized and increasingly managerialist development industry, in which development hopes are rearranged according to the internal logics of administration and organizational politics, and that is unchallenged by the ethnographic worlds of people for whom such professionals claim to speak or by the

contingencies of practice of the wider more basic moral vision of global justice and personal wellbeing, easily becomes a self serving organizational realm disconnected from the reality of its own effects. (Lewis and Mosse, 2006: 6)

Here, in this remote corner of India, the territory of modernity is visible, inscribing the borders between one policy regime and the next (Vazques, 2011). To adopt the language that I introduced earlier, there exists a policy assemblage that is based upon the right to a basic primary education, which understands this as including, among other things, schools as sites for learning, teachers as experts, commodified and assessed educational outcomes, and abstracted forms of learning.

> *Noémi Lendvai (NL):* Notions such as 'rights', 'education', 'schooling', 'knowledge', 'teaching' and 'individual pupils' are all deeply Westernised constructions. 'Rights', in particular, social rights, are associated with modern welfare state developments in the West. Education as a right draws attention to the 'legal' and the 'institutional', which is not only deeply displaced here, but, more importantly, assumes universal applicability that enables them to travel unproblematically across borders, reinforcing the taken for granted. What rights does Stanzin have?

Stripped naked, the complex social contexts of Western educational practices are reduced through cycles of simplification to a set of assumptions, where, in a different landscape, new realities are reassembled. These translations of education are based on assumptions of: the individualisation and commodification of knowledge through grading and certification; the static, institutional spaces of schooling; the abstracted nature of learning; and the dominance of the written over the spoken and the cognitive over the practical.

A language of policy assemblage, as outlined earlier, draws attention to the lived realities of education policies, suggesting that the life that Stanzin and her family live is not best understood as an unintended outcome of an education policy, nor as a quixotic translation or even mistranslation of an EFA agenda. Rather, a language of policy assemblage serves to acknowledge that considerable effort has been made to create this particular educational translation, and that rather than taking what exists for granted, we might seek to trace the lines of power that have enabled these efforts.

Paul Stubbs (PS): What may be the implications of the existence, both in theory and in practice, of similar critical articulations of commodified education, even within what you appear, here, to be constructing as a unitary 'West'? I am thinking, in particular, but by no means only, about Ivan Illich's influential work on 'deschooling' and experiments such as A.S. Neill's Summerhill School in the UK. Are there traces of these, in any form, in aspects of the EFA agenda? Is there any sense in which an understanding of these theories and practices may also help in the construction of an 'education otherwise'?

DB: Illich and Neill are, of course, examples of thinking about education differently, and might therefore be helpful to those engaged in translating education otherwise – but I have reservations. In the case of Illich, arguing for deschooling is only a first small step towards the more creative challenge of developing education otherwise. With regards to Summerhill, who is to say that a model of a democratic school (and, with it, particular understandings of childhood and learning) is nearer to achieving a more culturally sensitive mode of education? The argument of a translation lens is that these conversations should themselves take place in context – and the resources that are used should be the resources that are found in that context. Later in the chapter, I draw upon various local 'ways of knowing' to demonstrate how these might be effectively enrolled in such a task.

The paradox of translation

[U]nder a veneer of acceptance, the Other's knowledge is translated into familiar cultural forms in ways that construct it as possessing knowable characteristics able to be apprehended and controlled. These processes of Othering at once work to domesticate and subsume, while simultaneously separating and regulating the boundaries, preserving the integrity and authority of western science. (Gough and Gough, 2003: 12)

Translation is never neutral: some terms are translated, and some are not; some meanings are inscribed, while others are silenced. Policy translation, operating as it does on the borders between different epistemic territories, is inevitably caught up in this endless struggle between uniformity (reproduction) and creation (transposition). On the one hand, there is translation as an act of oppression, where dominant ideas are translated across the border into the language and territory of the subaltern, bringing epistemic violence in its wake. On the other hand, we have translation as resistance, a space where the dominant loses control over the meaning-making process, and where talking back is possible. To put it differently, even as translation inscribes a process of erasure as the meanings that are untranslated or unsayable are made invisible, so the possibility of a critical difference between what is and what might be opens up. So, maybe we are too quick to interpret meanings as being 'lost in translation', for, as Farquhar and Fitzsimons (2011: 653) argue, 'To be lost in translation is to accept both the contingency of language and our inability to fully encapsulate otherness within our frame of reference'.

These tensions between the oppressive and agentive possibility of translations runs through the translation literature. For some (Vazquez, 2011), this tension is understood in terms of translation as a process of epistemic violence (which takes place when translation takes place along the borders of modernity) and, on the other hand, a process of epistemic struggle. For Farquhar and Fitzsimons (2011: 657), translation is understood paradoxically, where being lost in translation is 'both our curse and our blessing as part of the human condition', in which 'translation is posited as a creative and interpretive act – involving neither image nor copy, but poetic transposition'.

I do not see these alternate conceptions of translation as competing. Rather, I understand both tendencies as being in play. Earlier in the chapter, I have shown how a particular translation of a universal policy, in its reassemblage of the social, leads to social rupture. At the same time, I am offering policy translation as an agentive expression of doing policy otherwise – offering directions for how we might conceptualise the potentiality of translation to think and act differently.

To this end, Emily Apter, in attempting to sketch out the possibility of rethinking translation away from linguistic and textual arenas into a broad theoretical framework, draws, in part, on the work of Alain Badiou, writing that:

> Badiou's view of translation as a disaster that nonetheless enables a singular comparatism of the Idea afforded an interesting paradigm: one based not on shared philological word-histories, but on the limitless and irreducible bounds of poesis. In the permission it grants to translate from divergent periods and traditions, Badiou's philosophy of the Idea introduces an enhanced democracy of comparison. (Apter, 2006: 9)

In this formulation, translation is not only that which limits, but also the potential inherent within the liminal slippage that is the process of translation. In a sense, it is the differences (of language, context, meaning) where translation is a struggle that opens up the potential for alternatives – of the making anew of poiesis.[4]

This chapter seeks to develop a language of assemblage and translation able to open up alternative directions for less violent translations of education. I have argued that the power of the language of assemblage and translation as a theoretical toolkit lies in the inherent multidimensionality and plurality of the world that is brought into being through it. This power is not only analytic, being able to critically analyse the forms of social and family reassemblage that certain translations of education create (as we saw earlier), but also to broaden the resources that might be brought to bear in seeking alternative translations of education that are less violent.

Critical to placing translation within a more transformative frame is understanding that the *potential* policy translations are always multiple, contested and constrained. In other words, a politics of translation suggests that there is a need to account both for how the broader field of potential translations emerges and how these then collapse into particular policy formulations. Translation, in this way, allows us to problematise and disentangle the complex relationship between policy production, knowledge production and social practices.

A translation perspective, then, emphasises policy translation as a process of *potential* struggle, and therefore struggles over the potential of policy translation. Policy transfer may take place in ways that are insensitive to context, creating social rupture, and yet, since 'all translation is local', translation processes are always anchored in local contexts, suggesting that translation is able to emphasise the specific rather than the general, diversity rather than uniformity, and divergence rather than convergence (Johnson and Hagstrom, 2005). This position argues not only that 'the translation process often should be regarded as a battle between competing interpretations vying for supremacy' (2005: 375), but also that behind the struggles that are visible, some interpretations do not get to 'vie for supremacy' – they are excluded, silenced or rendered archaic/out of time or place. In that sense, translation is always a political project, with a need for a

---

4   The term 'poiesis' is drawn from Ancient Greek, but revitalised by Heidegger. It is used here in the sense that Heidegger uses it: as a creative act that leads things into being (Whitehead, 2003). In this use, processes of translation open up the possibilities of poiesis.

critical research agenda to uncover what gets translated, who gets to translate and how alternative translations might assemble differently within a particular context.

This talks to the more creative dimensions of a translation toolkit. If we use translation here in emergent, culturally significant ways (How, say, might we find better ways to translate education for nomads in Ladakh?), then the generation of translations is more than a process where we need to be attuned to cultural sensitivities, or where we need to trace who gets to translate what, and in whose interest. It is a process in which particular translations, insofar as they 'become' in their reassemblage of the social, can be understood (and therefore judged, resourced, supported or resisted) through the forms of livelihoods and relationality that are brought into being by them. Furthermore, it is this focus on the becoming, and on agency within it, that the language of translation and assemblage offers the most. It points not only to the challenges of finding methodological ways to trace the reassemblage of the present by different translations (as a critical project), but, more crucially, to the task of multiplying both the field of potential translations and their enactments.

The remainder of this chapter turns to just this task: to develop the creative potential of this approach. Creativity, here, is a necessary element – as Escobar (2004: 16), echoing De Sousa Santos, notes, 'modernity's ability to provide solutions to modern problems has been increasingly compromised'. This creative project is not one that is attainable through deconstructive, or analytic, tools alone; it is a creation, a building up, an association, an interrogation and an imagination, and we need different tools for this. In searching for alternative lines of thought, I have been drawn both to the possibility of the encounter in place and to indigenous forms of theorising as ways to sketch out the possibility of 'educating otherwise' (Rojas, 2007).

PS: Is it possible to use terms like this in a non-essentialist way? Terms such as 'indigenous', 'traditional' and 'non-Western' suggest something separate and authentic that hides the ways that they are also constructed in power.

DB: That is a question close to my heart. For me, these terms are only meaningful in their relationality. The indigenous invokes the non-indigenous; the traditional invokes the modern. Rather than implying an essentialism, I am using them non-essentially to mark a distinction that calls attention to a directionality of counter-hegemonic possibilities. In a sense, I am trying to rescue these terms from essentialist understandings and to recognise them as dynamic terms that have been forged though dominant understandings. These terms point to a possible 'other' of modernising discourses that remain uncaptured and with potential for the creation of policy otherwise.

I have tried to develop themes (of silence, of place, of excess, of praxis, of narrative) that are emergent out of particular ethnographic encounters in Ladakh. Each weaves research narrative, reflection and theoretical readings, and can be understood to be attempts to formulate theorising in place – to do some work, as a Western academic, that does not 'lose respect for the other as placeholder for the origin(al)', and remains true to a politics of listening that seeks a fidelity to the original 'not because it's possible, but because one must try' (Spivak, 1985: xx).

The form of narrative is an attempt to challenge the usual relationship between the author and reader, and between theory and practice. In part, this is to allow the form of each to be coherent with the arena of possibility it explores in order to make its themes (landscape, silence, sculpture, etc) present within the texts; in part, it is to create more 'writerly' texts, where:

> The writerly text is a perpetual present ... the writerly text is ourselves writing, before the infinite play of the world (the world as function) is traversed, intersected, stopped, plasticized by some singular system (ideology, Genus, Criticism) which reduces the plurality of entrances, the opening of networks, the infinity of languages. (Barthes, 1990: 5)

The function of such a text is less to fully explicate and more to sow seeds that might evoke new lines of thought in the reader. The work that a more writerly text does in this chapter is to take seriously the aforementioned arguments: academic texts are also particular ways of knowing, and expanding, our ways of writing about, and comprehending other ways of knowing is one critical part of an ethic of translation and an ethic of listening. They are, in this sense, attempts to explore the form of a politics of translation.

Translation as praxis

In this chapter, in various ways, I am seeking to transpose translation into a form of praxis within education policymaking that is better able both to understand how education reassembles lives and livelihoods and how this understanding helps to open up new spaces for translating education otherwise. In conceptualising this transposition, I draw principal inspiration from Vegso's (2012) discussion of the praxis of translation. Vegso foregrounds the potentiality, plurality and materiality of translation, understanding that as 'a material praxis, translation is a contingent assemblage of diverse bodily and textual movements, a loose collection of apparatuses, a constellation' (Vegso, 2012: 62). Critical for my purpose, in this formulation, translation is an 'actualization', 'when one particular activity is realized from this original plurality' (Vegso, 2012: 55–6).

The ways that particular translations are actualised from their original plurality has important implications for the development of a politics of translation. Understanding translation as a form of praxis that reassembles the social, and thereby 'until we perform an act of translation, we do not know what translation *is*' (Vegso, 2012: 55–6, emphasis in original), does not mean that we are inevitably absent from contestation at the moment of actualisation. Rather, it repositions a politics of translation to one less concerned with which meanings are more valid or representative and, at a deeper level, more cognizant of the fact that translations are claims over the relation between what is and what is not translatable:

> The field of translation (as the field of translatability) comes about as a result of a primary exclusion. The untranslatable has to be excluded from the field of translation to establish what is translatable. But the excluded element does not disappear without a trace: the untranslatable constantly threatens the normal operation of translation.... But if the very separation of what is and what is not translatable has no essential identity, this very division becomes a question of practice: the very division between the two has to be produced by an act of translation. (Vegso, 2012: 58–9)

The distinction between the translatable and the untranslatable directs us to the primary exclusion that takes place when potential understandings go unheard, silenced or ignored. It directs us to look behind interpretations competing for meaning, to an expanded field of translation where new, as yet unknown, meanings might be found. As such, Vegso argues that translation participates less in theoretical debates over the opposition of a (modernist) universal language and the (post-modern) fetishisation of the untranslatable; instead, being better located both within a politics of translation as exclusion (of how particular translations create their own histories) and an ethics of translation.

Such a politics calls for two modes of operation. First, and most urgently, it calls for a commitment to expand the field of translation into new, less verbal and textual spaces and understandings – spaces that, in the context of this chapter, are occupied by non-Western 'ways of knowing'. This would suggest a politics of translation where education might be translated in ways that did not exclude myriad ways of knowing from its actualisation (as explored in Chapter Seven). However, it also calls for a second realignment: that since translation, in a reprise of Apter's earlier argument of the paradox of translation, is inevitable and inevitably a world-calling, then translation should be done lightly, with a thought to both the worlds that we thereby call into being and the worlds that we thereby silence.

The exploration of this expanded field of translation is necessarily empirical, as well as theoretical – in the sense that these rich excluded fields of potential translations are sites of praxis. I shall now explore one particular site, that of traditional sculpture in Ladakh.

Translating silence

> What happens to the theory of translation in an age when philosophy no longer considers language to be the ultimate horizon of being, yet reality constantly confronts us with situations that prove on a daily basis the urgency of translation? Whereas the former tendency might disorient our thinking with relation to translation, the second relentlessly reminds us of its inescapable necessity. It is this state of affairs that has led many of us to believe that translation has finally and irrevocably entered the domain of global politics. (Vegso, 2012: 47)

Traditional sculpture in Ladakh is a form of skilled practice that remains recognised within society, but is not part of the assemblage that is education – and, in this sense, I shall explore it as a site of exclusion, offering something to the search for translating education otherwise. Sculptural knowledge and skills remain largely acquired through apprenticeship, and both in its divergent pedagogy (from the modern assemblage of education) and its aesthetic practice, it seems one possible place to seek the seeds of alternate translations. I am taking traditional sculpture as one answer to Vegso's question of what might happen to the politics of translation in a world that while remaining framed by the discursive, recognises that life and our experience of it are not fully reducible to it – that we are confronted with the possibilities of translating ways of knowing that reside to a greater degree in the non-verbal and the experiential.

The sculptor was making a new god for a monastery, and the work took place in and around one of the prayer rooms in the monastery. As the most junior apprentice for a week, my job was to hammer the clay and fibre that would be needed for the sculpture. From a research perspective, this had started out as a way of becoming involved in an indigenous knowledge practice, with the expectation that this would allow for conversations to take place within an authentic space of knowing. It turned out to be a deeply personal transformative experience, leading to an understanding of the quality of silence and an ethics of listening. This exploration of silence, being not something devoid of language (and so of knowing), was an attempt to bring the non-verbal from a site of untranslatability to one that is understood to be filled with other ways of knowing, is an attempt to shift the line between the translatable and the untranslatable.

I was sitting in this high corner of a monastery to try to understand how traditional sculptural knowledge practices are responding to a world where development reassembles the processes and practices of knowing within this high mountainous desert in the northern tip of India, where knowing is being translated into something different entirely – into forms of schooling and practices of enclosure and dislocation.

We sit in quiet – me hammering clay in a high corner of a Buddhist monastery from sunrise to sunset, hammering the mixture of clay and fibre that will, in the more skilled hands of the sculptor, create a god. As we hammer and sculpt, words only intervene when strictly necessary – and it is largely only my ignorance of how to hammer properly that creates this necessity. The day's work proceeds with only a few words passing between us – as the body, then arms and legs of the god are slowly formed.

As the days pass, and I begin to experience differently, the silence itself seems to takes on its own substance as the few words gently frame our encounters and our activities. Words shift in their places – no longer the discursive substrata of life, but the negative space that surrounds the non-verbal – pointing to the silences that are filled with an excess of meaning, relationality and alternate ways of knowing.

Milarepa, an 11th-century Buddhist poet and saint, wrote:

In realising that the non clinging
  and illuminating mind,
  is embodied in bliss and transcends all playwords,
  one sees his mind's nature as clearly as great Space.

This is the sign of the consummation
  of the Stage of Away-from-Playwords.
  Though one talks about the stage of
  Away-from-Playwords,
  Still he is declaring this and that;
  In spite of illustrating what is beyond
  all words, Still he is but piling words on words.

He then, is the ignorant one,
  Who with the self-clinging Meditates.
  In the stage of Away-from-Playwords,
  There is no such thing as this. (Milarepa, quoted in
Chang, 1999: 98–9)

Of course, one cannot but offer an ironic, delightful smile at the wonderfully wordy way that this call to wordlessness has been crafted. This, just part of one of the *Hundred thousand songs of Milarepa* (Chang, 1999), written perhaps 1,000 years ago, is loved for its narrative mixture of story and song. The *Hundred thousand songs of Milarepa* is not unreflexive about its wordiness. It chooses, uses, provokes, leads us in, offers spaces and uncertainties, carries us forward, shocks, and confuses. Words are insufficient, yet they are all we have – our necessary illusions.

This move away from playwords is quietly joyful – at least I find joy at the way it humbles the Western episteme (though that was not its target of course). It speaks from a place that finds a humorous path through the paradox that while words are all we have – there are realms and (higher) ways of knowing that are only possible to follow by holding words lightly and going beyond them.

In that sense, although there is something rather critical about the text, its criticality feels, at least to my interpretation, to have a different quality to it than Western critical theory – a standpoint where, in poking fun at those who are still 'declaring this and that', it looks to a silent, vanishing, clarity that comes from letting go of our own sense of ourselves in the process of illumination, where, akin to a kind of Heisenbergian uncertainty, insight only appears as we ourselves disappear.

Silences, it seems to me, are particularly relevant here, in Himalayan Ladakh, where the meanings of words are somehow illusory, always slightly out of shape, always somehow insufficient, always somehow unable to capture all of the meanings that we might wish to convey – meaning alive within the negative spaces of our language. This is important here, on many levels – not just that we (academics, educators, policymakers) are often drawn to fetishise words, or that words are the material that policies, knowledge and experiences are all too often translated into, and not just that we know that words are slippery and purposeful, politicised and appropriated, and always insufficient.

Milarepa offers a text that places words differently – transposes language into translucent representations of knowing that stand beyond, behind or above. As we communicate, the space between one person and the next is opened up, and within this uncomfortable liminality, the illusion of understanding is troubled and we must accept that the words of another are words only of invitation.

In a Western academic frame, this relationship to language is perhaps best expressed by the wonderful work of Trinh T. Minh-ha:

> For the heart of the matter is always somewhere else than where it is supposed to be…. There is no pushing, no directing, no breaking through, no need for a linear progression which gives the comforting illusion that one knows here one goes. (Minh-ha, 1989: 1)

I love the writing of Trinh T. Minh-ha. Adopting Barthes' (1990) distinction between readerly and writerly texts, this is not so much the 'readerly', complex, post-colonial theorised writing of Spivak or Bhabha, but a more open, 'writerly', subtler, deeper form of expression that engages the heart, and the unconscious – you feel drawn in and carried by the language into new ways of thinking. When I read Minh-ha, I feel drawn to its beyond. Words written loosely enough that your mind's gaze slips past them, through them, into other ways of knowing.

If silence is understood not as empty space devoid of words, but as the gaps between words, through which we might see, we are inevitably drawn towards a different ethic. Western academia, taken as it has been by the discursive, has a politics that is concerned with 'talking back' and with 'how the subaltern can speak' (Spivak, 1985). I am arguing that the processes of hegemony are not only processes of silencing, for while voices must be silenced to be unheard, the experiences of others can simply be neglected, and in this neglect, in our simple carelessness to notice, are alternative mechanisms of hegemony – our sins of omission.

When we see past words and move beyond metaphors of voice to metaphors of recognition, then we come to a being for the other (Levinas, 2000) – a 'being for' that opens up new spaces to understand the limitlessness of our responsibility to hear. Surely, if we are ever to find ways to hear what the subaltern says, it must be by dwelling in quieter worlds.

I have used this ethnographic encounter to try to find inspiration for new directions for how we might translate education differently. My purpose is not to imagine a new educational assemblage, but, more modestly, to use ethnography and translation to highlight themes for knowing differently. I am arguing that assembling education in ways that include the richness of knowing that dwells in silences might offer a seed.

Placing narratives of knowing: crafting the present

Yet, even as we feel the potentiality of the pluriverse that is inherent within each moment of translation, we are faced with finding ways forward through a politics of translation. If, following Vegso's argument, translations are world-calling, reassembling through their very instantiation worlds that are only partially visible, how might we find a form of praxis that allows us to imagine the futures that might be assembled?

Gibson-Graham (2006) offers a useful way towards conceptualising such a possibility by contrasting two political imaginaries: the politics of empire (Hardt and Negri, 2001) and the politics of place. In a geographical reprise of Apter's analysis that language holds within it an excess of meaning that can never be fully contained by translation, so Gibson-Graham offers 'place' as a similar site of revolutionary imagination:

> place [became] that which is not fully yoked into a system of meaning, not entirely subsumed to and defined within a (global) order; it is that aspect of every site that exists as potentiality. Place is the 'event in space', operating as a dislocation with respect to familiar structures and narratives. It is the eruption of the Lacanian real, a disruptive materiality. It is the unmapped and the unmoored that allows for new moorings and mappings. Place, like the

subject, is the site of becoming, the opening for politics. (Gibson-Graham, 2006: 32–3)

In this articulation, 'Place is not a local specificity (or not that alone) but the aspect of potentiality … places always fail to be fully capitalist, and herein lies their potential to become something other' (Gibson-Graham, 2006: 33). Such a geographical imaginary helps to locate 'translation within place', where the verbal is not fetishised, or at least calls us to resist a dislocation from its site of articulation. In a similarly geographical turn within translation theory, Apter (2006: 193) usefully offers the idea of a critical habitat, '"located", so to speak as a margin of critique inserted in the space where this translation process occurs', where critical habitat is defined as 'a translation medium that links territorial habitat and intellectual habitus, physical space and ideological force-field, economy and ecology'.

The placing of translation within landscape offers new metaphors for the politics of translation, reframing the craft of politics. In a similar attempt to foreground the dynamic, unfolding world in the moment of instantiation, Ingold (2007) offers a distinction between fragmented and continuous lines of movement. While fragmented lines offer connection between different moments of experience, continuous lines are associated with what Ingold calls 'wayfaring', as 'development along the line of life' that changes the very being of the wayfarer (Ingold, 2007: 77), where wayfaring, as a practice of observation and engagement with the environment is understood as a process of ongoing place-making, 'where wayfarer and environment are shaped mutually and concurrently' (Ingold, 2007: 83). Pathways mediate this co-construction – pathways that are embedded (physically, culturally, habitually) in the landscape, and are deepened by each pass. Pathways invite a consideration of the social and cultural landscape, where resisting its habitual line of flow requires a conscious (or perhaps inadvertent) change of direction.

> *John Clarke (JC):* I am puzzled by the metaphor of pathways, since they point to routinised and even taken-for-granted lines of movement that have no necessary implications for attention to the social, cultural or geographical landscapes in which they are worn. So, the wayfarer may not be transformed, but turned into a creature of habit: a follower. More interesting is how – and why – do new pathways get started, new turnings get taken and new lines of possible movement and relation get created? How – to borrow Davina Cooper's (2013) phrase – do 'everyday utopias' come to be imagined and enacted?

DB: Maybe we have been on different paths! Walking in the mountains, it is easy to find oneself on paths that take you away from security and reproduction, or to find yourself on a path that faded as you walk along it as lines of connection shift, and you are forced to find new routes. The metaphor of pathways, therefore, offers a line in tension between the taken for granted and new lines of possibility. Paths are intrinsically dynamic – not only because they mark a shifting relationship with place and context, but also because landscape is itself dynamic and excessive, meaning that paths are doubly unstable, endlessly challenging us to re-inscribe them and ourselves differently. Paths are also important here in there semi-permanence – tracing past inscriptions in the landscape that are thereby available to be reclaimed.

It is this image of the 'craft' of translation that I am attempting to draw resonance with here. Translations, insofar as they are translations at all, are world-creating, and, as such, the politics of translation is less a matter of choice between competing understandings of the world and more the process of wayfaring – as we go one way, rather than another, we create the very places of our existence, and, in so doing, we both create and limit the future ways that we may go. The paradox that this image wishes to 'hold' is that the future is neither fully constrained by the past, nor fully free of it. Historical assemblages of power do not inevitably construct the future, nor can we proceed without acknowledging the ways that they shape the possibilities of what new translations might be formed.

I shall seek to further develop and interrogate the possibility of translation in place by reflecting on another ethnographic encounter – a day herding *dzo* (a cross between a cow and a yak). This reflection draws attention to how knowing is always located in landscape, and how processes that enclose and dislocate ways of knowing from their habitats inevitably create loss. It also draws attention to the narrated nature of ways of knowing, as Polkinghorne (1988: 160, quoted in Lewis, 2006: 832) notes:

Our lives are ceaselessly intertwined with narrative, with stories that we tell and hear told, with the stories that we dream or imagine or would like to tell. All these stories are reworked in that story of our own lives which we narrate to ourselves in an episodic, sometimes semiconscious, virtually uninterrupted monologue. We live immersed in narrative, recounting and reassessing the meanings of our past actions, anticipating the outcomes of our future projects, situating ourselves at the intersection of several stories not yet completed. We explain our actions in terms of plots, and often no other form of explanation can produce sensible statements.

The narrative turn in the social sciences (Polkinghorne, 1988; Clandinin and Connelly, 2004) understands narratives to be the medium by which we experience the world, and share these experiences with others. This trend no doubt has many reasons – perhaps among them a desire to recognise in academic texts the presence of the kind of unified, coherent and continuing self that people often feel themselves 'to have or to be' (Day Sclater, 2003: 324). However, this turn is not so much a turn away from post-structuralism, at least in my reading, but rather an attempt to add to it an understanding of the human subject as a site where social forces are played out. As Cohen and Shires (1988: 324) note, this turn is 'not to deny the insights and strengths of poststructuralist thought, but rather to reinsert the subject of the site of meaning and transformation'.

If we understand the narrated self as a site of inscription, a narrative understanding adds to, rather than detracts from or conflicts with, post-structuralist thought. As Michael Jackson (1996: 22) eloquently puts it:

> no matter what constituting power we assign the impersonal forces of history, language, and upbringing, the subject always figures, at the very least, as the site where these forces find expression and are played out [...] no matter what significance we attach to discourse or culture, the phenomenal world of human consciousness and activity is never reducible to that which allegedly determines the condition of its possibility [...] [the subject is] the very site where life is lived, meanings are made, will is exercised, reflection takes place, consciousness finds expression, determinations take effect, and had itself formed or broken.

Jackson, like Apter and Gibson-Graham, talks of excess – in this case, of the irreducibility of the phenomenal world to discourse. If words are our necessary illusion, then perhaps narrative is the way people have developed to use words in ways that point to our lives beyond them. Narratives find ways to hold this human excess visible – the experiential, the aesthetic, the empathetic, the felt and the intuited.

If so, they might provide another site of revolutionary imaginary that we might draw upon to create alternative translations of education.

> Oh, you beautiful beasts, your strong beast!
> Your tail is long, and your horns reach to the sky!
> Please plough our fields.
> Please work hard for us now,
> And we will take you to the pastures
> Where you can eat long grass and flowers
> And do nothing all day!
> Oh, you beautiful beast! (*Ladakhi song of dzo*, quoted in Norberg-Hodge, 2000: 26)

The path strikes its way up the valley through and then above Saboo village. A path that has been drawn by generations, connecting the village to the 'beyond' spaces above the '*phu*', the end of the village, the 'just', before the beyond. This path constitutes my experience that day. Up there, beyond the bridge, the path is still inscribed into the stone and sand and grass, a faint line in the brown landscape.

I have heard so many stories placed on this path in the mountains, in my conversations with people in the village. Stories of wealth, of desolation, of the everyday; but that particular day the path was all about the *dzo*. *Dzo*: a cross between a male yak and a female cow. A large working animal used for ploughing fields; hardy enough for the mountains.

> 'It might be interesting for you,' Nawang says, 'tomorrow, some people are taking their dzo up the mountain. There is no grass for them here, and if they get in other people's fields they cause trouble, so we send them up for the summer.'
>
> 'Do you have to go and fetch them again at the end of the summer?' I ask.
>
> 'They know when to come. My dzo is an old fellow, he knows. He just comes when it is time. Now he goes and enjoys in the mountains.' There is pride – the old dzo knows!

We chat as we walk, Nawang, Gyatso and I. There are three *dzo* altogether. Nawang's is the oldest, and carries himself like the leader at the front. His left horn is broken, his right marks his age. The other two curry behind, like teenagers, squabbling for position.

As we walk, stories emerge:

'Dorji, his Dad is good with *dzo*. My *dzo*, he broke his leg a few years ago, and Dorji's dad he set it. The doctors, they just put plaster on it, but that is not good for them.'

And:

If they eat poison grass, then we bleed the nose and they get OK, that's different from what a vet does. Vets they put a hole through to let the air out, we just bleed the nose."

There is knowledge here, indigenous knowledge. It is an easy label here – the knowledge brought up as contradictory, in opposition to that of the knowledge of the vet. What is the nature of this knowledge? Embodied? Enacted? Performed? I would not say that my own knowledge of this was only possible through participating in walking the *dzo* up the mountain that day, perhaps this knowledge would have emerged in interview, perhaps not. I only say that it was the walk, the *dzo* and these mountains that encouraged such things to be shared. This is important. There is fragility to this knowledge. Knowledge that perhaps only emerges, is possible to be revealed, shared and passed on, in these moments of being and talking within this landscape.

The *dzo* are more relaxed now, in the open ground. There is the sense that we are companions, we do this journey together, the *dzo*, Gyatso and I. At intervals, we stop, resting together upon the warm rocks and pleasant grass that each desires. We move. There is only a series of moments. It is supremely relaxing. There is a rhythm here. We meander from one side of the valley to the other. There is a line that we try and keep to. I always behind and farther away from the line than he. It is a strange dance, this: I the lighter, faster particle, circling, as he lumbers upwards.

There is no better word than dance. I dance with the *dzo*. We walk, we move. The illusion of causality disappears. It is no longer clear that the *dzo* goes ahead because I chase behind. Perhaps it is he who is leading me up the mountain. I laugh at this paradox – who can doubt that it must be the *dzo* who is being chased – for surely he would not move up the mountain otherwise. Yet, who can doubt that the *dzo* is leading us – for surely I would not walk unless he went in front.

I could interview cattle herders. I could ask them questions about what it is like to herd cattle, about the changing times, about what they see as cattle-herding knowledge, but I would not 'feel' this knowledge. I enjoy writing this, enjoy the swaying that inhabits me as I do so, knowledge that can only be poorly communicated, only felt. Knowledge enacted, but not verbally so. The moment allows me to feel such knowledge, only that.

We get back to the house at the bottom of the village around 2pm, tired. I sleep a while. In the evening, Nawang appears:

> 'You didn't do your job properly', he says, smiling.
> 'What? He came back? Who?'
> 'The dzo, he came back. He is there at our place.'
> 'Really?'
> He is there! He knows! He is getting old. It's cold up there this summer. He knows he can get fed here. Why to have a tough time up in the mountain?' I hear the humour and pride in his voice – the old dzo knows.

This points towards a different ethic, too. In the same way that the privileging of voice over silence creates the hegemony of omission, so, too, does a lack of recognition of place: our knowing creates a silent disregard as we pass by places and the knowledge that inhabits them. The merest shifting on the path takes us elsewhere, takes us away from these fragile places where knowing might take place. Indigenous knowledge should not be thought of as sitting in a repository of old people's heads or bodies, like a library, an archive. There are only moments of experience where knowledge is enacted or it is not. Ways of knowing forgotten about, passed over, unrecognised. Just as recognising the excesses within silence leads us to an ethic of listening, so, too, does a recognition of place lead us to an ethic of encounter and of story.

Conclusions: excessive translations

The analytic project goes beyond the historical or even contemporary analysis of how particular translations have functioned. It demands, but then goes beyond, the need to dwell in the translation process in order to make active choices about how different policies might be effectively translated. The beyond, here, has a different temporality – a sociology, to pay homage to De Sousa Santos's term (see De Sousa Santos, 2004: esp ch 7), a sociology of emergences, a sociology of the 'not-yet'. Such a sociology takes not what exists as its object, but rather what might be. In seeking to make choices about the multiple possible policy translations that would bring into being alternate policy assemblages, we have need for an analytic of what might be. As De Sousa Santos (2004: 24) puts it:

> The concept that rules the sociology of emergences is the concept of 'Not Yet', [a] more complex category because it expresses what exists as mere tendency, a movement that is latent in the very process of manifesting itself. The not-yet is the way in which the future is inscribed in the present. It is not an indeterminate or infinite future, rather a concrete possibility and a capacity that neither exist in a vacuum nor are completely predetermined. Indeed, they actively re-determine all they touch, thus questioning the determinations that exist at a given moment.

This sociology of emergences gives us a glimpse beyond the now, beyond, in this case, particular translations of education, How might we create the not-yet? What tools can we use to craft the alternatives that are so clearly needed?

Embracing the freedom to translate differently, perhaps the most developed attempt to create anew comes from the work of Gibson-Graham. The diverse economies research community that they write about attempts to create 'other worlds' through the practice of researching and theorising alternative economies. This work crucially positions itself where we might ask something different of theory:

> what if we were to accept that the goal of theory is not to extend knowledge by confirming what we already know, that the world is a place of domination and oppression? What if we asked theory instead to help us see openings, to provide a space of freedom and possibility? (Gibson-Graham, 2006: 7)

Exploring mundane forms of power, such an approach eschews strong, critical theory, and instead advocates 'weak theorising', where power is de-exoticised and a different relationship to analysis is sought:

> weak theory could be undertaken with a reparative motive that welcomes surprise, tolerates coexistence, and cares for the new, providing a welcoming environment for the objects of our thought. It could foster a 'love of the world' as Hannah Arendt suggests, rather than a masterful knowing or moralistic detachment. It could draw upon the pleasures of friendliness trust and companionable connection. There could be a greater scope for invention and playfulness, enchantment and exuberance. (Gibson-Graham, 2008: 619)

I have attempted to do this by weaving two ethnographic encounters with theoretical discussion on translation to try to develop a politics of translation that might be able to offer genuinely new ways to translate and assemble education otherwise.

The starting point for this has been a reading of translation that sees all translation as a closure, and a world claim. Translations enclose the world through an act of exclusion – between that which is translatable and that which is not. This reading of translation offers a particular understanding of the politics of translation as engaged in the process of shifting the dividing line to expand the field of what we take as possible to translate, in order that we might thereby translate differently.

Arguing that words are necessary illusions does not diminish the critical project of interrogating the operation of dominant discourses, such as education or development, but it does recast the directionality of their potential resistances. While words cannot be left behind, we do need ways to make present those other, quieter ways of knowing that make possible the enactment of human existence.

In order to do this, I have drawn upon two spaces outside the assemblage of modern education – outside the excess of the potentially translatable – dwelling within the rich worlds that are not commonly recognised as part of the contemporary educational assemblage, and which, in their excess, offer critical potential. This is where ethnography enters – how we might think of ethnography as a critical process of encountering outside contemporary assemblages to translate across (bring across) other ways of knowing.

The end points of these encounters are not, in this chapter, a new vision of what education could be in Ladakh, but rather possibilities for how ways of knowing might form part of an alternative education assemblage – an educational imaginary that consists of narrative, of place, of praxis, of landscape, of doing, of humour and of dancing, where gods and narratives cross paths across a landscape filled with ghosts and legacies, broken water wheels, and mountain streams as we dance away from playwords.

SEVEN

'Policy otherwise': towards an ethics and politics of policy translation

Introduction

In this final chapter, we return to thinking and writing collaboratively in order to develop our approach of 'making policy move' in several ways. First, we reflect on the four 'case study' chapters to draw out some general observations about what has been gained by putting our vocabulary for policy analysis to work. Then, we explore the implications of thinking through assemblage and translation for 'policy otherwise': asking what sorts of possibilities such an approach brings into view. In the third section, we take these concerns back to the case study chapters to ask what 'policy otherwise' might look like in those settings: how might they be assembled and translated differently? These comments are intended as brief reflections that point to the possibilities of 'otherwise', rather than programmatic statements, strategies or grand plans. Finally, we end – as our collaboration began – in conversation, with a transcription of a discussion at our last meeting (in Veszprém, Hungary) in February 2014. In that conversation, we explore some of the key issues and concerns that have shaped our work together and worry about some of their implications. This seems like an appropriately conversational and open-ended finale to an unfinished – and unfinishable – project.

Tales of translation and assemblage

In the four substantive chapters, we have put elements of our vocabulary of 'policy in motion' to work in exploring four very different cases: global education policy in Ladakh; policy consultancy in South East Europe; the translation of social inclusion between the European Union (EU) and Hungary; and the managerialisation of universities in England. These are diverse cases – in their subject matter, in their settings and in our approaches to them. Nevertheless, we are convinced that each of them bears witness to the value of examining policy through the lenses of assemblage and translation. Most obviously, approaching policy through translation illuminates what is at stake as policy travels from place to place. Ideas of policy transfer and diffusion largely ignore what happens as policy travels and transmutes in linguistic, symbolic and cultural forms – as it is actively translated between one site and another (in which the intimate relationships between language, culture, power and politics are always in play). Whether this involves the destruction of ways of life in the name of universalising (one model of) schooling or the 'fictions' involved in the creative writing of policy in translation as it passes from EU English to Hungarian (and back again), making translation visible illuminates the complicated relations of knowledge and power that make policy move.

Let us be clear: an approach through translation makes language(s) visible as a central thread of policy analysis. It draws attention to the imaginative, symbolic and affective work that takes place as policy is made to move from one place to another. However, we need to add some qualifications to this centrality of language. Translation, as we argued in Chapter Two, is not a technical process of trying to create the most functional exchange between a term in one language and the nearest equivalent in another. Indeed, as Chapter Five indicated, such functional equivalence may well not exist. It is more important to think of language as modelling the world, offering particular ways of thinking, knowing and feeling, and, not least, dispositions to act in and on the world. As such, language is intrinsically bound up with questions of power – authorised ways of thinking, knowing and acting that attempt to travel along with the words. This is visible in each of the chapters as the specific policy language carries orders, hierarchies, relationships and mappings of social space and time, and establishes ways of being and acting. Perhaps this is most visible in the chapter by John Clarke (JC), where everything appears to take place in one language – English. Indeed, this 'common language' sews together the US corporations where management was reinvented, the business schools, textbooks and inspirational handbooks that circulated 'new managerialism', and the advisory organisations, courses and workshops through which people were invited to recognise themselves as managers. Yet, this managerialism involves a distinctive 'managerial English' that creates positions and places, and ways of thinking and acting, and distributes varieties of power, authority and responsibility as it incites people and organisations to become businesslike, to achieve excellence or to be entrepreneurial, seizing opportunities wherever they are encountered.

It is in such linguistic moments that what Noémi Lendvai (NL) calls the 'consensus on consensus' is formed – the presumption of shared understandings and dispositions. This condition enables translation –

from language to language and from place to place – to proceed as if it is technical rather than controversial. In this way, we can see policy as typically involving a double process of 'rendering technical': policy itself forms a mode of 'taking the politics out of things'; and translation proceeds as if exchange between places and people is merely a matter of (technical) translation. Instead, we have drawn on other views of translation as an intrinsically political and contentious process in which forms and relationships of power are always at stake, even if processes of technicalisation try to make them invisible and inaudible. For that reason, post-colonial perspectives have played a particularly productive role in our work – not because we think that the only relations in the world are colonial ones, but because colonial relations (new and old) have often been conducted through the articulation of power, culture and language. Post-colonial perspectives have therefore helped us think about what happens as policy moves – about the presumptions of universality, reason and rationality, and progress and modernity that carry with them forms of domination and subordination, and processes of othering and orientalism. In particular, thinking of policy moving through many instances of what Pratt calls 'contact zones' has been helpful to us, both in drawing attention to the asymmetries of power that shape and condition such moments, and in her insistence that the encounters that take place are not wholly determined by those asymmetries – they are performative (in Butler's sense of being imperfectly scripted) and emergent.

Throughout the substantive chapters, we have tried to hold on to this sense of policy (and what it seeks to accomplish) being 'made up' in practice. Differently located groups of actors, differently derived imperatives and injunctions, and different senses of what might become are brought together in the crafting of policy. As Pratt insists, these moments of contact are both conditioned by asymmetries of power and have a quality of unpredictability, even if those asymmetries mean that such encounters are 'structured in dominance'. In the remainder of this book, we will become more and more engaged by this quality of unpredictability – the sense that things might be made up 'otherwise'. The continual struggle in the contact zones of policy is to inscribe the intended message, outcome and relations of power, while avoiding the possibilities of otherwise becoming visible and audible. Paul Stubbs' (PS's) chapter on policy in South East Europe makes it clear that this process of inscribing and ensuring the dominance of the dominant is hard work – a work of translation and articulation. Equally, Dave Bainton's (DB's) chapter is haunted by the possible forms of 'otherwise' that the globalisation of education policy displaces when installing a singular model of schooling, knowledge and modernisation. It is important that these possibilities are not merely rhetorical gestures on our part – just a place-marker for the resistance to domination (when it arrives). On the contrary, in the chapters by DB and PS, it is possible to see the traces – the marks – left by older and emergent ways of thinking and doing otherwise on the scenes of policy. These traces mark the presence of cultural practices, social habits and relationships, and imagined ways of being, that have to be displaced – silenced, rendered out of place or out of time – by the universalising logics of the would-be dominant. We return to 'otherwise' later in the chapter, but think it is vital to stress that possibilities are always embedded in, and enacted through, social practices and relationships (what Shannon Jackson [2011] calls the 'social work' that enables cultural production).

We have stressed the social conditions of translation (the hard work of inscribing domination; the embeddedness of alternatives) because with 'translation', there is always a risk that such analyses are dismissed as 'merely' about language or culture – as if these domains were separate from, and somehow less substantial than, social relations or material conditions. At various points in the substantive chapters, we have tried to indicate how the practice of translation is both socially embedded and intrinsically political. We have also used the idea of assemblage to explore ways in which policy is made – as well as made up – through bringing together a variety of elements. These include: texts and talk (the discursive forms); types of people and places (meeting rooms, offices, etc); infrastructures (telephones, computers, printers and translation equipment, such as the ubiquitous headphones); affective or emotional dispositions (from enthusiastic participation to resigned acquiescence); and forms of training, instruction and guidance. Many of these policy assemblings take place through encounters (from ministerial conferences to translating people into categories/cases at the 'front line'). In different ways, we have all tried to indicate how making policy move involves more than 'just words' (even though words are critical resources). Translation and assemblage enable us to see the conditions that are mobilised in making policy move – and that result from such movements. As NL argued, it is vital not just to take the textual forms in which policy appears as their sole form of existence (policies are enacted in practices, as well as being temporarily fixed in texts), and, as JC's chapter argued, what are also assembled as policy moves are the forms and relationships of power: managerial authority requires the displacement, exclusion or subordination of other modes of authority. In these ways and more, the previous four chapters have explored what happens if policy is examined through an analytic vocabulary of translation and assemblage. As Kingfisher (2013: 15) argues:

> Together, assemblage and translation point to the cut-and-paste processes of piecing together that are involved as policies travel up, down and sideways. It would be a mistake, however, to envision these processes as involving free-wheeling cutting-and-pasting by sovereign agents in completely open and constrained environments populated by unmoored, empty signifiers.... Although fluid and unstable, translation and assemblage are also constrained. Signs and practices can be disarticulated and set off on travels in any number of directions, and policy assemblages can indeed represent cut-and-paste experimentation, but what and how things are translated, cut-and-pasted, and experimented with is not completely arbitrary.

We believe that this move to thinking through translation and assemblage makes a profound difference to how policy – and its movement – can be grasped. In particular, we think that it enables us to see the complex and shifting politics of policy movement more clearly – and that this is increasingly vital as policy moves and subordinates new sites, spaces and settings. Not the least of these gains from looking through translation and assemblage is to reveal that which becomes lost in translation (excluded, forgotten, silenced) and to attend to what is absent from, though ruled by, new assemblages of policy. In Chapter One, we suggested that the challenge of understanding policy in motion involved four dynamics of 'unsettling':

- unsettling policy and its study;
- unsettling policy as transfer;
- unsettling policy as meaning; and
- unsettling policy in space and time.

Here, we reflect back on these dynamics and briefly consider how an approach through translation and assemblage provides a response to the issues at stake in them. First, then, we suggested that the movement of policy undermined some of the taken-for-granted foundations of policy studies: that 'policy' is a singular and complete object; that a simple distinction can be drawn between policymaking and the implementation of policy; and that policy can be studied as a technical and apolitical domain. The substantive chapters have shown –

compellingly, we hope – that policy is always 'in the making', that there are always struggles to fix (and 'contest') the meaning and consequences of policy. Defining the objects and objectives of intervention – *these* effects, in *these* places, changing *these* sorts of people – is, as the chapters have shown, a central feature of social inclusion or educational provision. Creating the authority to enact policy – whether in post-conflict regions or the space of the university – is always at stake and is one way in which the attempted distinction between policymaking and implementation is a critical, if contested, separation of powers. Claiming the authority to make policy (rather than 'merely' implement it) is a significant political move in the field of policy (we are strategic; we have the vision; we know what is needed ...; you should get on with it; be grateful; get with the programme ...).

Second, we argued that treating policy as translation was a more productive way of thinking about policy movement than treating it as a process of transfer, suggesting that the transfer view was framed by assumptions about the solidity of policy, the linearity of movement and the locatedness of agents and actors. In the course of Chapters Three to Six, we have tried to exemplify how policy as translation illuminates the unfinished quality of policy, its making and remaking as it moves from site to site and the ways in which lines of flow and (temporary) settlement demand our attention when thinking about policy in motion. The casts of actors in specific policy work are complex and complexly located (eg not just international versus local) and policy emerges in the 'contact zones' where actors encounter others (and the inequalities of power and authority that they embody and bring to bear on the situation). Linear views of the policy process miss the dynamics of 'bending and blending' visible in the Hungarian case, the performance of compliance in the face of international expertise or the disaffected consent engendered by the strategic claims of management.

We further claimed that policy in motion unsettled established views of policy as meaning. Translation makes visible the ways in which meanings may change – or be changed – as policy moves from one setting to another. This is only partly a linguistic question, as Chapter Four on universities showed. Meaning is linked to context and to the politics of meaning-making. Hence, we insist that it is not enough to be interested in policy as meaning because meaning is never singular or alone. In the Hungarian alignment with EU policies, in the invention of policies to improve South Eastern Europe and, most dramatically, in the development of education policy in nomadic spaces, policies in motion are about the entanglement of meaning with power and politics. The ideas of translation and assemblage (and other concepts we have borrowed) have enabled us to foreground these entanglements as integral to the practice of policy. In the process, they have helped us to see how the meanings of policy are made – and to see the meanings and possibilities that are suppressed, ignored and silenced in the process of meaning-making.

Finally, we argued that policy in motion unsettled established understandings of space and time. The effects and implications of these unsettlings have been visible across the four substantive chapters. It has become increasingly obvious that the old 'container' model of space – composed of contiguous but clearly bounded nation-states – cannot be sustained. Boundaries collapse and are redrawn. Policy flows across boundaries, helping to redraw them in the process – such that Hungary becomes 'European' or the regional space of 'South East Europe' is imagined as a potentially governable space, ready for 'helpful' intervention. Spaces that are defined as, in some senses, 'backward' are opened up for change – whether this is the educational 'lack' of Tibetan communities in Northern India or the 'ivory tower' backwardness of universities needing management to survive in the 'modern world'. Places, as Doreen Massey (2004) has argued, are condensations of relationships – and, as the relationships (and the power that shapes them) change, so places and spaces more generally are remade. Studying policy on the move demands attention to this unstable combination of flux and resettlement in how space is ordered. Policy moves across spaces and reorganises the relationships in the process – although (as we have consistently stressed) it might be better to say policy *tries to* reorganise relationships in the process, since it does not always succeed.

Policy also works on and through time. Policy studies has typically worked with a conventional understanding of time (as well as space) in which linear narratives of policy (discovering the problem, identifying a solution, creating the policy, implementing the policy, etc) proceed in a logical sequence. However, policy in motion bends this sense of time: pasts are narrated (failures, lacks, backwardness against 'modern' expectations). The present is defined as a moment of possibility, necessity or urgency ('we must act now …'), while improved futures are promised. Time is also enacted through policy: in claims about what is reasonable (versus alternatives dismissed as utopian or backward-looking); in the time frames of 'projects' through which policy is turned into practice; in the hyperactive invention of new policies (to demonstrate the will of governing authorities); and in the mixture of temporalities and rhythms in which a policy is often entwined – the slow pace of analysis and development, the time limits and pace of projectisation, the amnesia about past policies, the urgent resetting of goals and objectives, and the glacial slowness of resistant or recalcitrant institutions and fields of practice. All of these dimensions make time a complex partner in the entanglement of policy, power and politics.

For us, then, the cumulative effect of these 'unsettlings' demands an approach to policy studies that is attentive to the entangling of power, politics and policy in the ways that policy is made to move, and to the ways in which policy remakes people, places and power (and the relationships in which they are settled) as it moves. Translation and assemblage have provided us with concepts that enable this attention – they illuminate what is at stake when policy moves and what goes on in the processes of making policy move. However, these are not the only things that are at stake in thinking of policy as translation.

Beyond the 'not-yet': principles and practices for a critical policy praxis

In this section, we explore some of the implications of engaging in the process of making policy translation more visible. Our ideas, radically unfinished first steps, are offered less as definitive conclusions and more as a cautious iteration of a set of principles and practices that perhaps offer a take-off point for a critical policy praxis. Although we continue to insist on the primacy of context and conjuncture, we attempt, perhaps riskily, to move between the general and the specific, through an interrogation and reworking of notions of 'ethics' and 'politics' and a tentative recombination of the two in the form of a kind of 'ethico-political project' (Rojas, 2007: 585). The concept of 'policy otherwise', borrowed and adapted from post-colonial scholars' understandings of 'political economy and development otherwise' (Rojas, 2007), offers a way in to the full potentiality of a view of translation as a site of struggle. The praxis of 'policy otherwise' requires a multiplication of the possible policy assemblages that a reflexive translation may bring into being, and a dialogic talking and acting back that may have the potential not only to unsettle dominant policy conceptions, but also to open up meaningful spaces for contestation, resistance and positive alternatives that are not only different, but actually make a difference.

'Policy otherwise' is a way of addressing possibilities that derive from a recognition that policy translation is always concerned with multiple voices and diverse trajectories. Not only, then, is 'another policy world possible', but, in many ways, it is present already within existing policy translations and assemblages, despite attempts to marginalise, silence or suppress it. As a praxis, it is always searching for a connection to that which is 'beyond', what De Sousa Santos (2004: 24) has termed a sociology of emergences or the 'not-yet', which 'expresses what exists as mere tendency, a movement that is latent in the very process of manifesting itself'. This clearly goes beyond a kind of hyper-pessimism in which every alternative policy idea is inevitably and inexorably disciplined, stripped of any progressive intent and content, and incorporated into the dominant hegemony. Throughout the book, we have insisted on both the capacity of dominant structures to render the policy world, and the populations enrolled within it, technical, malleable and manageable, and the profound possibility of other practices and claims that escape, if only momentarily, the all-encompassing gaze and restrictive practice of those same structures. Hence, we have used the concepts of translation and assemblage as lenses, sensitising us to the multiple, the contradictory and the awkward in the policy process. What a policy studies orthodoxy sees as 'unintended consequences' or 'unforeseen scenarios', then, are not by-products, but, rather, systematic features and consequences of policy as it moves. The task here is to take this further, to articulate some of the ethical and political implications of a commitment to a double orientation to the movements of policy and power: to recognise plans and projects but to be attentive to their interruptions, disjunctures and complexities.

Analytically, a translation from 'pluralism' to 'pluriverse' is a necessary first step in the articulation of 'policy otherwise'. Crudely stated, pluralist understandings of 'the world of policy' and 'the policy world' tend to take for granted policy as a modernising project while largely denying the complex, multiple and changing lineages and linkages between modernity and coloniality. Policy, in this sense, is the epitome of a kind of 'modern epistemology' (Rojas, 2007: 574) that masks these linkages, in the process, marginalising alternative knowledges and rationalities. Even in the process of revalidating some of these alternative knowledges, often through a process of translation that renders them more understandable to, and manageable for, the dominant rationality, the possibility of going beyond what Gibson-Graham (2006) terms 'capitalocentric perspectives' is much reduced within pluralist, as well as neo-Marxist, analyses. In other words, while pluralist perspectives may expand an understanding of what is to count as modern and rational, this is still at the expense of really hearing, understanding and promoting those voices and discourses that lie outside what Rojas (2007: 576) terms 'the prevailing web of interlocutions'. Translating this distinction from an 'epochal' to a 'conjunctural' understanding is crucial in moving towards a conception of the 'pluriverse', going beyond a monolingual understanding of the totalising force of 'globalisation', which tends to collapse complex social realities into a singular conceptual and analytical framework (Escobar, 2010). As we noted in Chapter Two, in contradistinction to 'the modern ontology of One World – a universe', Escobar posits the 'pluriverse' as 'a different way of imagining life ... an other mode of existence', borrowing from the Zapatista movement the idea of 'a world where many worlds fit', suggesting that 'in the rising concepts and struggles from and in defense of the pluriverse' can be found 'a post-dualist theory and a practice of interbeing' (Escobar, 2011: 139).

Throughout this work, our concern has been to advocate for a policy praxis that is reflexive and framed by a kind of 'relational attentiveness' beyond the confines of a singular epistemological and ontological world. This is far from a call for policy relativism precisely because it is based on the need to trace power dynamics and to question unequal relations, uneven negotiations and the production of symbolic and real violence. Translation has an epistemic dimension, insofar as it never merely reflects and reproduces existing knowledge, but is itself a form of knowledge production, reminding us that 'translation has a potentially radical and activist edge' and 'is driven by ethical and ideological concerns' (Tymoczko, 2006a: 459). One part of an ethics of policy translation, then, involves literally 'changing the subject', revealing the 'metatext' or the 'text about text' (Tymoczko, 2006a: 447), treating translation as 'a significant medium of subject re-formulation and political change' (Apter, 2006: 6). Although radical discourse theorists might disagree, for us, 'changing the subject' or, perhaps more accurately, allowing space for 'other narratives' to be voiced and heard is both necessary and far from sufficient in the praxis of policy translation we advocate here.

Translation as a practice is important, then, in constructing a different narrative, a first step in the articulation of 'policy otherwise'. Translation questions what Gibson-Graham (2006: 60) calls 'the rules of syntax and grammar' of dominant structures, rendering them 'loose to the point of nonexistence, allowing for empirical encounters and creative expressions of the new, the unthought, the unexpected'. Expanding their understanding of the language or discourse of the economy to policy writ large, such a discursive double movement of de- and reconstruction can 'disarm and dislocate the naturalized hegemony' and 'make the space for new ... becomings' (Gibson-Graham, 2006: 60). Their focus on different kinds of *transactions*, different types of *labour* and different forms of *enterprise* can be expanded to cover diverse elements of policy – their form, substance, processes and practices – with the aim throughout to construct new 'incommensurabilities' challenging the supposedly immutable laws of policy. Challenging the equivalences that policy needs in order to perform its hegemonic work opens up not only a 'contested space of representation' (Gibson-Graham, 2006: 54), but also the possibility of what Judith Butler (1993: 4) has termed 'collective disidentification'. As we have argued throughout, a hegemonic discourse is always unstable, so that the task of policy translation is to uncover alternative narratives, events, actors and experiences that have been integrated, marginalised or silenced, in Gibson-Graham's (2006: 57) terms 'giving them space to fully "exist"'. In many ways, we share their view of the importance of 'weak theory', although we may baulk at their notion that this is 'little more than description' (Gibson-Graham, 2006: 8). Such weak theorising, akin to ethnography's 'capacity to surprise' (Willis and Trondman, 2000), refuses to know in advance 'that social experiments are already co-opted and thus doomed to fail or to reinforce dominance' or, conversely, 'that the world economy will be transformed by an international revolutionary movement rather than through the disorganized proliferation of local projects' (Willis and Trondman, 2000: 8).

Ethnography, broadly conceptualised, has offered the promise of seeing 'policy in motion': a means of tracing the relationships and practices through which policy is assembled, translated and enacted across its multiple locations. It is 'fit for purpose' in terms of tracing translations, capturing the multiple entanglements of policy in relation to power and politics. Ethnography offers an entry point for the study of how different forces, relationships and dynamics are condensed in particular locations, while also being capable of revealing connective practices – the ways in which different sites, scales and spaces of policy are articulated to one another. This double movement around a specific location (treating it as a site of condensation and articulation) is, for us, a critical feature of the ethnographic imagination.

Despite our enthusiasm for ethnographic investigation, however, we are left with some questions about whether it can be the sole method of inquiry in pursuing the questions we want to examine about policy. In particular, we are troubled about what cannot be revealed through the lens of ethnography. We might put this better as a double question. What escapes the ethnographic gaze? And what evades the ethnographic gaze? The former implies the limits of ethnography as a way of looking; the latter implies that at least some agents and agencies in the world may wish not to be looked at (by ethnographers and others).

We remain troubled by questions of analytic and political scale. Our concern has been with the practices of policy in motion and paying attention to the ways in which possibilities are realised (and rejected). Instances cannot be simply or directly deduced from larger-scale forces, interests or tendencies. This does not mean that we have no interest in such larger scales of analysis. These are, however, not readily commensurable with the contradictions, dynamics and flux of policy as practice. This incommensurability cannot be resolved through a false binary of a choice between 'macro' and 'micro' scales of analysis. Our current way of living that discomfort involves keeping questions of work/practice central to the making/unmaking of all objects (at whatever scale) at the core of what we see, and insisting on the 'unfinished' and heterogeneous character of all formations.

The creation of the possibility of 'equal dialogue' or a 'dialogue between equals' goes far beyond the idealism, and narrow Eurocentrism, of a bourgeois public sphere, most closely associated with Habermas (1991 [1982]). Mere acknowledgement of 'cultural diversity' is, therefore, profoundly insufficient, with ethical commitments to 'listen to the voice of the other' meaningless if 'the terms of the dialogue are dictated by capitalist rules' (Rojas, 2007: 577), akin to 'inviting the subaltern to a dialogue in which his [sic] position was secondary from the very beginning' (Chakrabarty, 2002: 33). Providing we acknowledge, as Chakrabarty himself does, that this maxim is easier to preach than to practice, it should be clear that, at its best, an ethics of translation is an attempt, never easy and rarely completely achieved, to ensure that 'languages and competencies ... of citizenship, of democracy, of welfare ... be made available to all' (Chakrabarty, 2002: 33). In a form that breaks down Eurocentric notions of a binary between micro- and macro-levels, Chakrabarty (2002: 34) continues:

> a dialogue can be genuinely open only under one condition: that no party puts itself in a position where it can unilaterally decide the final outcomes of the conversation. This never happens between the modern and the nonmodern because, however noncoercive the conversation between the transcendent academic observer and the subaltern who enters into an historical dialogue with him [sic], this dialogue takes place within a field of possibilities that is already structured from the beginning in favour of certain outcomes.

Although largely ignored by a new wave of post-colonial theorists, the Brazilian-born educator Paulo Freire inspires an ethically and politically informed conception of policy as transformative and liberatory praxis, not least because of his explicit distancing from the role of 'transcendent academic observer'. Freire stands as an early, and particularly significant, transnational activist for social and political change, directly implementing programmes of educational reform, primarily through mass literary campaigns underpinned by the building of critical consciousness, particularly in post-colonial Latin America and Africa. Freire provides an entry point for discussing the possibility of a radical policy praxis which is neither that of the fully fledged revolutionary political actor à la Che Guevara – much as Freire read, admired and cited him – nor that of the currently rather more ubiquitous persona of the technocratic transnational policy consultant. Crucially, Freire maintained a commitment to 'revealing the work as it progresses', exploring both 'activities being developed' and 'the theoretical problems that underlie them' (Freire, 1978: 6) across a large number of interventions over a significant period of time.

As with all policy interventions, Freire and his actions need to be situated within the particular social and political contexts in which they were embedded. His intellectual and political trajectory, involving as it did, over time, a marked move to the Left and an explicit identification with post-colonial liberation struggles, was very much of its time, if not of its place. The antinomies of his fusion of humanistic Marxism and Catholic liberation theology, as well as his appropriation and translation of, and, in some cases, critical dialogues with, diverse, and sometimes radically opposed, theoretical and political traditions and movements, including different feminist and radical black liberation ideas, have been extensively discussed elsewhere (cf McLaren and Lankshear, 1994). His concern with 'dialogue' based on 'love, humility and faith', creating a 'horizontal relationship of mutual trust' (Freire, 1998 [1970]: 72) as the basis of his critical pedagogy, resonates with later post-colonial conceptualisations. His emphasis on 'generative themes', derived from people's own perceptions of reality and views of the world, 'a complex of ideas, concepts, hopes, doubts, values, and challenges in dialectical interaction with their opposites, striving towards plenitude' (Freire, 1998 [1970]: 82), presents the need to start from and build upon people's understandings of their own material conditions as a key principle. Teachers, students and, by extension, policy interveners and their publics need to become 'critical co-investigators in dialogue' (Freire, 1998 [1970]: 62). Only by starting from people's own realities can they be empowered to act upon and change that reality.

While Freire tended to see identity primarily in class terms and within a notion of revolutionary class struggle, he also exhibited a strong aversion to forms of political indoctrination and demagogy, arguing, in effect, for a process of continuous dialogue and the avoidance of imposed political slogans or political closure. His view of subjectivities remains rather abstract or, in Spivak's (1988) terms, 'transparent', rather than formed through an understanding of the intersectionality of gender, race, class and ability. Nevertheless, Freire's thought 'illuminates the central question of political action in a world increasingly without universals' and can itself be translated through 'a more situated theory of oppression and subjectivity' (Freire, 1998 [1970]: 18). In his work in Guinea-Bissau in the late 1970s, Freire expressed concern about the insistence on using Portuguese as a 'unifying national language', stressing the need to liberate the people's own language 'from the supremacy of the dominant language of the colonizer' (Freire, 1978: 126), and noting the ways in which colonisers had labelled the language of the colonised as mere 'dialect' to demonstrate their own superiority and deny the colonised a history.

As a consultant to the United Nations Educational, Scientific, and Cultural Organization (UNESCO) and in his work with the World Council of Churches, Freire faced some of the dilemmas that are common to transnational policy actors today. His principled resistance to seeing his approach to mass literacy as a more or less pre-packaged, technical, method or system and, conversely, the way in which it was sometimes presented as such, not least through claims, from his early work in Brazil, that the 'method' could achieve results in 40 hours, is perhaps the clearest example of this. From Freire (1978: 12), we learn the importance of transnational policy actors working out 'the best way to see and hear, inquire and discuss' programmes to be created 'in dialogue with the people of the country, about their own reality, their needs, and the possibility of our assistance', rather than a project 'prepared in Geneva … with all of its points worked out in fine detail, to be taken … as a generous gift' (Freire, 1978: 8).

While perhaps Freire chose to intervene *only* in post-colonial settings where left-leaning national liberation movements had come to power, hence involvement as 'fellow militants' and 'true collaborators', rather than as 'neutral specialists' (Freire, 1978), the dilemma of how to understand context and what to do with that understanding remained. Indeed, it has been argued that his interventions in Guinea-Bissau were informed by an overreliance on the writings of Amílcar Cabral and, in particular, a shared overstatement of the extent of 'de-Africanization' (Kirkendall, 2010), illustrating the need for continued triangulation and for a multi-voiced critical reflexivity in understanding 'context' beyond the privileging of one account. Nevertheless, Freire's commitment that projects should be thought through by national educators enabled to reflect critically on their praxis in a revolutionary context within 'a constant effort to refuse to be bureaucratized', without the need for 'neutral specialists or cold technicians' (Freire, 1978: 12), is an important marker.

De Sousa Santos has argued for the importance of combining 'translation', which aims 'to create mutual intelligibility between diverse struggles and to encourage self-reflexivity among movements, campaigns and networks', while respecting 'the autonomy and diversity of practices' (De Sousa Santos, 2001: 192), with practices of 'Manifesto', which open 'paths towards an alternative society' (De Sousa Santos, 2001: 209). Similarly, Mignolo emphasises the importance of 'double translation', concerned with both 'delinking' or 'epistemic disobedience' and translation 'across struggles and experiences marked by subalternization' (Rojas, 2007: 584). In Escobar's (2001: 163) terms, translation 'sees as interwoven languages of biodiversity, sustainability, cultural rights, and ethnic identities and links identity, territory and culture', although his tracing of these linkages 'at local, national and transnational levels' risks reproducing rather orthodox and static notions of separate, nested, hierarchical levels.

In a sense, an ethics and politics of transspatial, translocal and transscalar practices presents one of the most difficult challenges for a 'policy otherwise' articulated through the lens of translation. The need to go beyond a crude structural political economy position that tends 'to render small and local changes useless' (Rojas, 2007: 575), while acknowledging, at the same time, that struggles that remain particular and local do not, in and of themselves, constitute a basis for 'policy otherwise', is a difficult balancing act. While a concept of 'place', avoiding the 'reification of space', appears, at times, to be a privileged site 'to think theory through from the political praxis of subaltern groups' (Rojas, 2007: 581), particularly when this concerns places that were never fully, or only, capitalist, this can reproduce a different reification unless used to articulate 'a network of local histories and multiple local hegemonies' (Mignolo, 2000: 22). In many ways, understanding translation and assemblage allows us to go beyond merely bringing 'different narratives into contact with each other', allowing 'the marginalized to reveal their own intepretation' and opening 'space for accommodation, contradiction, and resistance' (Rojas, 2007: 585) in the context of a structured variegation of resistance.

Although heavily 'capitalocentric', an understanding of variegated structures in recent work on 'neoliberalisation' pays attention to the systematic production of geo-institutional differentiation, which always involves 'combined and uneven development' and the 'polymorphic interdependence' of assemblages (Peck and Theodore, 2007: 33). In building on this work, we continue to insist that these assemblages cannot be reduced to a 'capitalist', much less a 'neoliberal', core. At the same time, a concern with 'neoliberalisation' rather than a unified 'neoliberalism' allows for an understanding of a much wider range of policy processes that are 'temporally discontinuous and spatially heterogeneous' (Brenner et al, 2010b: 208). There is, hence, a need to understand the 'vectors and circuits of ... regulatory practice' (Brenner et al, 2010b: 210), which are neither mechanistic and fully structured in advance, nor merely haphazard, accidental and spontaneous. A political articulation of 'policy otherwise' is always concerned, then, with the variegated 'conjunctural openings, political vulnerabilities, crisis points and strategic opportunities' (Brenner et al, 2010: 210) that dominant policy practices open up. A politics of variegation is concerned with relationality and multi-scalarity, insisting on the uneven co-constitution of multiple spatial scales and the multi-scalarity of transformation and restructuring (Lendvai, 2013). Here, 'it is not scale-levels in an absolute sense that matter, but the power-laden and shifting relations *between scales*' (Peck, 2002: 337, emphasis in original). Currently dominant hegemonic, inter-local and international 'rules of the game' (Peck and Theodore, 2007: 762) demonstrate a 'growing interdependence, interreferentiality and co-evolution of ... reform efforts among territorial jurisdictions, spatial scales and policy fields' (Brenner et al, 2010b: 209), as can be seen from the earlier substantive chapters. A politics of translation and assemblage becomes, to all intents and purposes, then, a search for a 'counter politics of connectivity' (Stenning, 2005), linking 'positions, imaginaries, [and] discourses' (Lendvai, 2013). A careful 'calibration of connections' and 'documentation of differences' (Peck and Theodore, 2007: 761) is, therefore, the analytical basis of an articulation of 'policy otherwise'.

James Ferguson's (2009: 166) plea for a progressive politics that rejects 'a project of resisting and refusing harmful new developments in the world' in favour of trying to 'get what you want' is highly instructional here. Although his discovery that the social has become 'transnational' seems rather belated and not particularly nuanced, his concern with the need to imagine, via a more open reading of Foucault, new 'arts of governance' that take advantage of transformations in the spatial organisation of government and welfare, based on a thorough analysis of 'the actual political processes at work' (Ferguson, 2009: 170), is pertinent to a politics of translation. Crucially, he argues that the '"arts of government" developed within First World neo-liberalism might take on new life in other contexts, in the process opening up new political possibilities' (Ferguson, 2009: 173), treating minimum income schemes in Brazil, South Africa and elsewhere not as 'the neoliberalism we love to hate', but as 'a set of much harder to place arguments that link markets, enterprise, welfare, and social payments in a novel way' (Ferguson, 2009: 178). Of course, grasping the specifics of these measures through a focused understanding of contexts and conjunctures, including the continued influence of a Freire-inspired politics in Brazil, is needed to take us beyond a notion of the 'polyvalency' of neoliberalism into a more nuanced understanding of policy assemblages that are always already much more than 'neoliberalising'. Via Collier (2005), his argument that there is no necessarily neat fit between a general neoliberalising political-economic project and specific techniques in specific sites is important, pointing to the 'polymorphously unstable' nature of policy assemblages as a basis for 'grounded political struggles'. Tania Li (1999: 298) makes a similar point in arguing that a 'project of rule' is not the same as 'the accomplishment of rule', although we would reframe her argument that 'policies are secure on paper but fragile in practice' with the idea that the former may also be more fragile than first appears.

By seeing policy translations and assemblages as 'part of the context of action' (Mosse, 2004: 664), a focus on 'policy otherwise' can make visible the 'hidden transcripts' (Scott, 1990) and result in a multiplication and scattering of the possible narratives in play. Inspired by an ethical vision, 'policy otherwise' aspires to create new 'loci of enunciation' (Rojas, 2007: 584) and, if only fitfully or partially, thereby increase the spaces for negotiation and for the possibility of a recognition of alternative rationalities, knowledges and practices. The search for an ethical vision based on values of equality, solidarity and social and environmental justice, or 'new social relations free of oppression and inequality' (Rojas, 2007: 585), may lead to a study of 'real utopias' (Olin Wright, 2010), such as the Mondragon cooperative in the Basque region of Spain, seen by Gibson-Graham (2006: 101, emphasis in original; see also Cooper, 2013) as a 'community economy … placing the issues of *necessity, surplus, consumption* and the *commons*, in the foreground of ethical deliberation and decision'. However, it is the prefigurative and transformative aspects, and the exploration of ways that they may be translatable to other contexts, which matter, rather than reproducing a familiar dichotomy of an oasis of hope set against a landscape of despair. Studying spaces 'in-between', including those initiatives that, at first glance, offer more limited transformatory possibilities, is crucial. As Mosse (2004: 666, emphasis in original) argues, via Latour, 'maximizing the capacity of actors to *object* to what is said about them' is a crucial part of this.

In summary, 'policy otherwise' takes advantage of the ways in which policies are constructed, contested, contradictory and constitutive (Clarke, 2004: 147) to explore 'the limitations, the refusals, the counter-tendencies, and the instabilities that constitute the conditions for *other* possibilities' (Clarke, 2004: 154). The importance of enlarging the possibilities of thought and action (Clarke, 2004: 157) throughout, not as a 'dislocated gesture at the end' (Clarke, 2004; 158), requires a commitment to both 'studying' and 'acting through' (cf Wedel, 2004) if translation is to be given an ethical and political force.

Glimpses of policy otherwise

Translation, then, has offered an analytic that is able to interrogate policy movement. We understand these practices of translation as being the dynamic that makes policies move, that makes assemblages appear and renders power visible in its variegated forms. These analyses are important because they raise questions that go beyond an analytic framing to make policy a crucial and urgent site not just of analysis, but also of politics and ethics.

In response to some of our papers at the American Anthropological Association conference in Montreal, Marilyn Strathern (2011) reminded us that 'there is translation and translation', so that our plea here should not be seen as another opportunity to turn a political commitment into a technical tool, much as has occurred in the world of development with approaches to 'drivers of change' and, lately, 'theories of change' (Warrener, 2004). Strathern (2011, emphasis in original) drew attention to the double movement of translation, pointing '*both* to the context-shifting character of policy goals that can be retrieved through analysis *and* to what is almost an injunction that accompanies this, the need for a translation process to take place'. In a sense, it is not whether, but rather how, 'translation should be part of policy' (Strathern, 2011) that most interests us.

In Strathern's reading of one paper (Bainton and Lendvai, 2011), she noted that:

> In fact they go so far as to imbue the concept of 'translation' with an ethical force: the way forward, they crucially suggest, is not to abandon the educational programme but to include within its conception just how it might get translated for any specific location. I find this – that

there might be a way forward – immensely encouraging.
(Strathern, 2011)

Our sense that we were, indeed, seeking 'an ethic of translation' has grown subsequently. There is something about our incursions into policy translations that are not simply a call for translation to be part of an analytic or political project, although we have argued that it should also be this. There is something more necessary, more fitting and more forceful about the need for an ethic of translation.

This is because policy translations, in our terms, are not present within a separated policy space, although such separations are inscribed and maintained. Rather policy translations are assemblages of the various aspects of people's lives; indeed, their lives, their conditions of existence and their social relationships are themselves reassembled in and through these processes. Such a transposition firmly places policy in the realm of the relational, and, hence, the ethical.

The idea that we might formulate a series of injunctions, a set of directives or imperatives, such as to expand the range of possible translations in play, to open up new narratives and to bring those marginalised or silenced into the policy process and work towards more equal social relations is certainly appealing. While this might capture something of our intent, we want to articulate a different form of ethics, based not so much on injunction, with its tendencies towards hierarchical relationality and observance of global formulations, but on a different, more non-hierarchical relational form, and one that, like translations themselves, operates in the moment. This might be formulated as a Levinasian relational ethic, based on the non-appropriating encounter with the 'face of the other' (Levinas, 2011), which seems to resonate with our sense of translation. We also felt that we needed to go beyond this, to bring in an understanding of how ways of knowing are enrolled in this – both in translation and its politics.

In imagining what this might look like for translation, the work of Rada Iveković offers some fruitful insights. What resonates here, in her work as a comparative philosopher, is her insistence on the inescapability of translation: that there is no place outside of translation where we might find the illusion of comfort. Rather, as she puts it:

> *translation is the original mother tongue* of humankind, in the sense that there is no language that does not reach out to the other (self, person, or group) and intend meaning even when monologic, as well as meaning a technique of negotiation and a strategy of survival in common and

in integration. The concept of translation as the mother tongue implies the *border as your country*. (Iveković, 2005: 2, emphasis in original)

This embracing of translation as 'a primal condition' places translation centre stage; it also has implications for its ethics and politics. Placing translation at the heart of being suggests not only that it is part of the functioning of hegemony, but, equally, that:

Translation, in this sense, is a vital form of resistance (through the differential critical expression of differences) to the hegemonic lines of imposition of the meaning (of a meaning), as well as a possible vehicle of power (but also its opposite). It is a whole field of degrees, nuances, divergences; a range of (im)possibilities of traversals of meaning. (Iveković, 2002: 1)

An ethics and politics of translation must engage with this paradox – that in this toing and froing of meaning, translation 'does not make anything impossible, but makes things otherwise-accessible' (Iveković, 2002: 3). The search for policy otherwise has been a search for ways to frame an ethics of translation that sits within this paradox – which at once refuses to close down meanings, while, at the same time, offering lessons that might escape, if only fleetingly and partially, the confines of individual contexts and moments. They do not create the general, but they do prefigure possible transjunctions – sets of issues to pay attention to in the complex entanglements of policy. In the same way that, in Chapter Two, a theoretical interrogation of translation led us to a conceptual repertoire, this search for an ethics of translation has suggested an ethical repertoire for a praxis of translation: *humility, listening, collaboration* and *heteroglossia.*

The four vignettes that follow are our attempts to re-place this discussion on policy otherwise into the messy entanglements of each of the case studies. As such, they perform multiple kinds of 'work'. In part, they help to unsettle the illusion of the neat imaginary of policy otherwise that precedes it – to throw some grit back in. In part, they represent attempts to take forward the discussion on what the process of a policy otherwise might be; there is only so far that this can be explored theoretically, thereafter, the imaginary must be formed, chiselled as it were, out of the existing contexts and assemblages.

These vignettes offer glimpses of what we imagine a process of policy otherwise might be. Some of these glimpses are already in existence –

fragments of a practice of translation that we feel a policy otherwise could be developed from; some are more imaginary glimpses of how we feel a policy otherwise might look. In both cases, we settled on the word 'glimpse' as the appropriate term to describe the kind of epistemological relationships with emergent practices that we are striving towards. We are not trying in these vignettes to prescribe policies, politics or practices per se. These need to be formed and forged in practice with people, in heteroglossic ways, with humility and in praxis. Perhaps it is no accident that humility is our starting point. We refuse to occupy the role of academics, saying 'you must', 'this must', 'it will'. Humility derives from knowing – and acknowledging – that we do not know what should be or will be. Each of our vignettes does no more than offer a glimpse of how a policy otherwise in translation is possible. Each, in its own way, is a miniature of struggling with the heteroglossic and humility. They suggest ways in which possibilities of expanding and changing the narratives, expanding and changing voices, and even possibilities for equality, justice and well-being might be glimpsed.

Social welfare reform otherwise (Paul Stubbs)

A glimpse of 'policy otherwise' in relation to consultancy and social policy emerged in February 2014 in precisely the geographical space discussed in Chapter Three, namely, Bosnia-Herzegovina. At that time (the present, as this is being written), street protests in a number of cities in Bosnia-Herzegovina, some of which, albeit briefly, included violence, were followed by plenums in a smaller number of cities, citizens' assemblies based on principles of 'direct democracy'. These have articulated a set of demands, some of which had an immediate effect in terms of the resignation of a number of politicians, and, even more crucially, some of these demands have been translated into policies and actions by district parliaments, which, if only momentarily, appear to have 'changed the nature of political discourse' (Sarajlic, 2014). The linkage between protests, plenums and demands offers a glimpse of a possibility of a different articulation, a different translation, working from the deconstruction of an authoritative and authoritarian voice to a different set of relationships, in which voices 'otherwise' are facilitated by practices of listening.

These events have been interpreted *ad absurdum* by all manner of commentators, analysts, experts and intermediaries, seeing in the protests that which they want, or do not want, to see. Few, if any, of these accounts have addressed the issue that these interpreters, in Bosnia's flexible arenas of governance, may also be a part of the problem, alongside corrupt politicians in dysfunctional political arrangements, and sections of the so-called international community. Some of the best texts have urged *listening* long and hard before jumping to conclusions, echoing Callon's (1986: 216) maxim, which we noted in Chapter Two, that 'To speak for others is to first silence those in whose name we speak'. In thinking through these events, there is a reluctance, here, to do more than urge listening, avoiding any generalisation or translation of events, in one place at one time, into any general discourse, whether about politics, democracy or, much less, so-called 'progressive' social policy, all of which are deeply troubled and troubling concepts.

At the same time, whatever happens in the future, the events[1] provide glimpses of 'policies otherwise' in at least two ways. Procedurally, it is significant that early demands from plenums for the formation of technocratic governments of experts, populated by 'uncompromised' people, quickly translated into a demand that these be answerable to the plenums, precisely to avoid the idea of 'politics as usual' and the importance of continued scrutiny of anyone in a position of power. Substantively, the events provided a glimpse, again, of the possibility of demands for equality, justice, dignity and fairness being able to be translated into winnable claims and sustainable social platforms. One form of expertised consultancy, existing as a colonial practice, might be translated, therefore, into the possibility of a different set of practices, multi-voiced, unfinished and generated in dialogue, of course, always risky, and always in danger of being closed down, appropriated and colonised again, but nevertheless worth pursuing. In other words, one moment reveals a stretched sense of the rupture in which other possibilities may appear. Plenums such as those occurring in February 2014 in parts of Bosnia-Herzegovina reveal, if only literally 'for a moment', the impossibility of sustaining a depoliticised consultancy practice. In such moments, policy otherwise is glimpsed and becomes a space of possibility for a different work of translation.

Regarding the other empirical case in Chapter Three, the glimpse of policy otherwise may, perhaps, be in terms of the need to combine a greater reflexivity with the creation of spaces and possibilities of disagreement, rather than the creation of rather slick consultations. Again, a translation perspective would continue to try to widen the narrative possibilities, widen the range of voices to be heard (users of services, their families and caregivers are important here) and avoid the labelling of any position in one-dimensional terms. How to fold the

---

[1] For a set of resources in English deriving from the protests and plenums, see: http://bhprotestfiles.wordpress.com/ (accessed 25 March 2014).

politics of change into a policy otherwise, without, in turn, rendering the politics rather technical, through constructing models of 'drivers of change' or 'theories of change', is crucial. At a more mundane level, engaging in translation exercises which ensure that concepts used are both understood and fit the cases being discussed is vital. In other words, the fact that 'statutory service', 'case management' and other key concepts proved difficult to translate or sustain across contexts should be the starting point for heteroglossic exchange, a cacophony of discordant understandings, not a reason for flattening and homogenising.

Rereading and translating Freire, it may be that one part of 'policies otherwise' would reject 'consultancy' as a standalone intervention governed by terms of reference and time-limited activities. The importance of working alongside political projects and social movements that one agrees with, in broad-brushstroke terms, at whatever scale, would seem to be central to any practice of policy otherwise, helping to tease out from experiments aspects of a different kind of policy, both procedurally and substantively, responsive to, and feeding back into, these movements as they develop and change. In this sense, knowing the Other in a colonial sense, thereby taming, containing and controlling it, may be displaced, if only in a glimpsed moment, by a practice of recognition that can be an entry point for a different, radically contingent, engaged, praxis otherwise.

Managing universities otherwise (John Clarke)

Chapter Four sets two different, if linked, problems for thinking and acting otherwise. The larger one concerns the challenge of universities otherwise; the smaller one, the challenge of managing otherwise. In these comments, I will mainly focus on the second – smaller – of these issues. However, it is important to at least register some of the other ways in which 'doing universities' has been imagined and enacted. There are many models for doing the university that already exist as practices, as experiments and even as abandoned schemes (teach-ins, the 'Occupy' universities, the Workers Educational Association, People's Universities of various kinds and even the origins of the Open University itself). These alternatives vary around questions of: access (Who is university for? Under what conditions can people participate?); the forms and styles of knowledge production, creation, distribution and exchange; and the relationships, methods and technologies of teaching and learning. Such alternatives also make visible the persistent tensions between hierarchical and collaborative relationships, between possessive and collective forms of knowledge, between closed communities and open access, between co-present and mediated interactions, and so on. In the present, most of these tensions are being reproduced (rather than resolved) in the obsession with Massive Open Online Courses (MOOCs) as educational consortia try to find ways of commodifying and monetising online education.

The second issue is more directly derived from the chapter: how might universities be managed otherwise? The question is not exactly separate from the larger issue: how the purposes, conditions and relationships of universities are imagined has consequences for how they are organised. However, it remains worth exploring because, again, 'otherwises' have existed, still exist and are constantly being invented (which seems to me to be the message of Gibson-Graham and others; see Gibson-Graham, 2006; see also Cooper, 2013; Newman, 2013b). Such forms of thinking and acting otherwise are not outside or beyond the world as it is lived, although they may occupy strained and difficult places, and uncomfortable relationships to the dominant forms (which often seek to neutralise, incorporate or even exploit their 'alternativeness').

Randy Martin's (2011) book (to which I referred in the chapter) returns to three forms of collective or collaborative organising: professional associations, trades unions and political parties. He uses them to refresh our collective memory and imagination – as ways in which we have found methods of doing organising and to underline the way in which organising (in all settings) is socially necessary labour. I think he tends to underestimate some of the (bad) lessons we learned about organising in these ways, but it is a potent reminder that past ways of thinking and acting are not necessarily dead to us merely because they have been displaced by the rise of new forms. Such ideas and practices persist because, as Raymond Williams (1977) says about 'residual' cultural forms, they pose questions that the current dominant forms cannot answer.

This is true for most of my examples of thinking and acting 'otherwise': they persist because contemporary dominant forms of 'managing' exclude vital issues, questions and demands. There has, for example, been a recent interest in cooperative forms of doing and managing universities, as reflected in the following article:

> At a time when many academics feel remote from their university's managers and strategic plans, the cooperative model, in which all staff have a stake, has obvious appeal. So, can the University of Mondragon, an established higher education cooperative in the lush green mountains of the

Basque Country in northern Spain, offer any answers for academies elsewhere? Founded in 1997 from a collection of co-ops dating back to 1943, the institution now has 9,000 students. The staff have joint ownership and the institution's culture and its model of governance are radically different from those of modern UK universities.

In 2011, three academics – Rebecca Boden of the University of Roehampton, Davydd Greenwood of Cornell University and Susan Wright of Aarhus University – visited the university and wrote that Mondragon was a 'highly successful' alternative to what they called 'neoliberalised university formations'.

'It is possible to create and manage successful universities that do not involve the exploitation of faculty as passive employees and the treatment of students as mere clients in a fee-for-service educational scheme,' they conclude in 'Report on a field visit to Mondragón University: a cooperative experience/experiment', published in the journal *Learning and Teaching*.[2]

Like the earlier 'otherwises', the cooperative model is not without its strains and troubles (about membership, about sustaining shared cultures and about the stresses of competitive survival), but its flattened and delegated management structures and practices form a striking contrast to their inflated and costly British equivalents. The cooperative model also bears traces of an older working-class conception of management as *stewardship* (and with echoes of the ecological view of stewardship, too). The working-class version (typically associated with working men's clubs) had managers employed by the elected members who run the organisation; indeed, they were sometimes literally known as stewards. However, their stewardship was subject to the judgement and evaluation of the members. This inverted view of management – as subordinated to the organisation and its members – also contrasts sharply with the hierarchical conception of the well-managed organisation that dominates university life now.

I would add the (unevenly) abandoned collegial/quasi-democratic model of the university as a self-governing body. This poses important

---

2   Source: http://www.timeshighereducation.co.uk/features/inside-a-cooperative-university/2006776.fullarticle

challenges to the current model of managerial authority, even if it has flaws (about who is recognised as participants in the democracy, about active participation and about the fantasy of an academic 'community'). However, such processes do form the ground on which we might pose questions about participation, forms of power, relationships of ownership and belonging that are silenced in current managerial discourse and practice.

All of these ways of thinking and doing otherwise are relatively silent about the relationships between students and staff – both in the ordering of learning and in the coordination of the organisation. Open University students once protested (in 2003) in the university senate about being addressed as 'customers' and expressed a preference in favour of being viewed and treated as 'members of the academic community'. However, here, we encounter the recurring paradox of community: what sorts of relationships make a community? What sorts of membership can be imagined and enacted? What happens in weakly bounded institutions, as universities are increasingly becoming? (Who from the 'outside' has a claim on the university-as-community?) More widely, how might a move from community to commons be imagined in reinventing the university?[3] For me, the importance of thinking otherwise is not to have '*the answer*', but to keep open the spaces of thought and dialogue in which alternatives can be voiced, discussed and practised in the face of a managerial monoculture.

Europeanisation otherwise (Noémi Lendvai)

'Europeanisation' has long been associated with policy diffusion, policy learning and discursive institutionalisation. The puzzle starts when 'other' languages, contents, techniques and technologies of social inclusion and its governing by the EU seem 'unfit to fit'. The puzzle starts when one comes to wonder whether Europeanisation is more about unlearning than about policy learning. If only we learn, we measure, we accumulate knowledge, we deliberate, we move (in a linear line) forwards, towards 'better policies'. What if unlearning or learning otherwise is more productive? What if the Europeanisation process is less about the cognitive, the technical, the textual and the discursive, and perhaps much more about the performative, the imaginary and the transformative? Or, when inclusion becomes 'togetherness', the certain becomes tentative, the single becomes more than one but less than many. It is also when sense instantiates nonsense, where meaning

---

[3] Thank you to Sam Kirwan for this way of reworking the problem of community.

is replaced by anti-meaning. Through these series of puzzles, I have come to argue in my chapter that 'Europeanisation' is enacted through fictions: fictions of strategic planning, policy actions, policy priorities or administrative practices. Fictions, here, are not the opposite of reality; quite the contrary, fictions sustain reality as they enact and perform policies. In particular, I argue the strategic reports and all kinds of policy documents, 'texts', are enrolled in fiction.

Policy otherwise, or Europeanisation otherwise, for me, would start with languages, not in a sense, as most EU studies scholars argue, that multilingualism is a key part of the project of EU integration, but, rather, in a sense that we need translation practices otherwise. Rather than confining translation practices as a highly technicalised, linguistic set of practices, we need new forms of translation praxis in which translation is recognised as a political project. Translation, then, is performed not only by translators (no matter how well-qualified they are), but by policymakers themselves. Translation, then, is not a prerequisite of policy, but rather the making of it. We need to reopen the box of 'social inclusion' and allow for multiple translations, connotations, associations, voices and relations to emerge (where, for instance, the Hungarian translation of 'societal togetherness' can be made visible and heard). Many more alternatives and different translations need to emerge, too. The 'pluriverse' of social inclusion governance needs to be populated by other voices and other translations. Rather than writing and reading 'National Reports', we need social inclusion reports by non-governmental organisations (NGOs), by local communities of all kinds, by professionals and by 'ethnic' communities, and, more broadly, we need to mobilise other channels and genres that are able to disrupt dominant fictions.

Rather than disregarding fiction, as 'non-compliance', 'weak implementation' and 'naming and shaming', or assign it as the work of 'laggards', let us see these dynamics as 'implementation otherwise', or 'inclusion otherwise'. Working with others, being with others, rather than endlessly telling them what they need to do in order to become European, might be a step towards Europeanisation otherwise. Through inclusion otherwise and its politics otherwise, one can move beyond both a particular kind of modernisation project and a colonial project. Insisting on not listening, not hearing and not engaging, is where Europeanisation (both as a policy space and an academic space) reproduces the discourse of backwardness. Learning otherwise, learning from other experiences, opening to possibilities of other voices, other relations and other imaginaries, is where I would imagine Europeanisation otherwise to be.

Reconfiguring, quite radically, both the academic and the policy language of EU and EU studies, what I call in the chapter 'epistemic modernism', is also needed. As long as academic knowledge production colludes in the construction of a 'common European space', either in the form of emphasising master discourses or discursive Europeanisation, or in the form of the assumed common space of neoliberal governmentality, the language of EU studies will remain singular, overdeterministic and unhelpful. Similarly, as long as EU policy English remains a highly bureaucratic, highly technicalised language, with its buzzing wizardry, it will remain not only fictional, but highly exclusionary as well. The barriers of languages and to the access to EU policy spaces need to come down not go up; barriers are already mountainous in terms of mastering, speaking and accessing both English and EU 'policy' English in order to engage and participate. This needs not only a multilingual Europe in a linguistic sense, but an EU that speaks many languages in a policy sense as well. Policies, then, are not the insistence on the common, but rather the working with the multiple; policies that are not singular, but rather heteroglossic in their languages. It is in this sense of languages and translation practices that a politics and ethics of translation of social inclusion policies might be worth thinking about.

Finally, I am calling for learning otherwise in difficult times. Throughout our collaborations in this book, PS has reminded me over and over again that, for some, unlearning is what is needed in the age of austerity, where economic logics dictate an unlearning of welfare, and telling times of new ages, where welfare belongs to 'old times'. Unlearning, here, is a re-engineering of states, institutions at a meta-scale, when policy otherwise becomes policy elsewhere. For me, however, both unlearning of welfare and policy elsewhere is produced by particular translation practices that sustain dominant fictions. Fiction as a dominant genre is perhaps broader than the social inclusion of the Open Method of Coordination (OMC); it more broadly reflects the social dimensions of EU integration.

Education otherwise (Dave Bainton)

We live in a pluriverse. Yet, this plurality of cultural practices, languages, religions and forms of livelihoods stands in marked contrast to the global commonality of educational practices. The intractability of translations of education as 'schooling' is perhaps made possible through its materialisation in the form of schools. In their solidity and visibility, schools divert our attention from the interpersonal and social aspects of education that might remind us that there are many knowledges and many ways to learn. Whatever the reason, education seems stubbornly resistant to the generation of alternative translations based on a less restricted engagement with the multiplicity of ways of knowing. It is this articulation between the plurality of existent ways of knowing and restricted educational assemblages that I want to explore here in order to glimpse the potential working of the spaces that education otherwise might emerge from.

Otherwises do not come easy. While we have outlined a politics and ethics of translation that grounds their possibility, what I want to consider here is the poiesis at work in their operation, and the resources that we might employ for such creative work. In various ways, all of the case studies have searched for ways to expand policy (and social science) beyond the textual and linguistic and have drawn upon ideas of the material, of practice, of the affective and of the performative as alternative resources for policy otherwise; I am taking 'ways of knowing' as part of this repertoire.

Ways of knowing (in the case study, these involved sculptural practices, walking, storytelling, meditation, hammering, introspection, etc) are assemblages, in the sense that we have used it – as forms of being, doing and sociality that produce ways of understanding the world. What attracts me to this conceptualisation as 'ways of knowing' (rather than simply labelling these practices, as one could, as assemblages) is their 'way-ness', which highlights both the human achievement of these forms and their distinctiveness – these are not just myriad assemblages that (can) know the world differently, they are historical achievements that offer difference. 'Ways of knowing' gives us pause to consider what one way offers that another might not, it gives us a way to consider what ways of knowing we are hearing and making visible in our policy translation. Or, to put it another way, what we need is not only an ethics and politics of translation, but an ethic of knowing.

The difficulty in imagining an ethic of knowing might perhaps be explained by the difficulty it seems that we have (in Western academia) to accept that we are not able to stand outside our knowing. This externalisation and objectification of our ways of knowing as 'knowledge' is, perhaps, an explanation of how, while there has been a fruitful embracing of epistemology, we struggle with imagining such an ethic of knowing. Yet, translation, as we have argued here, takes us to an ontology where our worlds are always in the process of embodied becoming and this inescapable 'doing-ness' of life (and our ways of knowing, therefore, as an inseparable part of it) opens up both the possibility and the hope of such an ethic.

So, what does this all mean for glimpsing education policy otherwise? What is glimpsed is not a different type of school. The radical implication that translation of other ways of knowing needs to be part of the policy process suggests that educational otherwises may well be outside such structures. Instead, what is glimpsed here is the range of expanded resources and ways of knowing from which an education otherwise might be assembled.

Chapter Six developed an analysis of translation that centred around issues of place and of narrative. In this revitalised policy process, we need to imagine how ways of knowing, such as these, which are enmeshed in the narratives and practices of place and sociality, might be recognised and translated to become part of an alternative education. In particular, this suggests that a politics of translation places the possibilities of resistance as particularly emergent from these extra-linguistic translations. As Iveković (2002: 1) puts it:

> There remains something unsaid in this situation, or again there is a residue of what has no language; which is more or less the same thing as saying that there is something unheard. This basic inequality, which is already political (before there is any such thing as politics), can still be aggravated by historical circumstances that have made one of the two dominant. Since Foucault, at least, but also as a result of work done by anthropologists and psychoanalysts, we know that in the last analysis it is a question of the body. And there are other disciplinary, and undisciplined, approaches, such as feminist theory, post-colonial studies etc., which tell us that what cannot be articulated or understood in conventional language also comes from the other, from the subaltern, from the immediate experience of repression, the limit of which is also very much the body.

If education policy otherwise is to become, it must do so as an ethic that embraces these embodied, 'immediate experiences of repression' as starting points for transformative translations. These other ways of knowing become a resource for the potential translation of education otherwise.

The imaginative horizons are generated not so much by these ways of knowing per se, but by the questions of how they might articulate with an educational assemblage. The work of what this might look like is something that would need to be done in place and in context, but this analysis would certainly suggest that educational experiences should be liberated in multiple ways: from the confines of a school building to embrace an enlarged landscape; from exchanges with a limited number of teachers to include people from across the community; from a transmission model of knowledge to one where storytelling is used as a core pedagogic practice; and so on. Each of these raises many questions, but they are also horizons – directions of possibility.

I am arguing here that indigenous practices offer possibilities for glimpsing educational otherwises. The intention here is not that these particular glimpses be understood as the most important, but, rather, to suggest how an engagement in the indigenous practices that function in the silences surrounding schooling might allow a glimpse of how education might be translated and assembled differently – in its modes of relationality, its forms of progression and its dynamics of inquiry.

Policy otherwise in conversation

We end this chapter and this book with an edited and annotated transcription of a conversation that we had towards the end of its writing. We have all been humbled by the sense of what has been made possible between us through conversations that have taken place in friendship and in collaboration. This conversation does not manage to give a sense of the sheer fun that has been had (the role of playfulness in a resistive politics has not been given enough attention in this volume), but it does evoke a sense of the forms of space that are associative and heteroglossic. It offers a strange echo of the sections of this final chapter that have been attempts, in different genres, to develop an understanding of what policy otherwise might be. This attempt offers, in a more performative and embodied way, this understanding.

As we have argued, there is no escape from translation, except through a violence that creates a closure of meaning. This, then, is a stopping, rather than an ending – a ceasing of a set of conversations that, we hope, might inspire other conversations to be had. This particular conversation took place shortly after the death of Stuart Hall. Stuart is almost a fifth presence here – continuing conversations that, for one of us (JC), had begun four decades previously. In outlining an ethic of translation that is based on humility, heteroglossia, listening and collaboration, we are therefore inevitably performing a contingency that is framed by the absent presence of Stuart Hall, and the variegated relationships that we had with him – for some of us personal, and for others through his work. We take this not as an undermining of the possibility of truth, but rather a celebration of the possibilities of doing otherwise that might emerge if we might encounter differently.

DB: "I was struck, John, in what you wrote for your 'policy otherwise' about how there are already examples of, or fragments of, policies otherwise, already existing."

JC: "Glimpses of policy otherwise [in the sense that Gibson-Graham explore other existing possibilities – JC]."

PS: "So what would they look like?"

DB: "I remember one day in Ladakh, I had been chatting with the village blacksmith in the morning, and then in the evening, a local academic was telling me about the meeting on promoting indigenous knowledge that he was organising. So, I suggested that he could invite the blacksmith along, and he just said that this wouldn't be possible."

PS: "Why?"

DB: "He said that it was because he didn't speak English. But, you know, there were people who could have translated for him. But there were other reasons, really – around the social position of the craft of blacksmithing in the village – but this was a glimpse of when something otherwise could have been done – bringing different people in to give different understandings."

PS: "'Bringing in different people', reminds me of something I picked out from an old study of consultancy companies on the EU Consensus Programme [De la Porte and Deacon, 2002]. It made a difference when they did not have a consultancy company where all consultants were coming from one country. Imagine a consultancy team, where someone comes from Bolivia, someone from Bosnia, someone from Belgium – they have to translate!"

DB: "Anti-consensus then?"

PS: "You are building in a need for a conversation through translation."

JC: "And that means that, if you get it, you only get a consensus through struggling for it, and two things: one is that it is quite a nice way of putting heteroglossia in, but it is also why I am realising increasingly that I want to go back to the issue of articulation and think that for Stuart Hall, articulation was always at least double, it wasn't just about voice, it was also about connection as well."

PS: "Which always works?"

JC: "But, you know, I was sitting feeling deeply unsatisfied, thinking: yeah, but everybody does voice, and I don't want to write a sentence which has the word 'voice' in it. So, heteroglossia is one way of getting it, but articulation is also an insistence that relations of connections are also at stake, so even if you got the blacksmith into the room, it's then about what's the work that goes into the relation of listening politely, because we know what voice means: 'Thank you very much for coming along, and telling us your story'."

PS: "Well, it gets worse because what emerges is this new group of brokers, intermediaries who acknowledge that public meetings involve people with different resources and different capitals, so their job is to ensure that they have a Habermasian dialogic space and it's a real issue, there's a real tension, I think, between modelling a world that is meant to be in the context where it isn't, and that is why redistribution remains important to me."

JC: "The same is true for states. You can't want to build a state that is not dialogic. And that means that states have to create spaces for conversation, even though they think they know things. They have to listen. And they have to produce a public because you can't think there's a public just waiting there with its views already; so, states are the only vehicle that we can think of that might equalise things.... States are the only vehicle that could exercise zero-tolerance on anti-public activities, people who steal the public realm, people who fail to pay taxes, so *we* are quite into state power."[4]

PS: "It reminds me of the debate on an audit of consultants which was a discussion in one of our seminars in Croatia. There is nothing wrong with audit when it is used on and against the powerful."

JC: "That remains an outstanding issue for me in arguments, where audit culture is criticised from the point of view of a victimised academic profession. You know, even with academics, just tell me how many black students make it to Cambridge or Oxford? Tell me about the class distribution, I might want an audit of this."

NL: "But John, is audit really doing that? Do top universities in the UK really care about their intake of students from working-class families?"

JC: "I don't know, but you would need a different form of audit here. My experience of audit is of stop-and-search policy in policing London. And you needed to know the massive overrepresentation of young black males. And you couldn't have done that without somebody counting, and I think that this is being rejected as a sort of governmentality. Yes, it's a governmentality, but it's got a different politics."

NL: "But can we think about the form of audit that would deliver that. I think that's an interesting question."

PS: "Audit doesn't deliver anything in one sense; audit is a tool for another purpose. So, there would have to be some different policy otherwise where audit could appear in a different way."

JC: "There's a really interesting book about, I think it's Paraguay, called *Guerrilla auditors* [Hetherington, 2011]. And it's about the mobilisation of people to map land claims

---

[4] A reference to a contribution written by Janet Newman and JC for the 'Kilburn Manifesto'. Available at: http://www.lwbooks.co.uk/journals/soundings/manifesto.html

differently against the authorities and so I think auditing is like that. Its potential is like that – you might actually want to know what these bastards are doing. It doesn't mean it gives you immediate possibilities. But that's the problem, it requires the political will to act on those things; so, the missing bit of our paper on the state [see note 4, p 220] is … the political will question."

PS: "One of the problems, I think, in the book is that all the things we say about the problem of translation are absolutely the problems of some of the Left as well; they are the problems of alternative discourses, too. And, so, we're kind of rescuing something without being able to rescue it."

DB: "You know we talk about how policymaking is enmeshed and entangled and policy otherwise is not the same as policy research otherwise."

JC: "No, it's different entanglements."

DB: "I have been kind of wearied by the impossibility of expressing in a small section at the end of the book the impossibility of a new political project."

JC: "And to join all this up – absolutely."

DB: "We are not going to achieve that, but policy research otherwise may be something that could be outlined."

JC: "It's important to note the salience that both policy research otherwise matters, and policymaking otherwise matters. But all of that is to say I don't want to write a book that ended with us saying, somewhat heroically (I need to stand up so I look like those statues of Lenin), 'that way now', because the shame and humiliation of that would be just impossible, and not saying anything is not a possibility."

DB: "So, what can we say?"

JC: "Modes of possibility, connection … what needs to be thought about in doing policy otherwise. It's not what policy otherwise is. It can't be the prescription of what the policy is; it has to be the doing, and challenging the silencing ..."

PS: "Or the not doing, or the avoiding of doing. That's right. In a weird way, those are injunctions!"

JC: "I don't mind doing those things as injunctions. I can imagine saying: okay – the creation of spaces, of debate, argument and possibility that are not entirely captured and institutionalised are important, the openness of the policy process to what comes out of such spaces is even more important. Part of that is arguing for a re-politicisation and the suspension of technocratic wizardry but another one would be that none of us are, though I don't think we say it, entirely romantic about the local/indigenous."

PS: "Running through what I've been trying to say in the chapter and then in my 'policy otherwise' is this. One of my early injunctions was 'trust the local' and it didn't take me long to realise that that was a naive thing to do – locals are not locals. They are enmeshed and enrolled and variegated, in which 'local' is another fiction. It's not the lowest common denominator. So, for instance, when you use the term indigenous knowledge, is that the blacksmith or is it the academic ..."

DB: "It is not easy – but you can unpick those enrolments and enmeshments ... certainly those that are not currently brought into those spaces of debate are those you want to have in."

PS: "Dragging them screaming reluctantly?"

DB: "No, not dragging them screaming – you take the conversations to them."

PS: "Indeed – Freire."

JC: "This is the structural dilemma because the elites are elites for a reason. And it's not because they're elite. It's because they control and command lots of resources. One of the dilemmas is about saying what is it in these processes that work around, displace, disrupt, established regimes of power?"

NL: "Indeed, displacement, for me, is central in understanding translation."

JC: "What are the modes of displacement and disruption? That's the question. I want to be both romantic and dead scared ..."

DB: "So far, we have talked about two things: the first is the doing of ... the search for the forms of doing, and then there was the goal of ... the displacement and disruption. One is a process and the other is how you would recognise that process to have taken place. So, would it not be sufficient to say 'this is how you could identify policy otherwise', or one way to attack this will be to say 'this is how you would identify policy otherwise'."

PS: "I have been reading a bit about the Situationists [Wark, 2011, 2013] and it became relevant partly because of some of this."

DB: "You'll have to say who the Situationists were."

PS: "They were an *avant garde* art collective whose view was that they would spot and disrupt any power wherever it went, and were very involved in the 1968 events in Paris. A famous clip[5] is when Lacan is doing one of his famous 40-minute lectures of being the sole authority, with the students being there to write down what he says, when he is disrupted by a Situationist who throws something at him, throws water at him, and Lacan deals with it in an interesting way, but what Lacan is trying to do is keep his power as the authentic voice. The guy gets escorted out saying, 'this is exactly what I mean, this is exactly why we need to challenge and disrupt'. My only point is challenging and disrupting is tiring, and not very productive of a fairer

---

5   Available at: https://www.youtube.com/watch?v=6aqGYYBwKbQ&feature=p layer_embedded http://htmlgiant.com/random/lacan-gets-punkd/ (accessed 25 March 2014).

world. And I watched a documentary on Mao, and the cultural revolution, and Mao did this, and millions died, and all of his comrades from the revolution were humiliated in front of huge crowds"

DB: "Are you saying Mao disrupted?"

PS: "Mao was a Situationist in a sense, although the only thing that could not be disrupted was the cult of Mao!"

DB: "So, not all disruption is good …"

JC: "I think what you're saying is that disruption is difficult to sustain without being damaging and without exhausting people. So, we talk a lot about unsettling and disrupting and I think it's possibly easy, easy is not the right word, it is possible to imagine this as an academic practice. You know, I've spent my life wandering around and unsettling taken-for-granted academic knowledge. But I think that's different to constantly trying to unsettle state apparatuses on a systematic basis. Disrupting the police can be a hard and painful process … standing in the way of the powerful in whatever way they appear is risky, painful and uncomfortable and the story of the Situationists and Mao is a reminder that not everybody who disrupts is someone you want as a friend."

DB: "Doesn't that bring in your third point of social justice? But don't you always need a place to judge from?"

PS: "But we can't. We have no places to judge in the book. There is no privileged position – there is only the dialogue in translation."

JC: "Alright, I'm going to make an argument now for social justice. I'm not sure it's the word I mean, but that it's not a judgement, it's not a position for judgement…. It is precisely one of the vocabularies that is mobilised in unending conversations in which you want to say, 'that's an interesting idea … what does it do to material inequalities and what does it do to gender relations?'"

PS: "But the four words that I used – justice, equality, hope, fairness – came from the plenum."

JC: "Those words are ... well ... somebody's going to say 'What do you mean by fairness?'... but they are about saying what might be at stake in conversations, not what the position of judgement is.... So, I'm prepared to have long conversations (as you know to your cost already) but, in those terms, it would be 'And what's the difference it would make if we do that?', 'What's the difference it would make to these things?'"

DB: "What things?"

JC: "The forms of inequality that we know and can document interminably."

PS: "This is why my plenum as policy otherwise was carefully chosen. I do not know what kind of social policy demands would come from it. There is an idea of 'a global social protection floor' [Deacon, 2013], which could be a starting point for debate at least. We suffered from the World Bank 'one-size-fits-all neoliberalism'. And now we suffer from the Bank saying 'there cannot be a policy that's not adjusted to context', which is, of course, true but also in danger of foreclosing possibilities."

JC: "'Responsive to local circumstances.'"

PS: "Humility is crucial in this, including humility in theory ..."[6]

---

6   Subsequent to this conversation, I discovered a text on exactly this theme by Shannon Mattern, which argued:

Rather than deifying the Big Men of Theory, assuming that they possess some greater truth that we must adopt wholesale ... let's recognize the theory and the theorists for what they are. They're models to help us make sense of things, frameworks to help us ask questions.... And they're often women ... and practitioners ... and more often than not, groups of people who develop their ideas collaboratively, over time, through processes that likely won't bring glory to any one of them.... Theory with a little 't,' like knowledge itself, erupts not from the heads of Great Men, but from collectives comprised of folks whose last names, unlike Derrida's and Deleuze's, aren't likely to get 'adjectivized' in

JC: "I'm going to talk about it endlessly, but that is one of the things that people kept saying about Stuart Hall – that he was humble! That he did not behave like a professor: he was likely to talk to anybody because he thought anybody would be interesting. I think the thing about ... humility is about the politics of articulation ... which is ... it can't work if you think politics is about telling somebody where they should move to ... unless you do it collectively, conversationally, engagingly."

DB: "So, we just say read Freire?"

PS: "No, because it was of its time and space as well ..."

DB: "Sure, but the mode and the drive and the relationality, and the collaboration are part of the same politics and ethics."

JC: "And if you can't take the time to do it with people, don't bother."

PS: "But Stuart Hall did this. I met him once and he answered one of my questions and I wanted him to go further but then he said 'I can see you nodding, so let's try a bit harder'."

JC: "I'm sorry, I'm obsessed by the Stuart question at the moment but it's also about heteroglossia. Stuart could sit in *New Left Review* with Perry Anderson, Tariq Ali and others, and he could do those conversations and he could do sophisticated work on the novels of Henry James but at the showing of the Stuart Hall project in Birmingham, this older black guy stood up and said 'I never met Stuart Hall but his ideas have entirely shaped my world ... I was one of the founder members of the movement of black probation officers' and then the next guy said, 'I met him

our everyday academic discourse. I think we'd all be wise to do what we can to ensure that 'little t' theory emerges through processes, through intellectual labor, that embodies the politics those theories ostensibly valorize. (Source: http://www.wordsinspace.net/wordpress/2012/05/07/theoretical-humility/ [accessed 25 March 2014])

though. I met him on an Open University summer school. Looking at me you can probably see that I'm black, but what you can't see so easily is I spent 30 years working as a police officer and the combination of these two is not exactly comfortable. At that summer school I was talking to Stuart, or more accurately he talked to me in police ways, in ways that I can understand, ways that made sense to me about my situation and how to act …'. And you just think: actually, that's heteroglossia and articulation! That's what heteroglossia does for you – it means you engage with people and work around, and with, the different voices that might be at stake."

References

Ackroyd, S. and Thompson, P. (1999) *Organisational misbehaviour*, London: Sage Publications Ltd.

Adam, B. (2005 [1998]) *Timescapes of modernity: the environment and invisible hazards*, London: Routledge.

Allen, J. (2003) *Lost geographies of power*, Oxford: Blackwell.

Allen, J. (2011) 'Topological twists: power's shifting geographies', *Dialogues in Human Geography*, 1(3): 283–98.

Althusser, L. (2005 [1965]) *For Marx*, London: Verso (original French edition *Pour Marx*, 1965; first English translation 1969 by B. Brewster).

Amelina, A., Negiz, D., Faist, T. and Glick Schiller, N. (eds) (2012) *Beyond methodological nationalism*, London and New York, NY: Routledge.

Andrić, I. (1995) *The bridge over the Drina*, London: Harvill.

Apter, E. (2001) 'Balkan Babel: translation zones, military zones', *Public Culture*, 13(1): 65–80.

Apter, E. (2006) *The translation zone. A new comparative literature*, Princeton, NJ: Princeton University Press.

Arandarenko, M. and Goličin, P. (2007) 'Serbia', in B. Deacon and P. Stubbs (eds) *Social policy and international interventions in South East Europe*, Cheltenham: Edward Elgar, pp 167–86.

Ashiagbor, D. (2005) *The European Employment Strategy: Labour market regulation and new governance*. Oxford: Oxford University Press.

Bainton, D. and Lendvai N. (2011) ''Unfit to Fit': ruptures and erasures in the translation of the global Education for All agenda in Ladakh, India', Paper presented to American Anthropological Association Congress, Montreal, December.

Ball, S. (2003) 'The teacher's soul and the terrors of performativity', *Journal of Education Policy*, 18(2): 215–28.

Ball, S. (2008) *The education debate*, Bristol: The Policy Press.

Baltodano, A. (1999) 'Social policy and social order in transnational societies', in D. Morales-Gómez (ed) *Transnational social policies: The new development challenges of globalization*, London: Earthscan; 19–41.

Barbier, J.-C. (2013) *The road to social Europe. A contemporary approach to political cultures and diversity in Europe*, Abingdon: Routledge.

Barbier, J.-C. and Colomb, F. (2011) 'The unbearable foreignness of EU law in social policy, a sociological approach to law learning', CES Working Papers.

Barry, A. (2013) 'The translation zone: between actor–network theory and International Relations', *Millennium: The Journal of International Studies*, 41(3): 413–29.

Barthes, R. (1990) *S/Z*, Oxford: Blackwell.

Basch, L., Glick-Schiller, N. and Szanton Blanc, C. (eds) (1993) *Nations unbound: Transnational projects, postcolonial predicaments and deterritorialized nation-states*, New York, NY: Routledge.

Beckert, J. (2010) 'Institutional isomorphism revisited: convergence and divergence in institutional change', *Sociological Theory*, 28(2): 150–66.

Benson, P. and Kirsch, S. (2010) 'Capitalism and the politics of resignation', *Current Anthropology*, 51(4): 459–86.

Best, J. (2012) 'Bureaucratic ambiguity', *Economy and Society*, 41(1): 84–106.

Bilić, B. (2012) *We were gasping for air: (post-)Yugoslav anti-war activism and its legacy*, Baden-Baden: Nomos.

Bilić, B. and Janković, V. (2012) 'Recovering (post-)Yugoslav anti-war activism: a Zagreb walk through stories, analyses and activisms', in B. Bilić and V. Janković (eds) *Resisting the evil: (Post-Yugoslav) anti-war contention*, Baden-Baden: Nomos, pp 25–36.

Blagojević, M. (2009) *Knowledge production at the semiperiphery: A gender perspective*, Belgrade: Institut za kriminološka i sociološko istraživanja [The Institute for Criminological and Sociological Research].

Blagojević, M. and Yair, G. (2010) 'The catch 22 syndrome of social scientists in the semiperiphery: exploratory sociological observations', *Sociologija*, 52(4): 337–58.

Blyth, M. (2013) *Austerity: The history of a dangerous idea*, Oxford: Oxford University Press.

Borghi, V. (2011) 'One-way Europe? Institutional guidelines, emerging regimes of justification and paradoxical turns in European welfare capitalism', *European Journal of Social Theory*, 14(3): 321–41.

Bourdieu, P. and Wacquant, L. (1992) *An invitation to reflexive sociology*, Chicago: Polity Press.

Bovens, M. and Zuoridis, S. (2002) 'From street-level to system-level bureaucracies: how information and communication technology is transforming administrative discretion and constitutional control', *Public Administration Review*, 62(2): 174–84.

Brennan, T. (2001) 'The cuts of language: the East/West of North/South', *Public Culture*, 13(1): 39–63.

Brenner, N. (2001) 'The limits to scale? Methodological reflections on scalar structuration', *Progress in Human Geography*, 25(4): 591–614.

Brenner, N., Peck, J. and Theodore, N. (2010) 'Variegated neoliberalization: geographies, modalities, pathways', *Global Networks*, 10(2): 182–222.

Brown, B.J. and Baker, S. (2012) *Responsible citizens: Individuals, health and policy under neoliberalism*, London: Anthem Press.

Buchs, M. (2008a) 'How legitimate is the Open Method of Co-ordination?', *Journal of Common Market Studies*, 46(4): 765–86.

Buchs, M. (2008b) 'The Open Method of Coordination as a "two-level game"', *Policy & Politics*, 36(1): 21–37.

Butler, J. (1993) *Bodies that matter: on the discursive limits of 'sex'*, London: Routledge.

Callon, M. (1986) 'Some elements of a sociology of translation: domestication of the scallops and the fishermen of St Brieuc Bay', in J. Law (ed) *Power, action and belief: a new sociology of knowledge?*, London: Routledge.

Carmel, E. and Paul, R. (2010) 'Il difficile percorso verso la coerenza nella governance UE della migrazione' ['The struggle for coherence in EU migration governance'], *La Rivista delle Politiche Sociali*, 1: 209–30.

Cerami, A. (2008) 'Europeanization and social policy in Central and Eastern Europe', in F. Bafoil and T. Beichelt (eds) *Européanisation. D'Ouest en Est*, Coll. Logiques Politiques, L'Harmattan: Paris, pp 137–68.

Chakrabarty, D. (2002) *Habitations of modernity: Essays in the wake of subaltern studies*, Chicago, IL: University of Chicago Press.

Chamberlayne, P., Cooper, A., Freeman, R. and Rustin, M. (eds) (1999) *Welfare and culture in Europe: Towards a new paradigm in social policy*, London: Jessica Kingsley,

Chang, G.C.C. (trans) (1999) *A hundred thousand songs of Milarepa*, Boston, MA: Shambhala.

Clandinin, D.J. and Connelly, F.M. (2004) *Narrative inquiry: Experience and story in qualitative research*, San Francisco, CA: John Wiley and Sons.

Clarke, J. (2004) *Changing welfare, changing states: New directions in social policy*, London: Sage.

Clarke, J. (2005a) 'Performing for the public? Desire, doubt and the governance of public services', in P. du Gay (ed) *The values of bureaucracy*, Oxford: Oxford University Press, pp 211–32.

Clarke, J. (2005b) 'Reconstituting Europe: governing a European People?' in J. Newman (ed) *Remaking governance: Peoples, politics and the public sphere*, Bristol; The Policy Press, pp 17–37.

Clarke, J. (2007) 'Citizen-consumers and public service reform: at the limits of neo-liberalism?', *Policy Futures in Education*, 5(2): 239–48.

Clarke, J. (2008) 'Governance puzzles', in L. Budd and L. Harris (eds) *E-governance: managing or governing*, London: Routledge.

Clarke, J. (2010a) 'Of crises and conjunctures: The problem of the present', *Journal of Communication Inquiry*, 34(4): 337–54.

Clarke, J. (2010b) 'So many strategies, so little time... making universities modern', *Learning and Teaching in Social Sciences*, 3(3): 91–116.

Clarke, J. (2012) 'The work of governing', in K. Coulter and W.R. Schumann (eds) *Governing cultures: anthropological perspectives on political labor, power, and government*, New York, NY: Palgrave Macmillan, pp 209–32.

Clarke, J. (2013) 'Contexts: forms of agency and action', in C. Pollitt (ed) *Context in public policy and management: the missing link?*, Cheltenham: Edward Elgar Publishing Ltd.

Clarke, J. (2014) 'Community' in D. Nonini (ed) *A companion to urban anthropology*, London and Malden, MA: Wiley-Blackwell; pp 46–64.

Clarke, J. (forthcoming) 'Stuart Hall and the theory and practice of articulation', *Discourse: Studies in the Cultural Politics of Education*.

Clarke, J. and Fink, J. (2008) 'Unsettled attachments: national identity, citizenship and welfare', in W. van Oorschot, M. Opielka and B. Pfau-Effinger (eds) *Culture and welfare state: Values and social policy in comparative perspective*, Cheltenham: Edward Elgar, pp 225–44.

Clarke, J. and Newman, J. (1993) 'The right to manage: a second managerial revolution?', *Cultural Studies*, 7(3): 427–41.

Clarke, J. and Newman, J. (1997) *The managerial state*, London: Sage Publications.

Clarke, J. and Newman, J. (2012) 'The alchemy of austerity', *Critical Social Policy*, 32(3): 299–319.

Clarke, J. and Stubbs, P. (2010) 'Making policy move: the challenge of tracing transnational translation', Paper presented to conference 'Beyond Esssentialisms', Ljubljana, November.

Clarke, J., Coll, K., Dagnino, E. and Neveu, C. (2014) *Disputing citizenship*, Bristol: Policy Press.

Clarke, J., Gewirtz, S., Hughes, G. and Humphrey, J. (2000) 'Guarding the public interest? Auditing public service', in J. Clarke, S. Gewirtz and E. McLaughlin (eds) *New managerialism, new welfare?*, London: Sage/The Open University, pp 250–66.

Clarke, J., Newman, J., Smith, N., Vidler, E. and Westmarland, L. (2007) *Creating citizen-consumers: changing publics and changing public services*, London: Sage.

Clarke, J., McDermont, M. and Newman, J. (2010) 'Delivering choice and administering justice: contested logics of public service', in M. Adler (ed) *Administrative justice in context*, Oxford: Hart Publishing, pp 25–46.

Clifford, J. (1997) *Routes: travel and translation in the late twentieth century*, Cambridge, MA: Harvard University Press.

Clifford, J. and Marcus, G. (1986) (eds) *Writing culture: The poetics and politics of ethnography*, Berkeley: University of California Press.

Coffey, A. (2004) *Reconceptualizing social policy: Sociological perspectives on contemporary social policy*, Maidenhead: Open University Press.

Cohen, S. and Shires, L. (1988) *Telling stories: A theoretical analysis of narrative fiction*, London: Routledge.

Collier, S. (2005) 'The spatial forms and social norms of "actually existing neoliberalism"', International Affairs Working Paper, The New School, New York.

Collinson, D. and Ackroyd, S. (2005) 'Resistance, misbehaviour and dissent', in S. Ackroyd, R. Batt, P. Thompson and P. Tolbert (eds) *The Oxford handbook of work and organization*, Oxford: Oxford University Press, pp 305–26.

Cooper, D. (2013) *Everyday utopias: The conceptual life of promising spaces*, Durham, NC: Duke University Press.

Cowen, R. (1996) 'Performativity, post-modernity and the university', *Comparative Education*, 32(2): 245–58.

Cowen, R. (2009) 'The transfer, translation and transformation of educational processes: and their shape-shifting?', *Comparative Education*, 45(3): 315–27.

Crapanzano, V. (2004) *Imaginative horizons: An essay in literary-philosophical anthropology*, Chicago, IL: University of Chicago Press.

Czarniawska, B. and Sévon, G. (eds) (1996) *Translating organisational change*, Berlin and New York, NY: De Gruyter.

Dagnino, E. (2006) '"We all have rights but …" Contesting concepts of citizenship in Brazil', in N. Kabeer (ed) *Inclusive citizenship: Meanings and expressions*, London: Zed Books.

Day Sclater, S. (2003) 'What is the subject?', *Narrative Inquiry*, 13: 317–30.

Deacon, B. (with Hulse, M. and Stubbs, P.) (1997) *Global social policy: international organizations and the future of welfare*, London: Sage.

Deacon, B. (2013) *Global social policy in the making: The foundations of the social protection floor*, Bristol: Policy Press.

Deem, R. and Parker, J. (2008) 'Leading change in semi-autonomous public universities in England: following government agendas or subverting them?', Paper for presentation at European Group for Organisational Studies (EGOS) conference, Amsterdam, 10–12 July.

De la Porte, C. (2007) 'Good governance via the OMC? The cases of employment and social inclusion', *The European Journal of Legal Studies*, 1(1): 1–43.

De la Porte, C. and Deacon, B. (2002) *Contracting companies and consultants; the EU and social policy of accession countries*, GASPP Occasional Paper 9, Helsinki: STAKES.

Deleuze, G. (2006) *Two regimes of madness*, New York, NY: Semiotext[e].

Deleuze, G. and Guattari, F. (1988) *A thousand plateaus*, London: Continuum.

De Sousa Santos, B. (2001) '*Nuestra America*: reinventing a subaltern paradigm of recognition and distribution', *Theory, Culture and Society*, 18(2–3): 185–217.

De Sousa Santos, B. (2004) 'The World Social Forum: a users' manual'. Available at: http://www.ces.uc.pt/bss/documentos/fsm_eng.pdf (accessed 4 February 2014).

De Sousa Santos, B. (2005) 'The future of the World Social Forum: the work of translation', *Development*, 48(2): 15–22.

Diez, T. (1999) 'Speaking "Europe": the politics of integration discourse', *Journal of European Public Policy*, 6(4): 598–613.

Dobbin, F., Simmons, B. and Garrett, G. (2007) 'The global diffusion of public policies: social construction, coercion, competition, or learning?', *Annual Review of Sociology*, 33: 449–72.

Dolowitz, D. and Marsh, D. (1996) 'Who learns what from whom? A review of the policy transfer literature', *Political Studies*, 44(2): 343–57.

Dolowitz, D. and Marsh, D. (2000) 'Learning from abroad: the role of policy transfer in contemporary policy-making', *Governance: An International Journal of Policy and Administration*, 13(1): 5–24.

Duffield, M. (1994) 'Complex emergencies and the crisis of developmentalism', *IDS Bulletin*, 25(4): 37–45.

Du Gay, P. (2000) *In praise of bureaucracy*, London, Sage.

Dunleavy, P., Margetts, H., Bastow, S. and Tinkler, J. (2006) *Digital era governance: IT corporations, the state and e-government*, Oxford: Oxford University Press.

Dunn, E. (2005) 'Standards and person-making in East Central Europe', in A. Ong and S. Collier (eds) *Global assemblages: Technology, politics, and ethics as anthropological problems*, Oxford: Blackwell Publishing, pp 173–94.

Dussauge-Laguna, M. (2012) 'The neglected dimension: bringing time back into cross-national policy transfer studies', *Policy Studies*, 33(6): 567–85.

Ellis, C., Adams, T.E. and Bochner, A.P. (2010) 'Autoethnography: An overview [40 paragraphs]'. *Forum Qualitative Sozialforschung / Forum: Qualitative Social Research*, 12(1), Art 10, http://nbn-resolving.de/urn:nbn:de:0114-fqs1101108.

Escobar, A. (1995) *Encountering development*, Princeton, NJ: Princeton University Press.

Escobar, A. (2001) 'Culture sits in places: reflections on globalism and subaltern strategies of localization', *Political Geography*, 20(2): 139–74.

Escobar, A. (2004) 'Beyond the Third World: imperial globality, global coloniality and anti-globalization social movements', *Third World Quarterly*, 25(1): 207–30.

Escobar, A. (2010) 'Latin America at a crossroads: alternative modernizations, post-liberalism, or post-development?', *Cultural Studies*, 24(1): 1–65.

Escobar, A. (2011) *Encountering development. The making and unmaking of the Third World* (rev edn), Princeton, NJ: Princeton University Press.

European Commission (2008) *Renewed social agenda: Opportunities, access and solidarity in 21st century Europe*, COM (2008)412 final, available at www.eur-lex.europa.eu, dowloaded on the 01/01/2015.

Eyben, R. (2005) 'Ethical and methodological issues in researching international aid organisations: note of a workshop held at the Institute of Development Studies', 8 December 2004. Available at: www.theasa.org/ethics/workshop.doc (accessed 10 February 2014).

Eyben, R. (2009) 'Hovering on the threshold: challenges and opportunities for critical and reflexive ethnographic research in support of international aid practice', in S. Hagberg and C. Widmark (eds) *Ethnographic practice and public aid: Methods and meanings in development cooperation*, Uppsala: Uppsala University Press, pp 71–98.

Fabian, J. (1983) *Time and its other: How anthropology makes its object*, New York: Columbia University Press.

Fairbanks, R. (2009) *How it works: Recovering citizens in post-welfare America*, Chicago, IL: University of Chicago Press.

Fanon, F. (1965) *The wretched of the earth*, New York: Grove Press. (First published [1961] as *Les Damnes de la Terre*).

Farquhar, S. and Fitzsimons, P. (2011) 'Lost in translation: the power of language', *Educational Philosophy and Theory*, 43(6): 652–61.

Ferge, Z. (2005) 'Ellenálló egyenlőtlenségek: A mai egyenlőtlenségek természetrajzához' ['Resilient inequalities: towards the topography of contemporary inequalities'], *Esély* 17(4) : 3–41.

Ferguson, J. (1994) *The anti-politics machine: 'development', depoliticization, and bureaucratic power in Lesotho*, Minneapolis, MN: University of Minnesota Press.

Ferguson, J. (2010) 'The uses of neoliberalism', *Antipode*, vol 41, supplement S: 166–84.

Ferguson, J. (2013) 'Declarations of Dependence: Labor, Personhood, and Welfare in Southern Africa', *Journal of the Royal Anthropological Institute* 19: 223–42.

Ferguson, J. and Gupta, A. (2002) 'Spatializing states: towards an ethnography of neo-liberal governmentality', *American Ethnologist*, 29(4): 981–1002.

Ferrera, M. (2005) *The boundaries of welfare*, Oxford: Oxford University Press.

Fine, G. (2003) 'Towards a peopled ethnography: developing theory from group life', *Ethnography*, 4(1): 41–60.

Fischer, F. (2003) *Reframing policy analysis: Discursive politics and deliberative practices*, Oxford: Oxford University Press.

Fischer, F. and Forester, J. (1993) *The argumentative turn in policy analysis and planning*, Durham, NC: Duke University Press.

Fischer, F. and Gottweis, H. (eds) (2012) *The argumentative turn revisited: Public policy as communicative practice*, Durham, NC: Duke University Press.

Fischer, F. and Gottweis, H. (2013) 'The argumentative turn in public policy revisited: twenty years later', *Critical Policy Studies*, 7(4): 425–33.

Frank, T. (2001) *One market under God: Extreme capitalism, market populism and the end of economic democracy*, New York, Anchor Books.

Fraser, N. (1995) 'Pragmatism, feminism, and the linguistic turn', in S. Benhabib, J. Butler, D. Cornell and N. Fraser (eds) *Feminist contentions*, New York, NY: Routledge, pp 157–72.

Frazer, H. and Marlier, E. (2010) 'Strengthening social inclusion in the Europe 2020 strategy by learning from the past', in E. Marlier and D. Natali (eds) *Europe 2020: Towards a more social EU?*, Bruxelles: P.I.E Peter Lang Publisher.

Freeman, R. (2004) 'Research, practice and the idea of translation', consultation paper. Previously available at: www.pol.ed.ac.uk/freeman

Freeman, R. (2009) 'What is translation?', *Evidence and Policy*, 5(4): 429–47.

Freire, P. (1978) *Pedagogy in process: The letters to Guinea-Bissau*, London: Writers and Readers Publishing Cooperative.

Freire, P. (1998 [1970]) *Pedagogy of the oppressed*, New York, NY: Continuum.

Froggett, L. (2002) *Love, hate and welfare: Psychosocial approaches to policy and practice*, Bristol: The Policy Press.

Gabay, C. (2012) 'The Millennium Development Goals and ambitious developmental engineering', *Third World Quarterly*, 33(7): 1249–65.

Gasper, D. (2000) 'Evaluating the "logical framework approach" towards learning-oriented development evaluation', *Public Administration and Development*, 20(1): 17–28.

Gebhardt, E. (1982) 'Introduction to Part III: A critique of methodology', in A. Arato and E. Gebhardt (eds) *The essential Frankfurt School reader*, New York, Continuum.

Geertz, C. (1973) 'Thick description: towards an interpretive theory of culture', in C. Geertz, *The interpretation of culture: selected essays*, New York, NY: Basic Books, pp 3–30.

Gibson-Graham, J.K. (2006) *A postcapitalist politics*, Minneapolis, MN: University of Minnesota Press.

Gibson-Graham, J.K. (2008) 'Diverse economies: performative practices for "other worlds"', *Progress in Human Geography*, 32(5): 613–32.

Giddens, A. (1990) *The consequences of modernity*, Cambridge: Polity Press.

Gilbert, J. (2009) Presentation at 'Culture (and Cultural Studies) After the Crunch', an event organised by the Pavis Centre for Social and Cultural Theory, the Open University and the Centre for Cultural Studies Research, University of East London, London, 4 February.

Gill, R. (2009) 'Secrets, silence and toxic shame in the neoliberal university', in R. Ryan-Flood and R. Gill (eds) *Secrecy and silence in the research process: Feminist reflections*, London: Routledge, pp 253–64.

Ginsberg, B. (2011) *The fall of the faculty*, New York, NY: Oxford University Press.

Goffman, E. (1959) *The presentation of self in everyday life*, New York, NY: Anchor Books.

Gottweis, H. (2007) 'Rhetoric in policy making: between logos, ethos and pathos', in F. Fischer, G. Miller and M. Sidney (eds) *Handbook of public policy analysis: Theory, politics and methods*, Boca Raton, London and New York: CRC Press, pp 237–50.

Gough, A. and Gough, N. (2003) 'Decolonising environmental education research: stories of queer(y)ing and destabilising', paper presented at the University of Bath, 6 August.

Gould, D. (2009) *Moving politics: emotion and ACT UP's fight against AIDS*, Chicago, IL: Chicago University Press.

Gould, J. (2004a) 'Introducing aidnography', in J. Gould and H. Secher Marcussen (eds) *Ethnographies of aid: Exploring development texts and encounters*, Roskilde: Roskilde University, Institute for Development Studies, pp 1–13.

Gould, J. (2004b) 'Positionality and scale: methodological issues in the ethnography of aid', in J. Gould and H. Secher Marcussen (eds) *Ethnographies of aid: Exploring development texts and encounters*, Roskilde: Roskilde University, Institute for Development Studies, pp 263–90.

Gregg, M. (2009) 'Working with affect in the corporate university', in M. Liljeström and S. Paasonen (eds) *Working with affect in feminist readings: disturbing differences*, London: Routledge, pp 182–92.

Grossberg, L. (2011) *Cultural studies in the future tense*, Durham, NC: Duke University Press.

Guillen, A. and Alvarez, S. (2004) 'The EU's impact on the Spanish welfare state: the role of cognitive Europeanisation', *Journal of European Social Policy*, 14(3): 285–99

Gupta, A. (1998) *Postcolonial developments: Agriculture in the making of modern India*, Durham, NC: Duke University Press.

Gupta, A. (2006) 'Blurred boundaries: the discourse of corruption, the culture of politics, and the imagined state', in A. Sharma and A. Gupta (eds) *The anthropology of the state: A reader*, Oxford: Blackwell Publishing, pp 211–43.

Gupta, A. and Sharma, A. (2006) 'Globalization and postcolonial states', *Current Anthropology*, 47(2): 277–307.

Habermas, J. (1991 [1982, in German]) *The structural transformation of the public sphere: An inquiry into a category of bourgeois society*, Cambridge: MIT Press.

Hajer, M. (2005) 'Rebuilding ground zero: the politics of performance', *Planning Theory & Practice*, 6(4): 445–64.

Hall, S. (1986) 'Gramsci's relevance for the study of race and ethnicity', *Journal of Communication Inquiry*, 10(5): 5–27.

Hall, S., Critcher, C., Jefferson, T., Clarke, J. and Roberts, B. (1978) *Policing the crisis: Mugging, the state and law and order*, London: Macmillan.

Hardt, M. and Negri, A. (2001) *Empire*, Cambridge, MA: Harvard University Press.

Hartwich, V. (2011) 'Students under watch: visa checks and the rise of surveillance in UK universities', The Manifesto Club. Available at: www.manifestoclub.com (accessed 14 August 2013).

Harvey, D. (1990) *The condition of postmodernity*, Oxford and Malden, MA: Blackwell Publishers.

Hetherington, K. (2011) *Guerilla auditors: The politics of transparency in neoliberal Paraguay*, Durham, NC: Duke University Press.

Higgins, V. and Larner, W. (2010) *Calculating the social*, London: Palgrave Macmillan.

Hill, M. and Hupe, P. (2009) *Implementing public policy: An introduction to the study of operational governance,* 2nd edn, London: Sage.

Hoggett, P. (2000) *Emotional life and the politics of welfare*, Basingstoke: Macmillan.

Holquist, M. (ed) (1981) *The dialogic imagination: Four essays*, Austin, TX: University of Texas Press.

hooks, b. (1989) *Talking back: thinking feminist, thinking black*, Boston, MA: South End Press.

Howarth, D. (2010) 'Power, discourse, and policy: articulating a hegemony approach to critical policy studies', *Critical Policy Studies*, 3(3–4): 309–35.

Hughes, G. and Lewis, G. (eds) (1998) *Unsettling welfare: The reconstruction of social policy*, London: Routledge/The Open University.

Hungarian Women's Lobby (2013) 'The Hungarian Women's Lobby's opinion on the Hungarian partnership agreement for the programme period 2014–2020', consultation paper.

Ingold, T. (2007) *Lines: A brief history*, London: Routledge.

Innes, J. (2002) *Knowledge and public policy* (2nd edn), New Brunswick, NJ: Transaction Publishers.

Ivanova, V. and Bogdanov, G. (2013) 'The deinstitutionalization of children in Bulgaria: the role of the EU', *Social Policy and Administration*, 47(2): 199–217.

Iveković, R. (2002) 'On permanent translation (we are being translated)', *Transversal*. Available at: http://eipcp.net/transversal/0606/ivekovic/en/ (accessed 20 March 2014).

Iveković, R. (2005) 'Transborder translating', *Eurozine*. Available at: http://www.eurozine.com/articles/2005-01-14-ivekovic-en.html (accessed 20 March 2014).

Iveković, R. (2008) 'Translating borders: limits of nationalism, transnationalism, translationism', *Transversal*, March. Available at: http://eipcp.net/transversal/0608/ivekovic/en (accessed 22 January 2014).

Iveković, R. (2009) 'Translating borders: translations, transitions, borders', notes for CIPh seminar; unpublished manuscript.

Jackson, M. (ed) (1996) *Things as they are: New directions in phenomenological anthropology*, Bloomington, IN: Indiana University Press.

Jackson, S. (2011) *Social works: Performing art, supporting publics*, London and New York, NY: Routledge.

Jambrešić Kirin, R. and Povrzanović, M. (eds) (1996) *War, exile, and everyday life*, Zagreb: Institute of Ethnology and Folklore Research.

Jeffrey, A. (2013) *The improvised state: Sovereignty, performance and agency in Dayton Bosnia*, Chichester: Wiley-Blackwell.

Jenkins, R. (1997) *Rethinking ethnicity: Arguments and explorations*, London: Sage.

Jenkins, R. (2006) 'Problematising policy: culture, modernity and government', Arbejdspapir 138-06, Århus: Center for Kulturforskning.

Jessop, B. (2002) *The future of the capitalist state*, Cambridge: Polity.

Jessop, B. (2013) 'The returns of the argumentative turn', *Critical Policy Studies*, 7(4): 434–9.

Johnson, B. and Hagstrom, B. (2005) 'The translation perspective as an alternative to the policy diffusion paradigm: the case of the Swedish methadone maintenance treatment', *Journal of Social Policy*, 34(4): 365–88.

Jones, M., Jones, R. and Woods, M. (2004) *An introduction to political geography: Space, place and politics*, London: Routledge.

Kapoor, I. (2004) 'Hyper-self-reflexive development? Spivak on representing the Third World "Other"', *Third World Quarterly*, 4: 627–47.

Kern, S. (1983) *The culture of time and space, 1880–1918*, Cambridge, MA: Harvard University Press.

Kibberd, D. (1995) *Inventing Ireland: Literature of the modern nation*, Vintage Press: London.

Kingfisher, C. (ed) (2011) *Western welfare in decline*, Philadelphia, PA: University of Pennsylvania Press.

Kingfisher, C. (2013) *A policy travelogue: Tracing welfare reform in Aotearoa/ New Zealand and Canada*, Oxford and New York, NY: Berghahn Books.

Kirkendall, A. (2010) *Paulo Freire and the Cold War politics of literacy*, Chapel Hill, NC: University of North Carolina Press.

Koskinen, K. (2008) *Translating institutions: An ethnographic study of EU translation*, Manchester: St. Jerome Publishing.

Kovacs, J. (2002) 'Approaching the EU and reaching the US? Rival narratives on transforming welfare regimes in East-Central Europe', *West European Politics*, 25(2): 175–204.

Kramsch, O.T. (2010) 'Camuspace: towards a geneaology of Europe's de-colonial frontier', in C. Brambilla and B. Riccio (eds) *Transnational migrations, cosmopolitanism and dis-located borders*, Rimini: Guarald, pp 87–118.

Kramsch, O.T. (2011) 'Along the Borgesian frontier: excavating the neighbourhood of "wider Europe"', *Geopolitics*, 16(1): 193–210.

Kroger, S. (2009) 'The Open Method of Coordination: underconceptualisation, overdetermination, de-politicisation and beyond', *European Integration Online Papers* 1(13): Art 5.

Kusa, Z. and Gerbery, D. (2007) 'Europeanisation of Slovak social policy', ESPANET conference paper.

Kvist, J. and Saari, J. (eds) (2007) *The Europeanisation of social protection*, Bristol: The Policy Press.

Larner, W. and Laurie, N. (2010) 'Travelling technocrats, embodied knowledges: globalizing privatization in telecoms and water', *Geoforum*, 41: 218–26.

Latour, B. (1987) *Science in action: How to follow scientists and engineers through society*, Cambridge, MA: Harvard University Press.

Latour, B. (2005) *Reassembling the social. An introduction to Actor-Network-Theory*, Oxford: Oxford University Press.

Lavinas, L. (2013) '21st century welfare', *New Left Review*, 84: 5–40.

Law, J. and Urry, J. (2004) 'Enacting the social', *Economy and Society*, 33(3): 390–410.

Leibfried, S. and Zürn, M. (2005) 'Reconfiguring the national constellation', in S. Leibfried and M. Zürn (eds) *Transformations of the state*, Cambridge: Cambridge University Press, pp 1–36.

Lendvai, N. (2004) 'The weakest link? EU accession: dialoguing EU and post-communist social policy', *Journal of European Social Policy*, 14(3): 319–33.

Lendvai, N. (2007) 'Europeanization of social policy? Prospects and challenges for South East Europe', in B. Deacon and P. Stubbs (eds) *Social policy and international interventions in South East Europe*, Cheltenham: Edward Elgar, pp 22–44.

Lendvai, N. (2009) *Critical dialogues: EU accession and the transformation of post-communist welfare*, Saarbrucken: VDM Verlag.

Lendvai, N. (2013) 'Permanent transitions: "variegated welfare capitalism" in post-communist Europe', mimeo.

Lendvai, N. and Bainton, D. (2011) 'Unfit to fit? Ruptures and erasures in the translation of the global Education for All agenda in Tibetan communities of Ladakh, India', Paper presented at the American Anthropological Association annual conference, Montreal, December.

Lendvai, N. and Stubbs, P. (2007) 'Policies as translation: situating transnational social policies', in S. Hodgson and Z. Irving (eds) *Policy reconsidered: meanings, politics and practices*, Bristol: The Policy Press, pp 173–90.

Lendvai, N. and Stubbs, P. (2009a) 'Globale Sozialpolitik und Governance: Standpunkte, Politik und Postkolonialismus' ['Global social policy and governance: positionality, politics and post-colonialism'], in H.-J. Burchardt (ed) *Nord_Sud Beziehungen im Umbruch: Neu Perpektiven auf Staat und Demokratie in der Weltpolitik*, Frankfurt: Campus Verlag, pp 219–44.

Lendvai, N. and Stubbs, P. (2009b) 'Assemblages, translation, and intermediaries in South East Europe', *European Societies*, 11: 673–95.

Levinas, E. (2000) *Entre nous: Essays on thinking of the other*, New York, NY: Columbia University Press.

Levinas, E. (2011) *Totality and infinity: and essay on exteriority*, Dordrecht: Kluwer Academic Publishers.

Lévi-Strauss, C. (1966) *The savage mind*, London: George Weidenfeld and Nicolson (French edition, 1962).

Lewis, P.J. (2006) 'Stories I live by', *Qualitative Inquiry*, 12(5): 829–49.

Lewis, D. and Mosse, D. (2006) 'Encountering order and disjuncture: contemporary anthropological perspectives on the organization of development', *Oxford Development Studies*, 34(1): 1–13.

Li, T. (1999) 'Compromising power: development, culture and rule in Indonesia', *Cultural Anthropology*, 14(3): 295–322.

Li, T. (2007) 'Practices of assemblage and community forest management', *Economy and Society*, 36(2): 263–93.

Lipsky, M. (1982) *Street-level bureaucracy: Dilemmas of the individual in public services*, New York, NY: Russell Sage Foundation.

Lowenhaupt Tsing, A. (2007) *Friction: an ethnography of global connection*, Princeton, NJ: Princeton University Press.

Lyotard, J. (1984) *The postmodern condition: a report on knowledge*, Manchester: University of Manchester Press (French edition published in 1979; translated by G. Bennington and B. Massumi).

Machiavelli, N. (2003 [1532]) *The Prince* (trans. George Bull), London: Penguin.

Maglajlić, R. and Stubbs, P. (2006) 'Social impact assessment', in Independent Bureau for Humanitarian Issues (ed) *Social policy conference, book of papers*, Sarajevo: IBHI, pp 4–8.

Maglajlić Holiček, R. and Rašidagić, E. (2007) 'Bosnia and Herzegovina', in B. Deacon and P. Stubbs (eds) *Social policy and international interventions in South East Europe*, Cheltenham: Edward Elgar, pp 149–66.

Maglajlić Holiček, R. and Rašidagić, E. (2008) 'The role of NGOs in societies facing war: experiences from Bosnia and Herzegovina', in S. Ramon (ed) *Social work in the context of political conflict*, Birmingham: Venture Press, pp 123–46.

Mahony, N. (2013) 'The work of public engagement', *Comunicazioni Sociali*, 3: 249–358.

Mangham, I. (1978) *Interactions and interventions in organizations*, Chichester: John Wiley.

Marcus, G. (1995) 'Ethnography in/of the world system: the emergence of multi-sited ethnography', *Annual Review of Anthropology*, 24: 95–117.

Marcus, G. and Saka, E. (2006) 'Assemblage', *Theory, Culture & Society*, 23(2-3): 101-106.

Martin, R. (2011) *Under new management: universities, administrative labor, and the professional turn*, Philadelphia, PA: Temple University Press.

Massey, D. (2004) 'Geographies of responsibility', *Geografiska Annaler*, vol 86 B, no 1, pp 5–18.

Massey, D. (2005) *For space*, London: Sage.

Massumi, B. (2002) *Parables for the virtual: movement, affect, sensation*, Durham, NC: Duke University Press.

Mayo, P. (2004) *Liberating praxis: Paulo Freire's legacy for radical education and politics*, Rotterdam: Sense Publishers.

McCann, E. and Ward, K. (2013) 'A multi-disciplinary approach to policy transfer research: geographies, assemblages, mobilities and mutations', *Policy Studies*, 34(1): 2–18.

McDonald, C. and Marston, G. (eds) (2006) *Analysing social policy: a governmental approach*, Cheltenham: Edward Elgar.

McFarlane, C. and Anderson, B. (2011) 'Thinking with assemblage', *Area*, 43(2): 162–4.

McLaren, P. and Lankshear, C. (eds) (1994) *Politics of liberation: paths from Freire*, London: Routledge.

Merton, R.K. (1936) 'The unanticipated consequences of purposive social action', *American Sociological Review*, 1(6): 904.

Meyer, J., Boli, J., Thomas, G. and Ramirez, F. (1997) 'World society and the nation-state', *American Journal of Sociology*, 103(1): 144–81.

Meyers, M. and Vorsanger, S. (2007 [2003]) 'Street level bureaucrats and the implementation of public policy', in G. Peters and J. Pierre (eds) *Handbook of public administration*, London: Sage, pp 153–64.

Midgley, J. (2004) 'Social development and social welfare: implications for social policy, in P. Kennett (ed) *A handbook of comparative social policy*, Cheltenham: Edward Elgar, pp 217–38.

Mignolo, W. (2000) *Local histories/global designs: coloniality, subaltern knowledges, and border thinking*, Durham, NC: Duke University Press.

Minh-ha, T.T. (1989) *Woman native other*, Bloomington, IN: Indiana University Press.

Mintzberg, H. (1992) *Structure in fives: designing effective organisations*, Upper Saddle River, NJ: Prentice Hall.

Mitchell, T. (1991 [1988]) *Colonising Egypt*, Berkeley, CA: University of California Press.

Mitchell, T. (2002) *Rule of experts: Egypt, techno-politics, modernity*, Berkeley and Los Angeles, CA: University of California Press.

Mol, A.M. (2010) 'Actor Network Theory: sensitive terms and enduring tensions', *Kölner Zeitschrift für Soziologie und Sozialpsychologie*, 50(1): 253–69.

Monti, E. (2009) 'Translating the metaphors we live by', *European Journal of English Studies*, 13(2): 207–21.

Morgan, J. (2011) 'Identity check: vice-chancellors' education and pay revealed', *Times Higher*, 24 March. Available at: http://www.timeshighereducation.co.uk/415610.article

Morris, M. (2006) *Identity anecdotes: translation and media culture*, London: Sage Publications.

Morris, T. and Lancaster, Z. (2005) 'Translating management ideas', *Organisation Studies*, 27(2): 207–33.

Mosse, D. (2004) 'Is good policy unimplementable? Reflections on the ethnography of aid policy and practice', *Development and Change*, 35(4): 639–71.

Mosse, D. (2005) *Cultivating development: an ethnography of aid policy and practice*, London: Pluto Press.

Mosse, D. (2007) 'Notes on the ethnography of expertise and professionals in international development', Ethnografeast III: 'Ethnography and the Public Sphere', Lisbon, 20–23 June.

Mosse, D. (2008) 'International policy, development expertise, and anthropology', *Focaal*, 52, Winter: 119-126.

Mosse, D. (2011) 'Introduction: the anthropology of expertise and professionals in international development', in D. Mosse (ed) *Adventures in Aidland: the anthropology of professionals in international development*, New York, NY: Berghahn Books, pp 1–31.

Mukhtarov, F. (2014) 'Rethinking the travel of ideas: policy translation in the water sector', *Policy and Politics*, 32(1): 71–88.

Muller, M. (2007) 'What is in the word? Problematizing translation between languages', *Area*, 39(2): 206–13.

Neave, G. (1998) 'The evaluative state reconsidered', *European Journal of Education*, 33(3): 265–84.

Newman, J. (2012) 'Beyond the deliberative subject? Problems of theory, method and critique in the turn to emotion and affect', *Critical Policy Studies*, 6(4): 465–79.

Newman, J. (2013a) 'Spaces of power: feminism, neoliberalism and gendered labor', *Social Politics*, 20(2): 200–21.

Newman, J. (2013b) 'Performing new worlds: policy, politics and creative labour in hard times', *Policy and Politics*, 41(4): 515–32.

Newman, J. (forthcoming) 'Interpretive approaches to social policy and social welfare', in R. Rhodes (ed) *The Routledge handbook of interpretive policy studies*, London: Routledge.

Newman, J. and Clarke, J. (2009) *Publics, politics and power*, London: Sage Publications.

Newton, T. (1996) 'Agency and discourse: recruiting consultants in a life insurance company', *Sociology*, 30(4): 717–39.

Ninković, R. and Papić, Ž. (2007) *Reforming the systems and structures of central and local social policy regimes in Bosnia and Herzegovina*, Sarajevo: IBHI and Tiri.

Niranjana, T. (1992) *Siting translation: history, post-structuralism and the colonial context*, Berkeley, CA: University of California Press.

Norberg-Hodge, H. (2000) *Ancient futures: learning from Ladakh* (rev edn), London: Rider.

Oke, N. (2009) 'Globalizing time and space: temporal and spatial considerations in discourses of globalization', *International Political Sociology*, 3(3): 310–26.

Olin Wright, E. (2010) *Envisioning real utopias*, London: Verso.

Ong, A. and Collier, S. (eds) (2005) *Global assemblages: technology, politics and ethics as anthropological problems*, Oxford: Blackwell Publishing.

O'Reilly, D. and Reed, M. (2010) '"Leaderism": an evolution of managerialism in UK public service reform', *Public Administration*, 88(4): 960–78.

O'Reilly, D. and Reed, M. (2011) 'The grit in the oyster: professionalism, managerialism and leaderism as discourses of UK public services modernisation', *Organisation Studies*, 32(8): 1079–101.

Ozga, J., Dahler-Larsen, P., Segerholm, C. and Simula, H. (eds) (2011) *Fabricating quality in Europe: data and education governance*, London, Routledge.

Ozkan, U.R. (2013) 'Translating travelling ideas: the introduction of unemployment insurance in Turkey', *Global Social Policy* 13(3): 239–60.

Pain, R., Kesby, M. and Askins, K. (2011) 'Geographies of impact: power, participation and potential', *Area*, 43: 183–8.

Palmary, I. (2011) '"In your experience": research as gendered cultural translation', *Gender, Place & Culture: A Journal of Feminist Geography*, 18(1): 99–113.

Palsson, G. and Rabinow, P. (2005) 'The Icelandic controversies: reflections on the transnational market of civic virtue', in A. Ong and S. Collier (eds) *Global assemblages: technology, politics and ethics as anthropological problems*, Oxford: Blackwell Publishing.

Pandey, G. (2005) *The construction of communalism in North India* (2nd edn), Oxford: Oxford University Press.

Pandey, G. (2006) 'The politics of community: Some notes from India', in G. Creed (ed) *The seductions of community*, Santa Fe: School of American Research Press.

Pandolfi, M. (2003) 'Contract of mutual (in)difference: government and the humanitarian apparatus in contemporary Albania and Kosovo', *Indiana Journal of Global Legal Studies*, 10(1): 369–81.

Peck, J. (2002) 'Political economies of scale: fast policy, interscalar relations and neoliberal workfare', *Economic Geography*, 78(3): 331–60.

Peck, J. (2011) 'Geographies of policy: from transfer-diffusion to mobility-mutation', *Progress in Human Geography*, 35(6): 773–9.

Peck, J. and Theodore, N. (2007) 'Variegated capitalism', *Progress in Human Geography*, 31(6): 731–72.

Peet, R. (2003) 'Ideology, discourse and the geography of hegemony: from socialist to neoliberal development in post-apartheid South Africa', *Antipode*, 34: 54–84.

Pennycook, A. (2003) 'Global Englishes, Rip Slyme, and performativity', *Journal of Sociolinguistics*, 7(4): 513–33.

Peters, T. and Waterman, R. (1982) *In search of excellence: lessons from America's best-run companies*, New York: Harper and Row.

Phillips, J. (2006) 'Agencement/assemblage', *Theory, Culture and Society*, 23: 108–9.

Phillipson, R. (2008) 'Lingua franca or lingua frankensteinia? English in European integration and globalisation', *World Englishes*, 27(2): 250–67.

Polkinghorne, D. (1988) *Narrative knowing and the human sciences*, New York, NY: New York Press.

Pollitt, C. (2008) *Time, policy, management: governing with the past*, Oxford: Oxford University Press.

Pollitt, C. (2013) '40 years of public management reform in UK central government: promises, promises ...', *Policy and Politics*, 41(4): 465–80.

Pollitt, C. and Sorin, D. (2012) 'The impacts of the New Public Management in Europe: a meta-analysis', COCOPS. Available at: http://www.cocops.eu/wp-content/uploads/2012/03/WP1_Deliverable1_Meta-analysis_Final.pdf (accessed 30 March 2014).

Pollitt, C., Girre, X., Lonsdale, J., Mul, R., Summa, H. and Waerness, M. (1999) *Performance or compliance? Performance audit and public management in five countries*, Oxford: Oxford University Press.

Power, M. (1997) *The audit society*, Oxford: Oxford University Press.

Pratt, M. (1992) *Imperial eyes: travel writing and transculturation*, Abingdon: Taylor and Francis.

Pratt, M.L. (1999) 'Arts of the contact zone', *Profession*, 91: 33–40.

Pugh, M. (2000) *Protectorates and spoils of peace: intermestic manipulations of political economy in South-East Europe*, Copenhagen: Peace Research Institute.

Pupavac, V. (2011) 'Punishing childhoods: contradictions in children's rights and global governance', *Intervention and Statebuilding*, 5(3): 285–312.

Radaelli, C. (2003) 'The Europeanisation of public policy', in K. Featherstone and C. Radaelli (eds) *The politics of Europeanisation*, Oxford: Oxford University Press, pp 27–56.

Rajaram, P.K. and Grundy-Warr, C. (eds) (2008) *Borderscapes: hidden geographies and politics at territory's edge*, Minneapolis, MN: University of Minnesota Press, pp 263–82.

Rašidagić, E.K. (2012) 'Politics of welfare reforms: lessons from Bosnia and Herzegovina', unpublished mimeo.

Riles, A. (2006) 'Introduction: in response', in A. Riles (ed) *Documents: artifacts of modern knowledge*, Ann Arbor, MI: The University of Michigan Press, pp 1–40.

Robinson, W. (2001) 'Social theory and globalization: the rise of a transnational state', *Theory and Society*, 30: 157–200.

Roggero, G. (2011) *The production of living knowledge: The crisis of the university and the transformation of labour in Europe and North America* (trs by E. Brophy) Philadelphia, PA: Temple University Press.

Rojas, C. (2007) 'International political economy/development otherwise', *Globalizations*, 4(4): 573–87.

Rose, N. (1999) *Powers of freedom: reframing political thought*, Cambridge: Polity Press.

Rose, R. (2005) *Learning from comparative public policy: a practical guide*, London: Routledge.

Sahlin-Andersson, K. and Engwall, L. (eds) (2002) *The expansion of management knowledge: carriers, flows and sources*, Stanford, CA: Stanford Business Books.

Sakai, N. (2006) 'Translation', *Theory, Culture and Society* 23(2–3): 71–8.

Salakhyan, E. (2012) 'The emergence of Eastern European English', *World Englishes*, 31(3): 331–50.

Sarajlic, E. (2014) 'The perils of procedural democracy: a lesson from Bosnia', *Open Democracy*, 18 February. Available at: http://www.opendemocracy.net/can-europe-make-it/eldar-sarajlic/perils-of-procedural-democracy-lesson-from-bosnia (accessed 20 February 2014).

Sassen, S. (2006) *Territory, authority, rights: from medieval to global assemblages*, Cambridge: Cambridge University Press.

Schmidt, V. (2008) Discursive institutionalism: the explanatory power of ideas and discourse. *Annual review of political science*, 11: 303–326.

Schmidt, V. (2013) Arguing about the Eurozone crisis: a discursive institutionalist analysis, *Critical Policy Studies*, 7:4: 455-462.

Scott, D. (2004) *Conscripts of Modernity: The Tragedy of Colonial Enlightenment*. Durham NC: Duke University Press.

Scott, J. (1985) *Weapons of the weak: everyday forms of peasant resistance*, New Haven, CT: Yale University Press.

Scott, J. (1990) *Domination and the arts of resistance: hidden transcripts*, New Haven, CT: Yale University Press.

Sharma, A. (2006) 'Crossbreeding institutions, breeding struggle: women's empowerment, neoliberal governmentality, and state (re) formation in India', *Cultural Anthropology*, 21(1): 61–95.

Sharma, A. and Gupta, A. (2006) 'Rethinking theories of the state in an age of globalization', in A. Sharma and A. Gupta (eds) *The anthropology of the state: a reader*, Oxford: Blackwell Publishing.

Shore, C. and Wright, S. (eds) (1997a) *Anthropology of policy: critical perspectives on governance and power*, London: Routledge.

Shore, C. and Wright, S. (1997b) 'Policy: a new field of anthropology', in C. Shore and S. Wright (eds) *Anthropology of policy: critical perspectives on governance and power*, London: Routledge, pp 3–39.

Shore, C. and Wright, S. (2011) 'Conceptualising policy: technologies of governance and politics of visibility', in C. Shore, S. Wright and D. Però (eds) *Policy worlds: anthropology and the analysis of contemporary power*, New York, NY: Berghahn Books, pp 300–14.

Simon, S. (2000) 'Gender in translation', in P. France (ed), *The Oxford guide to literature in English translation*, Oxford: Oxford University Press.

Sinclair, T. (2000) 'Reinventing authority: embedded knowledge networks and the new global finance', *Environment and Planning C: Government and Policy*, 18: 487–502.

Slack, J. (1996) 'The theory and method of articulation in cultural studies', in D. Morley and K.-H. Chen (eds) *Stuart Hall: critical dialogues in cultural studies*, London: Routledge.

Smith, V. (2011) 'Speaking of change: why discourse is key to the dynamics of policy transformation', *Critical Policy Studies*, 5(2): 106–26.

Solioz, C. and Stubbs, P. (2012) 'Regionalisms in South East Europe and beyond', in P. Stubbs and C. Solioz (eds) *Towards open regionalism in South East Europe*, Baden-Baden: Nomos, pp 15–48.

Spivak, G. (1985) 'Can the subaltern speak', *Wedge*, 7(8): 120–30.

Spivak, G. (1988) 'Can the Subaltern Speak', in C. Nelson and L. Grossberg (eds) *Marxism and the interpretation of culture*, Chicago, IL: University of Illinois Press, pp 271–313.

Spivak, G. (2000) 'The politics of translation', in L. Venuti (ed) *The translation studies reader* (3rd edn), London: Routledge.

Spry, T. (2009) 'Bodies of/as evidence in autoethnography?', *International Review of Qualitative Research*, 1(4): 603–10.

Stan, S. (2007) 'Transparency: seeing, counting and experiencing the system', *Anthropologica*, 49(2): 257–73.

Stenning, A. (2005) 'Post-socialism and the changing geographies of the everyday in Poland', *Transactions of the Institute of British Geographers*, 30(1): 113–27.

Stone, D. (1999) 'Learning lessons and transferring policy across time, space and disciplines', *Politics*, 19(1): 51–9.

Stone, D. (1988) *Policy paradox and political reason*. Berkeley and Los Angeles: University of California Press.

Stone, Diane (2002) 'Introduction: global knowledge and advocacy networks', *Global Networks*, 2(1): 1–11.

Stone, Deborah (2002) *Policy paradox: the art of political decision making* (rev 2nd edn), New York, NY: Norton and Company.

Stone, D. (2012) 'Transfer and translation of policy', *Policy Studies*, 33(6): 483–99.

Stone, D. (2013) 'Taking emotion seriously: the promise of interpretive policy', Keynote speech at 8th International Conference in Interpretive Policy Analysis, University of Vienna.

Strathern, M. (ed) (2000) *Audit cultures: anthropological studies in accountability, ethics and the academy*, London: Routledge.

Strathern, M. (2006) 'Bullet-proofing: a tale from the United Kingdom', in A. Riles (ed) *Documents: artefacts of modern knowledge*, Ann Arbour, MI: Michigan University Press, pp 181–205.

Strathern, M. (2011) 'Discussant's comments', American Anthropological Association Conference, Montreal, Canada.

Strathern, M. (2013) 'Learning to see in Melanesia: lectures given in the Department of Social Anthropology, Cambridge University, 1993–2008', *HAU Masterclass Series* 2, available at: http://www.haujournal.org/index.php/masterclass/article/view/319/354

Stubbs, P. (2002) 'Globalisation, memory and welfare regimes in transition: towards an anthropology of transnational policy transfers', *International Journal of Social Welfare*, 11(4): 321–30.

Stubbs, P. (2003) 'International non-state actors and social development policy', *Global Social Policy*, 3(3): 319–48.

Stubbs, P. (2005) 'Stretching concepts too far? Multi-level governance, policy transfer and the politics of scale in South East Europe', *Southeast European Politics*, 6: 66–87.

Stubbs, P. (2007) 'Civil society or Ubleha?', in H. Rill. T.Šmidling and A. Bitoljanu (eds) *20 pieces of encouragement for awakening and change: peacebuilding in the region of the Former Yugoslavia*, Belgrade: Centre for Nonviolent Action, pp 215–28.

Stubbs, P. (2013) 'Flex actors and philanthropy in (post-)conflict arenas: Soros' Open Society Foundations in the post-Yugoslav space', *Politička misao*, 50(5): 114–38.

Stubbs, P. and Maglajlić, R. (2012) 'Negotiating the transnational politics of social work in post-conflict and transition contexts: reflections from South-East Europe', *British Journal of Social Work*, 42(6): 1174–91.

Stubbs, P. and Maglajlić, R. (2013) 'Constructing "child care reform" in South East Europe: revisiting UNICEF's "Travelling Technicism"', paper for International Studies Association Annual Convention, San Francisco, California, April.

Stubbs, P. and Zrinščak, S. (2009) 'Rescaling emergent social policies in South East Europe', in K. Rummery, I. Greener and C. Holden (eds) *Social policy review 21. Analysis and debate in social policy, 2009*, Bristol: The Policy Press, pp 283–305.

Stubbs, P. and Zrinščak, S. (2012) 'Clientelism and social policy', in N. Zakošek (ed) *Zagreb Economic Forum*, Zagreb: Friedrich Ebert Stiftung, pp 5–18 (in Croatian).

Szalai, J. (2002) 'A Tarsadalmi kirekesztoes egyes kerdesei az ezredforulo Magyarorszagan' ['Reflections on social exclusion at the turn of the century in Hungary'], *Szociologiai Szemle* 4: 34–50.

Sziklai, I., Bugarszki, Zs., Eszik, O. and Soltesz, A. (2010) 'Egylepes elore, ketto hatra. A nagy letszamu intezmenyek kitagolasa es az onallo eletvitel tamogtasa Magyarorszagon, az Europai Unio strukturalis alapjainak felhasznalasaval' ['One step forward, two steps back. The deinstitutionalisation of large institutions and the support for independent life in Hungary, with the support of EU's structural funds'], mimeo, Budapest, ELTE University.

Tag, M. (2012) 'Universalizing early childhood: history, forms and logics', in A. Twum-Danso Imoh and R. Ame (eds) *Childhoods at the intersection of the local and the global*, Basingstoke: Palgrave Macmillan, pp 34–55.

Tag, M. (2013) 'The cultural construction of global social policy: theorizing formations and transformations', *Global Social Policy*, 13(1): 24–44.

Tews, K. (2005) 'The diffusion of environmental policy innovations: cornerstones of an analytical framework', *European Environment*, 15(2): 63–79.

Thompson, E.P. (1967) 'Time, work-discipline and industrial capitalism', *Past and Present,* 38(1): 56–97.

Todorova, M. (2009) *Imagining the Balkans* (updated edn), Oxford: Oxford University Press.

Tosi, A. (2005) 'EU translation problems and the danger of linguistic devaluation', *International Journal of Applied Linguistics*, 15: 384–8.

Towns, A. (2012) 'Norms and social hierarchies: understanding international policy diffusion "from below"', *International Organization*, 66(2): 179–209.

Travers, M. (2007) *The new bureaucracy: quality assurance and its critics*, Bristol: The Policy Press.

Tymoczko, M. (2006a) 'Translation: ethics, ideology, action', *The Massachusetts Review*, 47(3): 442–61.

Tymoczko, M. (2006b) 'Reconceptualizing translation theory. Integrating non-Western thought about translation', in T. Hermans (ed) *Translating others. Volume I*, Manchester: St. Jerome, pp 13–32.

UNICEF (United Nations Children's Fund) (2010) *Adopting a systems approach to child protection*, Working Paper, New York, NY: UNICEF.

UNICEF (2013) *Integrated social protection systems: enhancing equity for children*, Consultation Paper, New York, NY: UNICEF.

Vatanabadi, S. (2009) 'Translating the transnational', *Cultural Studies*, 23(5–6): 795–809.

Vazquez, R. (2011) 'Translation as erasure: thoughts on modernity's epistemic violence', *Journal of Historical Sociology*, 24(1): 27–44.

Vegso, R. (2012) 'The parapraxis of translation', *The New Centennial Review*, 12(1): 47–68.

Venn, C. (2006) *The postcolonial challenge: towards alternative worlds*, London: Sage.

Verdery, K. (1996) *What was socialism, and what comes next?*, Princeton, NJ: Princeton University Press.

Verdes, T. (2009) '"A haz az intezet tulajdona". A totalis intezmenyek lebontasarol, humanizalasarol es mondernizalasarol' ['"The house is owned by the Institute". The dismantling, humanisation and modernisation of totalitarian institutions'], *Esely*, 4: 92–114.

Waldow, F., Takayama, K. and Youl-Kwan Sung, Y.-K. (2013) 'Finland has it all? Examining 'Finnish PISA success' as a multiaccentual sign in Australia, Germany, and South Korea', *Research in International and Comparative Education*, 8(3): 307–25.

Wark, M. (2011) *The beach beneath the street: the everyday life and glorious times of the situationist international*, London: Verso.

Wark, M. (2013) *The spectacle of disintegration: situationist passages out of the twentieth century*, London: Verso.

Warrener, D. (2004) *Synthesis Paper 3: the drivers of change approach*, London: ODI. Available at: http://www.odi.org.uk/RAPID/Projects/R0219/docs/Synthesis_3_final.pdf (accessed 25 March 2014).

Wedel, J. (2004) '"Studying through" a globalizing world: building method through aidnographies', in J. Gould and H. Secher Marcussen (eds) *Ethnographies of aid: exploring development texts and encounters*, Roskilde: International Development Studies, pp 149–73.

Wedel, J. (2009) *Shadow elite: how the world's new power brokers undermine democracy, government and the free market*, New York, NY: Basic Books.

Wedel, J. and Kideckel, D. (1994) 'Studying up: amending the first principle of anthropological ethics', *Anthropological Newsletter*, 31(7): 37.

Wedel, J., Shore, C., Feldman, G. and Lathrop, S. (2003) 'Toward an anthropology of public policy', *Annals of the American Academy of Political and Social Science, vol. 600, the use and usefulness of the social sciences: achievements, disappointments, and promise*, New York, NY: Sage, pp 30–51.

Weiler, K. (1994) 'Freire and a feminist pedagogy of difference', in P. Mclaren and C. Lankshear (eds) *Politics of liberation: paths from Freire*, London: Routledge, pp 12–40.

Wetherell, M. (2012) *Affect and emotion: a new social science understanding*, London: Sage.

Whitehead, D. (2003) 'Poiesis and art-making: a way of letting-be', *Contemporary Aesthetics*, Vol 1 (http://quod.lib.umich.edu/c/ca/7523862.0001.005/--poiesis-and-art-making-a-way-of-letting-be?rgn=main;view=fulltext).

Widerberg, K. (1998) 'Translating gender', *NORA*, 6(2): 133–8.

Williams, R. (1977) *Marxism and literature*, Oxford: Oxford University Press.

Willis, P. and Trondman, M. (2000) 'Manifesto for ethnography', *Ethnography*, 1(1): 5–16.

Wise, J. MacGregor (2005) 'Assemblage' in C. Stivale (ed) *Gilles Deleuze: Key concepts*, Chesham: Acumen: 77–87.

Wright, S. (2004) 'Markets, corporations, consumers? New landscapes of higher education', *LATISS – Learning and Teaching in the Social Sciences*, 1(1): 71–94.

Wright, S. and Boden, R. (2011) 'Markets, managerialism and measurement: organisational transformations of universities in the UK and Denmark', in J.E. Kristensen, H. Nørreklit and M. Raffnsøe-Møller (eds) *University performance management: the silent managerial revolution in Danish universities*, Copenhagen: DJØF.

Wright, S., Greenwood, D. and Boden, R. (2011) 'Report on a field visit to Mondragon University: a cooperative experience/experiment', *Learning and Teaching: The International Journal of Higher Education in the Social Sciences*, 4(3): 38–56.

Yanow, D. (1996) *How does a policy mean?*, Washington, DC: Georgetown University Press.

Yanow, D. (2000) *Conducting interpretive policy analysis*, Newbury Park, CA: Sage.

Yanow, D. (2004) 'Translating local knowledge at organizational peripheries', *British Journal of Management* 15 (special issue): 9–25.

Yanow, D. (2007) 'Interpretation in policy analysis: on methods and practice', *Critical Policy Analysis*, 1: 109–21.

Yanow, D. (2011) 'A policy ethnographer's reading of policy anthropology', in C. Shore, S. Wright and D. Però (2011) *Policy worlds. Anthropology and the analysis of contemporary power*, New York, NY: Berghahn Books, pp 300–14.

Yazici, B. (2011) 'Tracing welfare policy in Turkey: political rhetoric, state policy and precarious lives', paper presented at the American Anthropological Association Conference, 'Interest Group for the Anthropology of Public Policy', Montreal, Canada, November.

Zeitlin, J. (2005) 'Social Europe and experimentalist governance: towards a new constitutional compromise?', European Governance Papers, No C-05-04, Available at: www.mzes.uni-mannheim.de

Index